Challenges to Democracy

This book is dedicated to the memory of Tomas Hellén

Challenges to Democracy

Eastern Europe Ten Years after the Collapse of Communism

Sten Berglund

Professor of Political Science, University of Örebro, Sweden

Frank H. Aarebrot

Associate Professor of Comparative Politics, University of Bergen, Norway

Henri Vogt

Researcher, Finnish Institute of International Affairs, Helsinki, Finland

Georgi Karasimeonov

Professor of Political Science, University of Sofia, Bulgaria

Edward Elgar
Cheltenham, UK • Northampton, MA, USA

Published by
Edward Elgar Publishing Limited
Glensanda House
Montpellier Parade
Cheltenham
Glos GL50 1UA
UK

Edward Elgar Publishing, Inc.
136 West Street
Suite 202
Northampton
Massachusetts 01060
USA

Reprinted 2002

A catalogue record for this book
is available from the British Library

Library of Congress Cataloguing in Publication Data

Challenges to democracy : Eastern Europe ten years after the collapse of
communism / Sten Berglund ... [et al.].
    p. cm.
  Includes bibliographical references and index.
  1. Europe, Eastern—Politics and government—1989– 2. Post-communism—
Europe, Eastern. 3. Democratization—Europe, Eastern. I. Berglund, Sten, 1947–

JN96.A58 C49 2001
320.943—dc21

2001018768

ISBN 1 84064 293 9

Printed and bound in Great Britain by MPG Books Ltd, Bodmin, Cornwall

Contents

Figures

Tables

Maps

Notes on the Authors

Frank H. Aarebrot (b. 1947) is Associate Professor of Comparative Politics at the University of Bergen, Norway. He is the author and co-author of numerous articles and chapters within the field of comparative politics, among others: 'Analysis and Explanation of Variation in Territorial Structure' (in Stein Rokkan et al., eds, *Centre–Periphery Structures in Europe,* Frankfurt/Main 1987), *The Political History of Eastern Europe: The Struggle between Democracy and Dictatorship* (with Sten Berglund, 1997). He has published *The Handbook of Political Change in Eastern Europe* (co-edited and co-authored with Sten Berglund and Tomas Hellén 1998) and *Politics and Citizenship on the Eastern Baltic Seaboard* (co-edited and co-authored with Terje Knutsen, 2000).

Sten Berglund (b. 1947) is Professor of Political Science at the University of Örebro, Sweden. His previous publications include *The Scandinavian Party Systems* (with Ulf Lindström, 1978), *Democracy and Foreign Policy* (with Kjell Goldmann and Gunnar Sjöstedt, 1985), *The New Democracies in Eastern Europe: Party Systems and Political Cleavages* (co-edited and co-authored with Jan Åke Dellenbrant, 1991 and 1994), and *The Political History of Eastern Europe: The Struggle between Democracy and Dictatorship* (with Frank Aarebrot, 1997) and *The Handbook of Political Change in Eastern Europe* (co-edited and co-authored with Tomas Hellén and Frank Aarebrot 1998).

Georgi Karasimeonov (b. 1949) is Professor of Political Science at the University of Sofia, Managing Director of the Institute for Political and Legal Studies in Sofia, and President of the Bulgarian Political Science Association. His main research interests and publications are in the fields of political parties, political institutions, post-communist transition and constitutional law.

Henri Vogt (b. 1967) is currently affiliated with the Finnish Institute of International Affairs as a researcher within the framework of the project *Conditions of European Democracy,* funded by the Tercentenary Fund of the Swedish National Bank. He has written and published widely on issues related to the revolutions of 1989 and to subsequent developments in East Central Europe. His doctoral dissertation *Between Utopia and Disillusionment* will be published in 2001.

Preface

This book is the last one in a set of three volumes on the political development of Eastern Europe, all published by Edward Elgar. The first, *The Political History of Eastern Europe*, sets out to analyse the struggle between democracy and dictatorship in the 20th century from a macro-sociological perspective. The second, *The Handbook of Political Change in Eastern Europe*, offers country-specific analyses of political cleavages in ten Central and East European countries along with information on constitutions, elections and government formations between 1989 and 1997. The current volume, *Challenges to Democracy*, provides an in-depth account of how the new democracies of Central and Eastern Europe have coped with challenges such as political fragmentation, nationalism and xenophobia, lack of respect for human rights, and poorly developed civil society organizations. The analyses draw heavily on available survey data such as the Central and East European Barometers (CEEB). The authors want to avail themselves of this opportunity to thank the Central Archive (ZA) in Cologne and the Norwegian Social Science Data Services (NSD) in Bergen for providing them with the raw material without which this book would not have been possible.

A team of four authors from different countries – Sten Berglund (Sweden), Frank Aarebrot (Norway), Henri Vogt (Finland) and Georgi Karasimeonov (Bulgaria) – share responsibility for this volume, but it would have remained unwritten without a certain division of labour. The introductory and concluding chapters were drafted jointly by Frank Aarebrot and Sten Berglund. The former also drafted the chapter on nationalism, and the latter the chapters on human rights and civil society. Henri Vogt wrote the first draft of the chapter on social and political fragmentation, and Georgi Karasimeonov wrote the first version of the chapter on consolidation. Sten Berglund, Henri Vogt and Frank Aarebrot carried out the editorial work.

Tomas Hellén (Helsinki), who passed away on 26 March 1998 after having completed his work on *The Handbook of Political Change in Eastern Europe*, was to have been one of the co-authors. This book is dedicated to the memory of this young, talented political scientist and dear friend of ours.

The authors wish to express their gratitude to the research assistants, whose dedication and technical skills made it possible to finish the book in time. Mr Joakim Ekman (Örebro) and Mr Terje Knutsen (Bergen) were part of the process all along, Ms Satu Sundström (Helsinki) and Mr Jonas Linde (Örebro) became part of it towards the end.

The authors are also indebted to the Tercentenary Fund of the Swedish National Bank. The book was initiated within the framework of one research project, sponsored by the Tercentenary Fund, and completed within the framework of another project, also financed by the same foundation.

Sten Berglund　　　　　　*Frank Aarebrot*
Henri Vogt　　　　　　　*Georgi Karasimeonov*

1. Introduction

Few, if any, would expect the process of democratization in Central and Eastern Europe following the demise of Communism to be without problems. Yet this was sometimes the impression conveyed by politicians and observers alike in the euphoria in the aftermath of the dramatic events of 1989–90. But euphoria soon gave way to a more realistic outlook, bordering on pessimism, as rising expectations largely remained unfulfilled by the fledgling democratic regimes. The new democracies of Central and Eastern Europe were increasingly seen as being confronted by a variety of challenges, including extreme multipartyism, right-wing radicalism, legal arbitrariness and weak civil society organizations, to name but the most prominent ones. With the benefit of hindsight, we can establish that none of these challenges, important as they may be, has been sufficient to topple democracy as such in any but a few cases, mainly within the Commonwealth of Independent States (CIS).

On the face of it, the democratic regimes would seem to have been able to cope with the challenges, but they certainly cannot afford to relax in an ever changing environment. Optimists, pessimists and realists alike have embraced the term 'challenges' with equal enthusiasm, but they use the term for very different purposes. Pessimists see challenges as barriers to positive change. For optimists challenges are there to be overcome. Realists consider challenges to be part and parcel of governance in all polities since time immemorial.

This book represents an attempt by four political scientists to analyse the impact of a set of challenges with a historical as well as a structural record of destabilizing democracy (Berglund and Aarebrot 1997; Berglund, Hellén and Aarebrot 1998). We are particularly interested in the following challenges:

- party and political fragmentation
- xenophobia and nationalism
- absence of legal and bureaucratic traditions sustaining human rights

1

- weak civil society organizations

These are by no means the only challenges, as evidenced by the following chapter on the process of consolidation in the region, but we have reason to believe that they are crucial. They have a common denominator in what may be referred to as their dual focus. On the macro level, they are seen as detrimental to the functioning of a democratic system. On the micro level, they represent behavioural patterns and mass attitudes conducive to political efficacy. Thus, party fragmentation is a systemic problem to the extent that it inhibits the formation of stable, majority governments, but it also presupposes a complex cleavage structure encouraging voters to spread their ballots among a number of parties (Sartori 1976). Nationalism and xenophobia may serve as tools of political mobilization for aspiring political entrepreneurs, but they would be futile as instruments of mobilization if it were not for firmly embedded belief structures among substantial parts of the public. Ambitious political leaders see legal bureaucratic governance as an impediment, but sadly this is more often than not reflected in a desire for strong leadership within the electorate, contemporary Russia being a good case in point. On the systemic level, lack of civil society organizations makes governance less complicated by reducing public influence to the electoral process and occasional plebiscites, but this would not be possible without the widespread atomization within the 'flattened societies' of Central and Eastern Europe (Wessels and Klingemann 1994). It is hardly coincidental that much of the literature on the breakdown in inter-war Europe revolves around several of these issues.

We have devoted a chapter to each of these four challenges. But the distinction between the challenges should not be exaggerated. They serve as analytical constructs and they are more often than not intertwined. The citizenship laws in Estonia and Latvia enacted in the early 1990s, limiting the political rights of the Russian speaking minorities, constitute a case in point. The two emerging democracies were clearly faced with a challenge, but this challenge comprises a *combination* of the rule of law, human rights and nationalism. In Lithuania, on the other hand, we have a different combination of challenges associated with nationalism: weak civil society organizations among national minorities. Citizenship legislation is less relevant in the Lithuanian case – it has remained liberal.

Party fragmentation was perceived as a major challenge in the founding elections throughout Central and Eastern Europe. A large number of political parties and independent candidates competed for the favour of the voters. Ten years later there are few, if any, indications of increased party fragmentation in the region. Two different combinations of challenges account for this outcome – legal instruments in the form of creative electoral engineering or civil instruments in the form of organizational mergers, coalitions and fronts. Poland is an example of the former. The challenge of party fragmentation was solved in combination with legal instruments by the introduction of a 5 per cent clause. Bulgaria is an example of the latter. A plethora of anti-socialist civil organizations succeeded in forming a united front – the Union of Democratic Forces.

*

Challenges seldom appear alone; they tend to occur at the same time particularly in the aftermath of drastic political change. This kind of *agglutination* is in fact a prominent feature throughout the entire region. Contemporary Russia may serve as an excellent example of this phenomenon. President Yeltsin had to contend with a highly fragmented *Duma* from the day he was sworn in. And Russia has indeed been described as the very epitome of party fragmentation (Dawisha 1999). Private investors in Russia constantly complain about unpredictable bureaucrats and diffuse laws. The nationalist and xenophobic Liberal Democratic Party of Vladimir Zhirinovski had established itself as the second largest party in the *Duma* by the mid 1990s. With the possible exception of the Communist Party and affiliated organizations, civil society in general tends to be less than developed. The difficulties facing ordinary citizens when promoting their rights may serve as yet another example of agglutination. The obvious impediment of a weak legal framework is exacerbated by the lack of strong civil society organizations. The manifestation of several of these challenges at the same point in time has contributed towards aggravating the political situation in Russia. It may for instance be remembered that Yeltsin resorted to military force rather than legal arbitration, when trying to come to terms with a recalcitrant and fragmented parliament.

The universal presence of agglutination notwithstanding, there is variation. In Poland several of the challenges emerged already during communism. Laws protecting private property existed; the Solidarity movement with its 9.5 million dues-paying members as early as 1980 was a quite formidable civil society organization; and a well established nationalist faction within the communist party – the so called patriots – was a force to be reckoned with throughout the entire post-Stalinist era (Hellén 1996). Agglutination is a problem in Poland as well, but Poles have had the advantage of being able to deal with the challenges over a long period of time and across political regimes.

The capability of the political system to deal with challenges varies across the region, not only as a function of democratic institutions and structures established after 1989–90, but also as a consequence of differences between communist and even pre-communist regimes. Eastern Europe is often sweepingly defined as the former Warsaw-Pact countries, conjuring up the image of a communist monolith. Such a definition hides more than it reveals: important differences between communist systems as well as crucial differences in democratic heritage from the pre-communist era are blurred. Inhabitants of the Central European lands, once ruled by the Habsburg or German empires, experienced working democratic institutions before the turn of the 19th century. In the wake of the First World War, democratic constitutions were adopted throughout the entire region, albeit with varying durability and success. Even the short interlude between the Second World War and the cold war (1945–49) featured relatively free elections in parts of Eastern Europe (Berglund and Aarebrot 1997). Thus, the historical exposure to democracy varies across the region, from cases like Czechoslovakia involved in all the democratic periods mentioned above to cases such as Russia and Albania where hardly any serious attempts were made to establish mass democracy until the 1990s. The communist regimes also varied over time and space in terms of indulgence, from the 'goulash communism' of Hungary, sometimes referred to as the 'happiest barrack of the entire camp' to Nicolae Ceauşescu's sultanastic regime in Romania. These differences may not go far towards accounting for the breakdown of communism and the inception of the democratic transition process, but we have reason to believe that they are important for the understanding of the way in which challenges affect democratic consolidation today.

*

Much of the literature so far on the third wave of democratization has focused on the dramatic concepts of breakdown and crisis. There is a continuity among prominent students within this field, most notably Juan Linz and Philippe Schmitter, from an interest in the breakdown of authoritarian regimes in Spain, Portugal and Latin America to theory building on democratic transition and consolidation. This focus has its definite merits, but may have led to an overemphasis on dramatic events such as institutional crises and even regime breakdown. In this book, however, we apply a different perspective by concentrating on the more mundane concept of political challenges in an attempt to understand in what way the Central and East European democracies are coping with democratic consolidation. We would argue that the political systems of the entire region have been able to cope with the challenges they are facing, at least in general terms. Failure to cope conjures up the spectre of institutional crisis. The failure by Prime Minister Vladimir Mečiar's nationalist government to live up to Slovakia's pledge to human rights initiated such an institutional crisis between the government and the President of the Republic, who intervened in his capacity as constitutional protector and defender of human rights. Ultimately, such an institutional crisis may polarize the population and/or influential segments of the political elite, seriously weakening and possibly destabilizing the democratic regime. The situation in Belarus is another good case in point. President Lukashenko 'solved' the crisis between himself and the legislative body by dissolving the elected assembly and replacing it with a parliament of more or less his own choosing.

But these are exceptions and not the rule. The 1990s have been characterized by an increasing propensity to deal with challenges so as to preclude institutional crises. Indeed, this is reflected in attitudes measured by several European surveys. In the early 1990s, there were basically two kinds of East European democratic regimes in terms of leadership. In most countries, the new leaders were either former dissidents or former members of the communist *nomenklatura*, who had broken with the party during the communist regime. In a few countries, the communist party successfully managed to retain power under modified party labels, Ion Iliescu's government in Romania being a case in point. As the century drew to a close, almost all countries had experienced a change of guards as a direct result of the electoral process, Serbia being the sole exception. The normalization of the cleavage structure through the re-emergence of left-wing politics constitutes another clear trend. Countries as different as the Czech Republic and Croatia have moved from a situation where left-wing parties were virtually non-existent – reformed communist and social democratic parties alike – to a situation where left-wing parties have succeeded in coming out on top. This is epitomized by the fact that the Croats opted for the last President of the former Yugoslav Federation – Stjepan Mesić – when electing a successor to the late Franjo Tudjman. We would therefore argue that the West European style cleavage structure with a distinct left/right cleavage is the rule rather than the exception in contemporary Eastern Europe.

The changing attitudes towards European integration represent yet another trend. With the exception of the CIS countries and the countries directly affected by the Balkan wars, the countries of Central and Eastern Europe are now all EU candidate countries; Poland, Hungary and the Czech Republic have already been accepted as members of NATO and most of the other East European countries want to follow suit. There is in fact widespread consensus across the left/right divide about the importance of being part of European integration, Poland being a possible exception.[1] This is not so in Western Europe, where there is widespread scepticism towards NATO among left-wing parties and growing EU scepticism among right-wing parties.[2]

*

This book sets out to analyse popular attitudes to perceived challenges. There is a relationship between the systemic changes during the 1990s and popular attitudes. The first few years of the 1990s were marked by gradual erosion of the initial euphoria that eventually gave way to increasing disenchantment with the new regimes. The normalization of the cleavage structure, the change of governments as a direct result of the electoral process and the prospects for European integration have served to reverse this negative trend and have replaced it with a trend towards growing confidence in the ability of the systems to cope with challenges.

Hungary may serve as an example. After the founding election, Hungarian politics was dominated by a new brand of politicians. The voters marginalized the reformed communist party and other left-wing groups. The main difference between the winning parties – the Hungarian Democratic Forum (HDF) and FIDESZ – boiled down to subtle variations on a nationalist theme during the electoral campaign. HDF presented itself as slightly more keen on standing up for Hungarians in diaspora in neighbouring countries, while FIDESZ focused on issues of market economy and European integration. The voters were more attracted to the former than the latter. The nationalist rhetoric was further enhanced when the new HDF based government became involved in a dispute with the nationalist government of Slovakia over the impact of an electric power plant in the Danube and expressed concern for the plight of the ethnic Hungarian minority of Romania. The following election brought the reformed communists back to power. European integration and market reform became dominant issues on the political agenda. Today, with Hungary within NATO and a date for EU membership approaching, the nationalist challenge has more or less evaporated. Whether left or right, the political parties correctly view the re-emergence of nationalist politics as detrimental to Hungary's European aspirations; and Hungarian voters are probably more concerned about their prospects in a European labour market than about fellow Hungarians in neighbouring countries. The issue of capital punishment in Lithuania may serve as another example. The popular support for retaining the death penalty (80 per cent) was probably higher in Lithuania than it is in the United States. When abolishing the death penalty, the Lithuanian leadership gave in to international pressure towards harmonization of European human rights legislation. This might have been frustrating, but Lithuanian leaders were probably correct in assuming that NATO and EU membership would be more important to the voters than the death penalty.

*

The impact of political challenges is the main theme of this book. The next chapter is therefore devoted to an overview of the state of democratic consolidation throughout the region, followed by analyses of our selected set of challenges in four consecutive chapters.

NOTES

1. The agricultural sector constitutes the most serious stumbling block in the upcoming negotiations between the EU and the East European candidate countries. But as of now, Poland stands out as the only country in the region with a vocal rural opposition against membership in the European Union. In the Polish case, the opposition is at least partly a function of historical memories and experiences. Western Poland was part of Germany until 1944–45, and many Poles are afraid that the EU might pave the way for a Germanization of territories once lost by Germany.

2. In Northern Europe, however, the opposition against the European Union tends to be fuelled by the parties of the left who are inclined to see the European Union as the very incarnation of the capitalist structures of the West.

REFERENCES

Berglund, Sten and Frank H. Aarebrot (1997), *The Political History of Eastern Europe in the 20th Century: The Struggle Between Democracy and Dictatorship*, Cheltenham, Edward Elgar.

Berglund, Sten, Tomas Hellén and Frank H. Aarebrot, eds, (1998), *The Handbook of Political Change in Eastern Europe*, Cheltenham, Edward Elgar.

Dawisha, Karen (1999), 'Electocracies and the Hobbesian Fishbowl of Postcommunist Politics', in *East European Politics and Societies*, Volume 13, No. 2.

Hellén, Tomas (1996), *Shaking Hands with the Past: Origins of the Political Right in Central Europe*, Helsinki, The Finnish Society of Sciences and Letters and the Finnish Academy of Sciences and Letters.

Sartori, Giovanni (1976), *Parties and Party Systems: A Framework for Analysis*, Cambridge, Cambridge University Press.

Wessels, Bernhard and Hans-Dieter Klingemann (1994), 'Democratic transformation and the prerequisites of democratic opposition in East and Central Europe', Wissenschaftszentrum Berlin für Sozialforschung, FS III, 94–201.

2. Consolidation of Democracy

After ten years of post-communist transformation, only a small minority of East Europeans reject the idea and ideal of democracy, at least if the alternative were something even distantly resembling communism. For this reason, the main concern regarding future development of democracy in Eastern Europe is not whether there should be a democratic system of government or not, but rather the practical realization of democracy, the degree and nuances of democracy, problems related to certain aspects of democracy. In other words, the question is not of the possibility of democratic breakdown, but of creating the conditions for an unchallenged deepening of democracy or, more pessimistically, of preventing democracy from erosion.

Bearing this in mind, we explore the problems of the practical realization of democracy through the notion of democratic consolidation – a notion widely used to depict countries that have already passed the initial stages of democratization, usually called 'transition'. Through this exploration we try to provide the reader with an overall picture of the present state of democracy in the post-communist countries. This picture will also provide a framework for understanding the subsequent chapters.

In the first part of the chapter we will briefly reflect upon the use of the concept of democratic consolidation, particularly in the post-communist context. In the second, and main part of the chapter, we will try to assess the present level and nature of consolidation through a number of different factors. This assessment will be based on an elementary – and in many ways rather traditional – distinction between institutional/procedural and attitudinal/social consolidation. The chapter will end with a few concluding remarks about the state of democracy in Eastern Europe, particularly in relation to its Western counterpart.

The Notion of Democratic Consolidation

Democratic consolidation has become one of the central concepts for assessing the development and level of democracy in a certain country, particularly in connection with a political transformation from some sort of authoritarianism to democracy. The meanings of the notion vary considerably, however – even to the degree that its analytical value can be questioned. Scholarly literature abounds with its derivatives, such as 'sufficiently consolidated', 'partially consolidated', 'substantially consolidated', 'fully consolidated', or 'delayed consolidation', to name but a few. It is also easy to list attributes that are basically used as synonyms for describing democracy in a 'consolidation phase': democracy can be for example 'limited', 'partial', 'unstable', 'insecure' or, perhaps somewhat confusingly, it can be strong, stable, and secure. Moreover, consolidation can denote different processes, such as institutionalization, internalization of democratic principles, or the creation of trust between individuals, or it can include concrete tasks, such as the passing of new legislation, reorganizing local governments or providing financial possibilities for civic organizations (Plasser et al. 1998, 11–12; Schedler 1998; Przeworski et al.1996).

In spite of this array of different meanings, and the consequent analytical vagueness, the notion of consolidation seems suitable for our purposes. Consolidation can, perhaps better than any other term, capture the nature of the process whereby a state and its citizens gradually assume democratic ideals and practices and cultivate these ideals and practices, while they are simultaneously constrained by, or at least aware of, other, less democratic possibilities and practices. But let us try to clarify what may be subsumed by this notion.

First of all, there is the question of time and timing: *when* is a country's democracy in the state of consolidation? In most scholarly texts consolidation is seen as the 'second' phase of regime change, as the phase that comes after the actual transition (Linz and Stepan 1996). In this respect we no doubt belong to the main-stream: in this book consolidation refers to a situation where an elementary agreement of the need for democracy has been achieved among major social actors, groups and individuals, that is when there is a consensus about the idea of and need for democracy, and when the first concrete steps towards it have been taken. Consolidation comes after turbulence.

This definition requires a great deal of specification. First, it is obvious that different social spheres move from transition to consolidation at different paces. For example all necessary constitutional changes may already be in place, while only a few readjustment measures have been taken in the country's economy. In constitutional terms it thus sounds almost belittling to speak about consolidation, while the economic system has hardly passed the transition period. Yet, in a stable democracy most societal spheres should be at about the same level of development; even one underdeveloped sphere can destabilize the entire system. For this reason, we can still talk about a consolidation period in a certain country even though most, but not all, central societal spheres of the country appear to be firmly embedded in democratic principles. This line of argument is essentially similar to that of Juan Linz and Alfred Stepan, who in their influential 1996 study listed five elementary arenas of democratic consolidation: a free and lively civil society; an autonomous political society; the rule of law; a functioning state bureaucracy; and, finally, an institutionalized economic society. In their view, in order for a democracy to be 'fully consolidated' all these spheres should have achieved a certain, albeit unspecified, level of consolidation (Linz and Stepan 1996).[1]

This implies another central problem as regards the timing of democratic consolidation: when can we actually say that the period of democratic consolidation has come to its end? We are inclined to argue that no such point of time actually exists; consolidation cannot refer to an end station. Hence, for example such expressions as the 'only game in town' and 'fully consolidated' seem rather senseless: the name of the game may already be different tomorrow; and a 'fully consolidated democracy' is a paradox in itself – in our understanding it actually depicts a fully immobile system, autocracy rather than democracy. Yet, it is obvious that there is no point in talking about democratic consolidation in such stable democracies as, say, Sweden and Switzerland, not at least as long as the situation in these countries appears to be more or less 'normal'.

This leads to the most important aspect of our definition of democratic consolidation. *Democratic consolidation essentially refers to the process by way of which democracy is intensely tested and as a result becomes firmer.* In other words, it is only through various kinds of 'tests' – 'real' or 'perceived' threats and challenges that have an *exceptional* nature – that the quality and strength of democracy in a country becomes visible, can be measured, and can become stronger (or weaker, which is the antithesis of consolidation). This also means that in temporal terms consolidation of democracy denotes those periods of time when democracy seems to be tested or challenged in one way or another. Even a stable, old democracy can occasionally find itself in the process of consolidation, although young democracies usually face many more threats and challenges than old. Consolidation in this sense becomes a never-ending story, but it is not always 'active' or 'acute'; during these 'normal' times it does not make any sense to use the notion.

Austria after the parliamentary election of autumn 1999 might be a good case in point. Democracy in Austria may possibly be in a state of consolidation, considering that one of the governing parties, the Freedom Party (FPÖ), has openly expressed ideas that may easily be classified as racist – ideas that have reasonably little to do with the attractive idea of democratic pluralism. The answer to this implicit query must be in the negative. The Freedom Party became a serious political player, eligible to assume government power, through fully democratic processes. Nothing in the country gives reason to believe that the future existence of these processes would be in danger. Yet it may be argued that Austria currently finds itself in a phase of democratic consolidation to the extent that the debate about the Freedom Party tests the limits of democracy in Austria. The fact that Austrians have been forced to reflect upon the nature of their democracy much more than usual may actually have contributed to a further consolidation of democracy in the country – and even elsewhere in Europe following the discussion that the 'problem' of Austria has engendered.

The second central issue, to which we want to draw attention, is the close relationship between democratic consolidation and the legitimacy of democracy. In many scholarly texts consolidation is actually defined through the notion of legitimacy – in other words, consolidation would essentially imply that democracy becomes an ever more legitimate way of organizing society. 'Fully consolidated', in turn, would mean that democracy has become the only legitimate principle of government. However, this perspective on consolidation reduces the notion into a purely attitudinal matter; the concrete tasks that it includes would be ignored. Hence, the little that we can reasonably safely argue is that legitimacy is a central goal of the consolidation process – the more legitimate a democracy stands out to be, the less likely it is for serious systemic challenges to emerge. It should also be emphasized that the concept of legitimacy must not be over-psychologized (Di Palma 1990). In the final analysis, the legitimacy of democracy is something very simple and straightforward; it often boils down to a question of support for, or loyalty towards, the democratic system where one happens to live.

Thirdly, there is the question of 'the actors of consolidation', that is among whom consolidation takes place and who carries it out. The most elementary distinction is naturally that between the elite and mass levels. From the perspective of the masses the problems of democratic consolidation may indeed look rather different than they do when approached from an elite perspective. By way of example, elite level actors tend to be significantly more positive in their evaluation of the party system – no doubt an important aspect of democratic consolidation – than citizens at large. Some issues of consolidation are mostly a concern of the elite level actors. Above all, they are usually responsible for the institutional arrangements of democracy. However, even the etymological meaning of the term consolidation, from Latin *consolidare*, 'to make firm together', suggests that consolidation must take place on all social levels, and that it is a matter of cooperation, of mutual feedback, between these levels; the masses have to learn to use the democratic institutions. This principle of mutual 'cooperation' is of course one of the general requirements of a functioning democracy.

Two final notes still deserve to be made. The first note can be derived from our claim that consolidation is a never-ending story: we do not want to argue that there would be only one preferable sort of consolidation; on the contrary, consolidation must always be understood within its specific historical context. This means that external ready-made models – in the case of Eastern Europe for example models from the West – are not necessarily suitable for the conditions of any consolidating country. Secondly, self-evident as it may be, in our vocabulary consolidation is predominantly a political concept, that is having a consolidation perspective means that things are looked upon from a political point of view. Hence, although we will touch upon economic and 'purely' social factors as well, they are meaningful only in so far as they are conducive to the development of a democratic political order.

*

There are naturally a number of factors with which to assess, or even to measure, the level of democratic consolidation in a certain country. In the following presentation we have divided these factors into two groups in a fairly simple, traditional way (Di Palma 1990). We refer to the first group as *institutional and procedural consolidation*; it treats, as it were, the formal forms of democracy. The other group seeks to analyse the overall societal, cultural, and economic issues that influence the state of democracy in a given country. It is therefore called *attitudinal and social consolidation*. This distinction closely resembles that of Geoffrey Pridham, who identifies two major types of regime transition theories – *functionalist* versus *genetic* theories (Pridham 1990; 1999). The latter emphasize the institutional aspects of democratic consolidation, while the former pay more attention to the prerequisites – economic and cultural – of consolidation.

Four factors or elements of institutional/procedural consolidation seem particularly important in the context of Central and Eastern Europe's post-communist transformation:

- constitutional framework
- functioning of the political system (including electoral legislation, party

system, and government stability)
- elite relations
- international environment

Another set of four factors seems to capture the most important aspects of attitudinal/social consolidation:

- social cohesion and the level of modernity
- people's ability to cope with differences (for example differences of opinion or ethnicity)
- coping with political freedoms and human rights
- civil society and political culture

Admittedly, these eight elements of consolidation cannot be distinguished from each other in a clear-cut manner; instead, they, and particularly the latter set of factors, are often interdependent and even overlapping – a fact that complicates the analysis in many respects. Moreover, even though we made the basic distinction between the categories of institutional vs. attitudinal consolidation, both these forms of consolidation are at least somehow present in all eight elements. For example the level of modernity is clearly also an institutional matter, and elite relations have certainly very much to do with a country's political culture. In spite of this, each element appears overwhelmingly more important from the point of view of the main category where we have placed it. The difference is often a matter of elite level vs. mass level perspectives. Institutional consolidation is a matter of a top-down process, whereas attitudinal consolidation seems to start off from below.

Obviously someone else might list completely different elements, remove some elements or add new ones (for example Linz and Stepan's five arenas above). However, and as we hope to show below, through these eight aspects we can capture the most essential features of democratic consolidation in Central and Eastern Europe. Finally, it must be noted that the order in which we present these factors is by no means accidental. They may be seen as forming a circle: constitutional changes in a sense kindle the process of change, but without a functioning civil society and political culture the constitutional framework would be rather meaningless in the long run.

Institutional and Procedural Consolidation

Many analyses of democracy are overwhelmingly dominated by questions pertaining to the institutional and procedural arrangements of political systems; in fact, according to a 'minimalist' definition of democracy, the institutional and procedural components are fully sufficient for a system to be called as democracy (Dahl 1971). As will be seen below, most aspects of institutional consolidation primarily concern political elites, but it is also crucial to achieve a sufficient level of *responsiveness*, that is that the new democratic institutions, and the procedures these institutions follow, comply with the skills, expectations and ideas of the whole population. Responsiveness is also important when it comes to the constitutional framework – the first of our four factors of institutional consolidation – although in a negative sense: when the stipulations of the constitution are not followed, 'ordinary' citizens are likely to react.

The Constitutional and Institutional Framework

As a rule, the former communist countries adopted completely new constitutions during the early 1990s, usually by the end of 1992 (see Table 2.1). Before this they usually used a revised version of the old constitution. The symbolic meaning of these new constitutions was overwhelming: through them the countries of Eastern Europe formally declared their break with the old regime and adopted the principles of liberal democracy. Indeed, often this symbolic aspect appeared more important than the idea of providing the new democratic order with clearly defined rules and thereby long-term stability. The symbolic aspect was also the primary reason why the quick pace of adopting new constitutions became possible in the first place.

Perhaps somewhat surprisingly, of the old states of the area, Bulgaria and Romania were the first to introduce new constitutions. The most likely reason for this was that the field of politics was overwhelmingly dominated by ex-communist or left-oriented parties that could phrase the new constitution without having to pay attention to any major opposing opinions. The process was facilitated by the virtual absence of civil society in Romania and Bulgaria before the collapse of communism – there were thus very few societal actors that could have articulated alternative views on constitution building. In Romania, along with Estonia and Lithuania, the new constitutions were approved through referenda.

There were also countries where adopting a new constitution proved complicated, notably Hungary, Poland and Albania. In Hungary, the old, communist-era constitution was amended in the autumn of 1989 and the summer of 1990, as a result of the agreements in the National Roundtable Talks and the agreement between two new central political groupings, the Hungarian Democratic Forum (HDF) and the Alliance of Free Democrats (SZDSZ). This constitution was still in use in the summer of 2000, but it has been amended some 15 times during the past decade. The fragmentation of the political field has stopped the adoption of a completely new constitution.

In Poland, the so-called Short Constitution of 1992 brought together the amendments that had been made between 1989 and 1991, and in 1997 a new comprehensive constitution was passed by the National Assembly.[2] This 'delay' of several years was due to differences of opinion between the *Sejm* (lower chamber) and the Senate, and the existence of a relatively lively civil society, with a great variety of differing views – even Solidarity had fractionalized by 1991. The Polish case is also generally interesting from a comparative perspective. In most East European countries the new constitutions became quite open-ended, as they were drafted and passed very quickly; there were not yet any political procedures for the constitution to follow. In Poland, on the other hand, the drawn-out making of the new constitution made it possible to adopt a reasonably closed constitution that also corresponded to the political practices that had emerged during the transformation period. Poland may therefore turn out to be 'better consolidated' in this respect than most other East European countries. The Albanian situation resembled that of Poland. An interim constitutional law was adopted in 1991, but due to the delay of the whole transitional process and the very high level of political confrontation, a comprehensive new constitution was not adopted until 1998.

Yet another group of new constitutions worth mentioning are those of the countries that became independent in the aftermath of the collapse of communism: the former Soviet Republics, Slovenia, Croatia, Macedonia, Yugoslavia, and Slovakia.[3] There is hardly any doubt that the symbolic meaning was even more significant in these countries than elsewhere: adopting a new constitution was a formal sign that the country belonged to that highly exclusive group of independent states (albeit in the two former Czechoslovak republics many people had mixed feelings about whether the disintegration of Czechoslovakia actually made any sense). Unfortunately, these constitutions, particularly those of the former Yugoslavia, were also expressions of nationalist sentiments. The first words of the Croatian constitution (1990) are highly illuminating: 'The millennial national identity of the Croatian nation and the continuity of its statehood...' The Slovak constitution, in turn, begins as follows:

> We the Slovak nation, mindful of the political and cultural heritage of our forebears, and of the centuries of experience from the struggle for national existence and our own statehood, in the sense of the spiritual heritage of Cyril and Methodius and the historical legacy of the Great Moravian Empire...'[4]

In addition to these nationalist tendencies in some of the new East European constitutions, there are a number of other conspicuous features in these new constitutions. The central role of democratic ideals and the emphasis on human rights are particularly striking, not surprising given the historical experiences of these countries; in fact, in most cases a long chapter is devoted to human rights issues. Latvia is an interesting case in point. The country re-adopted its original, inter-war constitution of 1922 with amendments in 1991 and simultaneously passed a constitutional law, entitled 'The Rights and Obligations of a Citizen and a Person'. The bulk of this law became integrated into the 'real' constitution as chapter VIII when it was significantly amended in 1998.

Table 2.1: Governmental system

Country	Year of Adoption of Constitution	Type of Government	Structure of Parliament	President elected by
Albania	1991/1998	Parliamentary	Single chamber	Parliament
Belarus	1994/1996	Presidential	Two chamber	Electorate
Bulgaria	1991	Parliamentary	Single chamber	Electorate
Croatia	1990	Semi-presidential	Two chamber	Electorate
Czech Republic	1992	Parliamentary	Two chamber	Parliament
Estonia	1992	Parliamentary	Single chamber	Parliament
Hungary	1989*	Parliamentary	Single chamber	Parliament
Latvia	1922/1991/1998	Parliamentary	Single chamber	Parliament
Lithuania	1992	Semi-presidential	Single chamber	Electorate
Macedonia	1992	Parliamentary	Single chamber	Electorate
Poland	1992/1997	Parliamentary	Two chamber	Electorate
Romania	1991	Parliamentary	Two chamber	Electorate
Russia	1993	Presidential	Two chamber	Electorate
Slovakia	1992	Parliamentary	Single chamber	Parliament
Slovenia	1991	Parliamentary	Two chamber	Electorate
Ukraine	1996	Presidential	Single chamber	Electorate
Yugoslavia	1992	Parliamentary	Two chamber	Parliament

* Major amendments to the constitution of 1949 adopted.

The division of power between the government and the president on the one hand, and the executive and the parliament, on the other, are possibly among the most important relations regulated by any constitution. In this respect, however, it is difficult to find a general East European pattern – individual historical and cultural factors played a significant role when the articles regarding these issues were formulated. As demonstrated by the table below, most countries adopted parliamentary forms of government, and thus opted for a relatively weak presidency (Bulgaria, Hungary, the Czech Republic, Poland, Slovakia) or even for a ceremonial presidency (Estonia and Slovenia). But there are also countries closer to a presidential or semi-presidential form of government (Lithuania, Romania, Croatia, Macedonia, Russia, Belarus, Ukraine). The fact that most countries preferred parliamentary systems no doubt reflects the post-revolutionary need to give more space for party pluralism and diverse interests and values in general, as well as the fear that strong presidents might abuse their power.

It is worth keeping in mind that the actual division of power may be significantly different from the letter of the constitution. Many East European presidents with limited formal powers have had considerable moral and political clout by virtue of the central role they had played in the anti-communist opposition. Václav Hável of Czechoslovakia, Zhelyu Zhelev of Bulgaria, Lennart Meri of Estonia, and Lech Wałęsa of Poland are all cases in point. It is may also be noted that almost half of the East European countries opted for the bicameral form of parliament.

*

The constitutional order and the political system of a country are closely related: a political system prepares and adopts the constitution, which in turn serves as the legal basis for that very system. A political system is a multifaceted entity, which is why we have to confine ourselves to paying attention to only three aspects – particularly important from a consolidation perspective, namely the electoral system, party structure, and government stability.

The adoption of new electoral laws was one of the central issues discussed at round tables during the revolutionary struggles of the late 1980s. It proved by no means to be an easy issue: it was to have a crucial influence on what the political landscape would look like after the first few parliamentary elections. For the disgraced communist parties it was literally a matter of life or death. Indeed, the election laws effectively shaped the early development of the new party systems.

As may be gauged from Table 2.2, post-communist countries opted either for a form of proportional system or for a mixed system of single-member-constituencies and proportional representation (PR). This choice was of course natural given the ideal of political pluralism that prevailed after the revolutions. All significant political forces, including the ex-communists, were to be given the opportunity to win parliamentary seats. PR also made it possible for ethnic minority parties to gain parliamentary representation. The idea of an inclusive system undoubtedly had a positive impact on the level of social cohesion.

But pure proportional representation may lead to extreme multipartyism and to political fragmentation (Sartori 1976). This risk was well understood in Central and Eastern Europe. Electoral thresholds were introduced in most countries from the very outset, Poland and Romania being the most notable exceptions. By the second democratic elections, even these two deviant countries had incorporated a threshold into their respective electoral laws after an interlude of extreme fragmentation. It may be noted that most countries opted for d'Hondt's method of proportionality that counteracts party fragmentation by benefiting the bigger parties.[5]

Table 2.2: Electoral system (lower houses; as of 31 May 2000)

Country	*Electoral system*	*Number of seats* *S = single-member* *constituency* *P = proportional;* *E = for ethnic minorities*	*Method of vote counting** *(proportional seats)*	*Threshold (parties/ coalitions)*
Albania	Mixed	S = 115 (two rounds) P = 40 (party lists)	A complex counting system that favours the two biggest parties	2%
Belarus	Majority	S = 110 (two rounds)	–	–
Bulgaria	Proportional	240	Simple quota; d'Hondt nationally for remaining seats	4%
Croatia	Proportional	140 + 5 (E) + out-of-country seats (6 in 1999 elections)	d'Hondt	5%
Czech Republic	Proportional	200	Haggenbach–Bischoff in the electoral districts (d'Hondt nationally for the remaining seats)	5/**7–11%
Estonia	Proportional	101	Simple quota for electoral districts; modified d'Hondt for national compensation mandates	5%
Hungary	Mixed	S = 176 (two rounds) P = 210	Haggenbach–Bischoff in the electoral districts (d'Hondt for national compensation mandates)	5%
Latvia	Proportional	100	St Lagüe	5%
Lithuania	Mixed	S = 71 (two rounds) P = 70	Simple quota (Droop-formula)	5/7%
Macedonia	Mixed	S = 85 (two rounds) P = 35	d'Hondt	5%

Table 2.2: continued

Poland	Proportional	391 in multi-member constituencies + 69 nationally allocated	Simple quota on the constituency level; d'Hondt nationally	5/ 8% (7% for nat. seats)
Romania	Proportional	1 per 70,000 electors + each national minority 1 (343 in total in 1996)	Simple quota; d'Hondt nationally for remaining seats	5/**7–10%
Russia	Mixed	S = 225 P = 225	Simple quota (one district)	***5%
Slovakia	Proportional	150	'Haggenbach–Bischoff' (one district); preference vote	5%
Slovenia	Proportional	90 in total E = 2	Simple quota in electoral districts; remaining seats: d'Hondt nationally	****
Ukraine	Mixed	S = 225 P = 225	Simple quota (one district)	4%
Yugo-slavia	Mixed	1 per 65,000 voters; min. 30 per each state (138 in 1996)	d'Hondt	5%

* Simple quota: counted by dividing the total number of relevant votes by the number of seats; each party list thereby obtains as many seats as given by this quota; Haggenbach–Bischoff: same as the simple quota but the number of votes is divided by the number of seats + 1. d'Hondt: comparison figure for each candidate of the list counted by dividing the total number of votes of the list by 1, 2, 3 etc. – the candidate with the highest number of votes on the list gets the highest comparison figure etc. St Lagüe: otherwise same as d'Hondt but the divisor 1, 3, 5, 7 etc. ** Depending on the number of parties in the coalition. *** No threshold if one list gets more than 50% of the vote. **** Lists numerically entitled to at least 3 seats nationally are eligible for distributed remainder seats.

The transition to democracy and especially its level of consolidation are greatly influenced by political parties. Some commentators have even seen the emergence of new parties, and the stabilization of their position as the most important aspect of democratic consolidation.

Unlike the electoral systems, which took on their present forms relatively quickly, the party systems have been subject to a great deal of between-country variation. In the Czech Republic and Hungary the system basically assumed its present character within two or three years after the collapse of communism. In Bulgaria, Estonia, Romania, Poland, and Slovakia this process took a significantly longer time, but at the moment their party systems look fairly stable. Finally, there are countries where changes of party structure from one election to another still seem to be significant (Russia, Belarus, Ukraine, Croatia, Albania, Macedonia). Russia's most recent *Duma* election in December 1999 may serve as an extreme example. The *Unity* party, supported by Vladimir Putin, was founded in as late as October 1999, that is only two months before the election. In spite of this, the party came out as the second biggest political force in the country, only one percentage point behind the communists.

The way the former communist parties adapted to the new democratic rules constitutes yet another important milestone along the path towards democracy. In Hungary and Poland the ex-communist parties transformed into loyal (social) democrats relatively quickly while for example in Bulgaria and Romania debates concerning the true identity of these parties still go on. The Communist Party in the Czech Republic, which never transformed itself into a social democratic party, remains a deviant case.

Ethnic minority parties may also play an important stabilizing role in a country's political system. Indeed, in those countries and regions where these parties have been marginalized by majority parties, tensions tend to remain high. Ethnic minority parties do exist in most East European countries, but – as may be inferred from Table 2.3 – their electoral success has remained relatively low. Non- or anti-democratic and radical (nationalistic, xenophobic, and so on) parties make up yet another important group of parties. They are represented in most post-communist countries, but their popular support has usually remained low. In this sense they only pose a potential threat to democratic consolidation.

The different paces notwithstanding, and as demonstrated by Hellén, Berglund and Aarebrot (1998, 373), the party systems of Central and Eastern Europe resemble one another in many ways. Above all, most of these systems include parties that represent the cleavage between the national and the cosmopolitan, or between protectionism and free-market, or between the former communist party apparatus and the former dissidents in the anti-communist opposition fronts. In other words, the major post-communist cleavage between the urban, cosmopolitan, pro-market and the young, on the one hand, and the rural, national, protectionist and the old, on the other, is well reflected in most post-communist party systems. This division line will continue to have a major impact in the future politics of these countries.

Finally, let us note that the stability of the party systems does not necessarily mean that the parties enjoy wide support or trust among the electorate. In fact, the main problem of the political system in virtually all these countries is the highly critical public attitude towards parties. According to the *New Democracies Barometer V* that surveyed 12 East European countries, alarmingly few of the respondents, an average of 13 per cent, expressed trust in the political parties (Rose and Haerpfer 1998, 59). Thus, although the party systems already function reasonably well in institutional terms, a lot remains to be done to reassure the public of the good intentions of politicians and party leaders. We will return to these questions in the following chapter.

Government stability is particularly significant for democratic consolidation. There is indeed little doubt that East European countries with high scores on governmental longevity, most notably the Hungarian and Czech republics, profited greatly from their stability. But it is sometimes argued that the Czech Republic lost momentum on some essential reforms during the long term of Václav Klaus' cabinet from 1992 to 1997. Russia in the late 1990s is a rather extreme example of how weak governments may undermine the entire political system and erode all attempts at sustainable reform.

Table 2.3: Electoral strength of ethnic minority parties and radical nationalist parties

Country	Last elect-ions	Ethnic Minority	Electoral results	Radical/ Nationalist	Electoral Results
Albania	June 1997	Human Rights' Unity Party	2.8%	National Front Party of National Unity	2.3% 1 Seat
Belarus	May 1995			Liberal Democratic Party of Belarus	1 seat
Bulgaria	April 1997	Union for National Salvation (MRF was the major coalition party)	7.6%		
Croatia	Jan 2000	Serb National Party Hungarian Democratic Community of Croatia	1 Seat 1 Seat	Croatian Party of Rights	3.3%
Czech Republic	June 1998			Rally for the Republic/Czeco-slovak Republican Party	3.9%
Estonia	March 1999	Estonian United People's Party Russian Party in Estonia	6.1% 2.0%		
Hungary	May 1998			Hungarian Justice and Life Party	5.5%
Latvia	Oct 1998			Latvian Unity Party Popular Movement for Latvia (Siegerist Party)	1.7%
Lithuania	Nov 1996	Election Action of Lithuania's Poles Lithuanian Russian Union Alliance of Lithuanian National Minorities	3.0% 1.6% 2.4%	Lithuanian National Party 'Young Lithuania'	3.8%

Table 2.3: continued

Macedonia	Oct 1998	Democratic Prosperity Party Democratic Party of Albanians Union of Roma in Macedonia	jointly 19.3% 1 seat		
Poland	Sept 1997	German Social and Cultural Society Opole Silesia	2 Seats		
Romania	Nov 1996	Hungarian Democratic Alliance of Romania	6.6%	Party of Great Romania Romanian National Unity Party	4.5% 4.4%
Russia	Dec 1999			Bloc *Zhirinovskogo*	6%
Slovakia	Sept 1998	Party of the Hungarian Coalition	9.1%	Slovak Communist Party Slovak National Party	2.8% 9.1%
Slovenia	Nov 1996			Slovenian National Party	3.2%
Ukraine	March 1998				
Yugoslavia	Nov 1996	Party of Democratic Action Hungarian Party of Voivodina	0.3% 1.9%	Serb Radical Party	17.9%

The data at hand (Table 2.4) make it abundantly clear that governments have fallen relatively often in most countries of the region. But compared with Italy's track record, for example, the pace has been relatively modest, which is why we are inclined not to claim that there is cause for alarm. The real problem is that government crises in-between elections have far too often been moral rather than political in nature. In Estonia, three of the governments of the 1990s fell owing to financial/moral scandals, but the unfolding of the Albanian investment funds in 1997 probably represents the most striking scandal of this kind.

Another central issue regarding government stability is whether changes of government – as a result of parliamentary elections or moral scandals – actually lead to policy changes. In some of the countries under scrutiny, we can in fact see a normal democratic swing of the pendulum. In Poland and Lithuania, the overall thrust of the government changed from 'right' to 'left' in the second post-communist election and then back to 'right' in the third.

The fact that former communists, now appearing as social democrats, could reassume power so quickly gave rise to many worried comments. We would be inclined to interpret the change of guard as a measure of people's ability to co-opt governmental policies and, more importantly, as an indication that voters have the impression that their votes truly count.

Table 2.4: Average term of office of Central and East European post-communist governments

Country	Average longevity of cabinet
Albania	15 months
Belarus	42 months
Bulgaria	9 months
Croatia	16 months
Czech Republic	23 months
Estonia	15 months
Hungary	22 months
Latvia	15 months
Lithuania	15 months
Macedonia	46 months
Poland	14 months
Romania	28 months
Russia	16 months
Slovakia	18 months
Slovenia	19 months
Ukraine	11 months
Yugoslavia	24 months

The relationship between different societal elites in a given country is an extremely complex issue – an issue that probably defies most between-country generalizations: the cultural heritage of individual countries may in the end determine the nature of elite relations. For example, in the South East European countries under scrutiny, the clientilistic traditions may undermine all formal efforts to institutionalize the relations between different elites. There are, however, many issues that deserve special attention from the perspective of post-communist democratic consolidation.

First of all, there is the problem of the confrontation between the elites of the communist era and the new elites, that is those who actively opposed the former system or who came of age during the 1990s. This distinction permeates all social elites, be they politicians, businessmen, media people, or intellectuals. It basically boils down to the question of how to deal with the communist past or to what is referred to as *Vergangenheitsbewältigung* in the German context. As is well known, strategies of coping with this problem have varied significantly across the post-communist world, from lustration laws as in Czechoslovakia to rather mild measures in Poland. In the worst cases, the result has been the 'tyranny of the majority', and 'witch hunts', which still take place, to various degrees, in Albania, Romania, Bulgaria, Croatia, not to mention Yugoslavia.

The former political elites often transformed their power into the economic sphere (Řeháková and Vlachová 1995). Many people, even on the elite level, consider it highly unjust that the communist *nomenklatura* has been given the possibility to get away from their possible misdeeds in the past and to make fortunes under new circumstances – particularly as it seems that they do not use their economic success to the benefit of the entire society. The issue is more complex than this, though. In fact, it may have made the transformation process easier for these societies: the former *nomenklatura* could acquiesce in its new role relatively smoothly as long as it seemed economically more prosperous than their previous position (Higley et al. 1996). Be that as it may, the problem remains and there may be no good solution to it – unless one wishes to see forgiveness as such.

Finally, let us say a few words about the media and the role of intellectuals. The position of the media has been a difficult issue in many post-communist countries. In particular the future of the state-owned TV-channels has raised stormy debates in most of these countries (on the Bulgarian and Hungarian cases see Reljić 1998). By the end of the year 1999, however, most post-communist countries had adopted new media laws that basically guarantee the independence of the media. In spite of this, there are plenty of examples where freedom of the press has been jeopardized either by economic or political interests. Boris Berezovsky's media monolith in Russia is undoubtedly a good case in point.

In the case of the intellectual elites, the main problem of post-communism has been existential. With the disappearance of the Enemy, they no longer seem to have a real role in society. Besides, as George Schöpflin has remarked, in those countries where intellectuals have assumed important government positions, they have more often than not proved rather incapable of making necessary political decisions (Schöpflin 1993). This has led to further disillusionment among them.

The international context constitutes the last of our four factors of institutional consolidation. It is of course a two-way street. On the one hand, the international community – in practice what used to be called the First World – sets rules or gives recommendations as to how the countries of Central and Eastern Europe should adjust their policies and their legal, economic and bureaucratic frameworks in order to become true members of the 'international community'. On the other hand, these countries themselves try to comply with the true or imagined requirements of the international community, being at the same time constrained by domestic cultural traditions. It is also worth bearing in mind that the countries of the region by no means lived in an international vacuum under communist rule – one can hardly understand the collapse of communism without taking the international context into account. By way of example, the CSCE process with its emphasis on the human rights dimension was essentially important for the emergence of the East European opposition movements, and the ideological warfare that the West pursued throughout the years of communism did play an important role in de-legitimizing the communist system. No wonder, then, that the 'return to Europe' was an elementary idea in most Central and East European countries at the time of the revolutions.

After the collapse of communism, institutional arrangements designed to bring the region into Europe and the world rapidly got under way. Most countries became members of the Council of Europe within a couple of years, Hungary as the first East European member state in November 1990 and Russia as a late-comer in 1996. Membership was granted to some former Soviet republics even though it was obvious that these countries had problems meeting the human rights criteria set by the Council.

The most central – and the most difficult – change of institutional arrangements has no doubt been the integration of the countries of the region into the European Union – a goal that was spelled out by most of the Central and East European countries already within the first months and years of the transformation period. From the perspective of democratic consolidation, the most important aspect of possible EU-membership is that the integration criteria require the candidate members to harmonize their legislation with that of the EU. This process is well under way in the applicant countries (see Table 2.5) at the moment, and it is obvious that it is proceeding very fast indeed even considering the serious political problems facing many of the applicant countries. It has been particularly fast in the 'first' group of applicants that were accepted for membership negotiations in 1998. Popular support for EU membership has generally been widespread.

But EU integration also entails a number of risks. It may create new walls within the continent and between the former communist lands; no one really knows what would happen if the Czech Republic were to become a member, but Slovakia not. At the moment things look reasonably good, as all former communist states outside the Soviet Union plus the Baltic states have been accepted for accession negotiations. Still, the question of the Eastern border of the EU – or indeed of the very notion of 'Europe' – remains. There are also many social groups for whom integration would spell painful adjustment; the vast farming sector in Poland is often cast as an example. Moreover, if integration is pursued with too much arrogance by the old EU-members – and many people in the Balkans sense this at present – the result may be increasing nationalism and patriotism.

The latter point is particularly relevant as regards NATO enlargement – another central integration issue for most of the region, though politically it is much more difficult. Before the war in Kosovo support for NATO membership was on a fairly high level, generally between 50 and 80 per cent (Kostadinova 2000, 242; Haerpfer et al. 1999, 1008), but after the war in Kosovo, popular opinions have become much more divided and also less supportive, particularly in South Eastern Europe (excluding, of course, the Albanians and the Kosovars). We have not found any comparable post-Kosovo data that cover all the countries under scrutiny. The Czech Republic, which joined NATO in 1999, only a few days before the bombing of Kosovo started, saw a 56 per cent approval rating of NATO drop to 35 per cent from February 1999 to the end of the Kosovo campaign (Culik 1999); in Bulgaria a meagre 27 per cent thought that NATO's policy was right (*National Human Development Report* 1999, 21).

In the Baltic countries, the Kosovo question has not played as important a role. The support for NATO membership has remained on a fairly high level – in recent polls usually between 50 and 60 per cent. The need for security guarantees is particularly strong in these countries owing to the historical traumas of continuous foreign occupations. From NATO's point of view, Baltic membership is a sensitive question; Russia's security should not be jeopardized.

In pure economic terms, the countries of Eastern Europe have had to restructure their economies into an increasingly global and competitive setting. In practice this has meant that such organizations as the World Bank and the IMF have played crucial roles in the process of economic readjustment. How these newly opened economies have survived the global competition can be measured in various ways. One common measure is the level of foreign investments, which in the East European context no doubt gives a fairly reliable picture of the level of economic stability and the advancement of economic reforms. But there are great between-country variations: the Central European countries, Hungary, Poland, the Czech Republic, Slovenia and the Baltic states have been far more successful than Southern Europe and the Slavic countries of the former Soviet Union. It is an interesting question indeed whether EU membership will widen this gap further.

Table 2.5: Indicators of Eastern Europe's international position

Country	Foreign Direct Investment 1998 (net US$ millions)[a]	Foreign Direct Investment Per capita (net 1998)	Integration into the EU	% of people with a positive/ negative impression of the EU[b]	Relation-ship to NATO[c]
Albania	95	$28.3	Applied for association	61.4 / 1.5	PfP MAP
Belarus	50	$4.8	Not applied for association	38.5 / 5.7	PfP
Bulgaria	300	$36.6	Invited to negotiate, 1999	50.5 / 2.8	PfP MAP
Croatia	450	$95.7	Applied for association	43.3 / 8.9	PfP
Czech Republic	1275[e]	$123.8	Invited to negotiate, 1997	35.4 / 6.6	Joined in 1999
Estonia	200	$142.8	Invited to negotiate, 1997	31.6 / 7.1	PfP MAP
Hungary	1500	$147.1	Invited to negotiate, 1997	42.5 / 6.6	Joined in 1999
Latvia	344	$148.3	Invited to negotiate, 1999	38.4 / 5.6	PfP MAP
Lithuania	800	$223.5	Invited to negotiate, 1999	36.8 / 5.6	PfP MAP
Macedonia	45	$22.5	Applied for association	43.5 / 8.9	PfP MAP
Poland	4000	$103.6	Invited to negotiate, 1997	59.9 / 4.1	Joined in 1999
Romania	900	$40.4	Invited to negotiate, 1999	59.5 / 4.6	PfP MAP
Russia	1500	$10.2	Not applied for association	28.6 / 6.0	PfP[d]
Slovakia	220	$40.7	Invited to negotiate, 1999	45.9 / 5.0	PfP MAP
Slovenia	200	$101.5	Invited to negotiate, 1997	45.2 / 6.4	PfP MAP
Ukraine	700	$14.1	Not applied for association	25.3 / 4.2	PfP
Yugoslavia	N/A.	N/A	Not applied for association	35.3 / 18.6	

a: *Source*: *Women in Transition* (1999), Regional Monitoring Report, No. 6, UNICEF, page 139.

b: *Source*: CEEB 8 (Bulgaria, Czech Republic, Estonia, Hungary, Latvia, Lithuania, Poland, Romania, Slovakia, Slovenia; conducted in 1997) and CEEB 7 (all others; conducted in 1996). Respondents were asked about their impression of the EU, and given four options: 'positive', 'neutral', 'negative' or 'do not know'.

c: PfP = Partnership for Peace, launched in January 1994; most countries joined within a year. MAP = Membership Action Plan, launched at the NATO Summit in Washington in April 1999; assists candidate countries in preparing for membership, but does not guarantee it.

d: Russia froze its relations with NATO as a result of the Kosovo crisis. The relations were resumed in February 2000, but Russia will not take part in PfP military exercises in the year 2000.

e: in 1997.

Be that as it may, at the moment there is very little doubt that the dominant political elites in most countries under scrutiny – with the exception of Belarus, and possibly Yugoslavia – are resolutely guiding their countries towards Western and international institutional arrangements. And even as regards the problem cases, the present difficult situation may depend on a few leading politicians, as the example of Slovakia would seem to suggest: the country was more or less an international outcast under the leadership of Vladimir Mečiar, but the situation changed almost overnight after he lost the elections of September 1998, and a new pro-Western government assumed power. All in all, judging by the willingness to cooperate with the international community, there is indeed cause for optimism with respect to the future of liberal democracy in these countries.

Attitudinal and Social Consolidation

Let us now turn to the second major category of democratic consolidation, namely to what we call attitudinal and social consolidation. The four elements that we will discuss in this section all pertain to people's ability to adapt to the new circumstances and to cope with them – with the new freedoms, with modernity, with an increasingly complex civil society and with social and ethnic strife. Our perspective thus shifts more clearly towards the masses, the ordinary citizens. The general statement in the first section of this chapter about the relevance of these items for the legitimacy of democracy is well worth keeping in mind: citizens who respect basic human and political rights, who are open to the challenge of modernity, who are ready to participate in civic activities, and who are inclined to perceive social, political and ethnic diversity as an asset rather than a drawback, may indeed be said to have a democratic frame of mind.

'Social cohesion and the level of modernity' is undoubtedly the most general of the factors that seem to determine the success of democratic consolidation in Central and Eastern Europe. Arguably this is not just *one* factor: social cohesion and the level of modernity can be seen as completely different things. In our view, however, both are major denominators of the overall development of society; the question is essentially of a 'balanced' social situation between people and groups of people. For example, the emergence of social cleavages related to the use of modern technology mastered by some but not by others, may pose a challenge to the consolidation process.

Needless to say, social cohesion is often an economic matter. As regards post-communist Europe, after the economic shock of the first few years of transformation, it may rather safely be argued that overall economic performance as such no longer constitutes the major problem. Most economies are growing well at the moment – inflation rates seem to be under control – and as Centeno and Rands have remarked, most people have been able to maintain their previous levels of material consumption even under new conditions (Centano and Rands 1996). In fact, GDP figures, in most cases still under the level of 1989, do not necessarily tell the whole story about real material conditions; the secondary or 'hidden' economy plays an increasingly significant role.

The main problem then – a problem truly affecting the social organization of society – is the increasing inequality between people. Unemployment, a virtually unknown phenomenon under the old rule, is on a fairly high level, and tends to grow in some countries. The distribution of earnings has become much more unequal during the past ten years, and particularly the visibility of *nouveaux riches*, some of whom had close connections with the former ruling parties, is an endless source of annoyance (see Table 2.6). Poverty seems to become ever more common, as are poverty related problems, such as crime and the absence of security. Moreover, available economic resources increasingly determine the kind of health care and education people can afford. The societies were hardly prepared for these phenomena when the communist regimes fell. No wonder, then, that satisfaction with the economic performance has generally been on a clearly lower level than satisfaction with democracy (Rose and Haerpfer 1998).

These serious shortcomings notwithstanding, it should be kept in mind that the 'objective' economic indicators may not do justice to the real situation under such extraordinary conditions as those of Eastern Europe under transformation. We should also take into account such factors as people's expectations during the old system, and at the moment, their personal values, their ability to learn and to adapt to the new conditions, and whether, or to what extent, they perceive the new social inequality as just. By way of example, a certain amount of inequality is actually seen as highly just in the context of contemporary Central and Eastern Europe – inequality, or its companion, full freedom, is perceived as much more fair than the coerced equality of the communist era. The notion of patience provides us with another example; in the words of Feiwel Kupferberg:

> It seems that individuals in Eastern Europe have much more patience than one would assume. Partly because they were raised in a regime that always postponed the glorious times to an indefinite future, partly because there is still some optimism left that things will eventually improve, people in Eastern Europe have a time perspective which any Western politician could only dream of (Kupferberg 1999, 242; Vogt 2000, Ch. 4).

Table 2.6: Macroeconomic indicators for Central and Eastern Europe[6]

Country	GDP in 1998, % of the level of 1989	GDP per capita in US$ in 1998	GDP, % change in 1998	Regist. unempl oyment in 1997	Gini co-efficient in 1989[6]	Gini co-efficient in 1997[6]	Inflation 1991	Inflation 1998
Albania	87.2	929	9.0	13.9	N/A	N/A	35.5	21.9
Belarus	74.7	1,396	5.0	2.8	N/A	N/A	98.6	50.0
Bosnia	N/A	972	30.0	N/A	N/A	N/A	114.0	5.0
Bulgaria	65.7	1,315	4.0	14.0	0.212[c]	0.291[b]	333.5	25.0
Croatia	79.2	4,820	4.2	17.5	N/A	N/A	123.0	5.8
Czech Republic	97.0	5,479	-1.0	4.3	0.204	0.259	56.6	11.0
Estonia	77.1	3,593	5.0	4.0	N/A	N/A	210.5	11.0
Hungary	94.6	4,730	4.6	10.4	0.293	0.348	35.0	15.0
Latvia	58.4	2,622	4.0	7.4	0.244	0.336	172.0	5.3
Lithuania	62.8	2,890	3.0	5.9	0.260	0.345	224.7	5.5
Mace-donia	59.2	1,548	5.0	41.7	0.223	0.259	114.9	1.3
Poland	117.6	3,887	5.2	11.5	0.207	0.300	70.3	11.0
Romania	78.1	1,695	-5.0	8.8	0.155	0.422	161.0	60.0
Russia	55.7	1,867	-5.0	2.8	0.271	0.483[b]	92.7	40.0
Slovakia	100.2	3,793	5.0	12.9	N/A	N/A	61.2	7.5
Slovenia	102.9	9,779	4.0	14.4	0.219	0.307	117.7	8.5
Ukraine	37.2	846	0.0	3.1	0.249	0.413[b]	91.0	11.0
Yugo-slavia	50.3[a]	1,630[d]	7.5[a]	25.7[b]	0.323	0.338[b]	122.0	23.2[a]

a = 1997; b = 1996; c = 1990; d = figure from IMF Annual World Economic Outlook.
Sources: Women in Transition (1999), Statistical Annex; The column 'GDP per capita': EBRD Transition Report 1999 (estimates).

Although increasing inequality is the general pattern in Eastern Europe, there are also significant differences between countries, either regarding the ability of the transformed economic systems to deliver welfare to people or in the ways people actually cope with the new economic situation. The Baltic states are good cases in point as regards the latter alternative. The return to independence has been much more important to the citizens of Estonia, Latvia and Lithuania than the material problems that they have been faced with. These 'nationalist' sentiments have produced a relatively high level of social cohesion despite the everyday problems of economic transformation. In terms of economic performance, the Central European forerunners for EU-membership are better off. They will have much better chances to combat inequality than the countries of Southern Europe and the Slavic republics of the former Soviet Union. Table 2.6 suggests that income inequality is a particularly serious problem in Russia, Romania and the Ukraine.

As will be seen in the next chapter, the level of modernity in a given country hardly lends itself to a nutshell analysis. But it is of particular importance from the post-communist perspective that the *level* of modernity can be measured in relation to the level somewhere else – in the case of Eastern Europe with Western Europe. Indeed, the implication is that the notion of modernity is always a relational matter: it is a question of how people adapt and react to various macro-sociological phenomena that seem to determine the nature of today's Europe and the world, such phenomena as social fragmentation, atomization, individualism, globalization, information technology, consumptive hedonism, to name but a few. In general, Eastern Europe's chances to cope with these challenges seem positive. During the decades of communism the East European countries in many respects became truly modern. They became industrialized nations and introduced a system of mass education. A qualified working class and a new middle class emerged. But all this may not be enough to counteract the problem of inequality: some, or maybe most, people are truly able to learn what the modern world requires, but there is a significant number of people who are not – a problem that pertains to all other 'stable' democracies as well, but may be even more serious in Eastern Europe owing to the challenges the transformation itself has posed.

Our second factor of attitudinal/social consolidation is closely related to the first one. It is obvious that people's ability to cope with human differences – whether ethnic, national, sexual, or simply attitudinal – is contingent upon the level of social cohesion, the sense of social justice, and the level of modernity. In principle, the more 'modern' a country is, the more specific and individualistic people's life patterns tend to be – the more tolerance among people there should be, at least ideally, given the multiplicity of modern life styles. Human differences are endemic to all societies, but in one sense the present situation in Eastern Europe is truly different from what it was under communism: the communist systems imposed a kind of uniformity upon the individuals, and it was not possible to articulate different views as freely as it is now. The obvious common goal of democratic societies is for this articulation to take place within the political system, and not through violent means.

Nationalism and ethnic hatred, the theme of Chapter 4 of this book, is perhaps the most widely analysed, and one of the more serious problems as regards people's ability to cope with their differences in post-communist Europe. Formally the situation appears to be rather positive: most constitutions include articles of minority rights and in many countries a system that guarantees minority representation in the legislative body is in place; there are also ethnic minority parties in most countries. Moreover, as Table 2.3 above suggested, the electoral support of radical nationalist parties of the ethnic core population is by no means threatening.

Alas, reality seems far less rosy. Social exclusion due to ethnicity is commonplace in today's Eastern Europe, the relative ethic homogeneity notwithstanding. Moreover, available evidence clearly suggests that the number of racially motivated acts of discrimination against other people has indeed been increasing – a trend that unfortunately also makes itself felt in the West. The range of these acts naturally varies a great deal, from discrimination in the working place to racially motivated acts of violence – or even to war and ethnic cleansing as in the case of Bosnia and Kosovo.

In Estonia and Latvia, the large Russian minorities pose a real challenge to the development of democracy. There are serious efforts to integrate Russians into these societies, but some of these efforts can be seen as abusive rather than merciful. To give an example, in Estonia the official target is for 60 per cent of the instruction in Russian language secondary schools to be given in Estonian by the academic year of 2007–8. If this policy contributes to significantly better Estonian language skills among the Russian population, it may truly enhance the opportunities for ethnic Russians in Estonian society, but, on the other hand, this policy may deprive them of fluency in their mother tongue. It is a moot question whether this kind of formal arrangement made by the majority can actually remove the historical prejudices between the ethnic groups; at the moment interaction between them remains at a low level. In the final analysis, it is a question of mutual cooperation and understanding – whatever policies are pursued they should be pursued with mutual consent. These points are certainly also relevant in the case of the large Hungarian minorities in Slovakia and Romania, the Turks in Bulgaria, and the Albanians in Macedonia.

Without neglecting the difficulties of the above-mentioned minorities and excluding the nations of the former Yugoslavia, the Roma stand out as the most common target of racial discrimination, the scapegoat of the transformation problems, of the entire region. Slovakia, the Czech Republic, Hungary, Romania, and Bulgaria all have Romany minorities of several hundred thousand people – in Romania the estimated figure is as high as around two million – who often live under appalling conditions. Concomitantly, the chances of the Roma in the job markets are significantly worse than those of the rest of the population. For example in Hungary approximately 70 per cent of the Romany population are unemployed; in some Slovak villages virtually all (*Report on the Situation of the Roma and Sinti in the OSCE Area* 2000, 31). The recent flow of Roma to Western countries is a natural consequence of these problems.

Coping with human differences is not only a question of nationality or ethnicity, but of many other issues of otherness. One might list such issues as attitudes to sexual minorities or disabled people, or the opportunities of the 'other' gender – in many post-communist countries women's relative position in society clearly deteriorated during the 1990s. Moreover, in some cases the former communists have truly come to represent the Other, or even the Enemy. Indeed, even coping with different pasts and different opinions and different degrees of success may prove difficult in a situation where most previous safety nets have collapsed, and where the Other therefore seems to be a particularly serious threat. Democracy, and democratic civility, proves particularly important when we encounter something strange or alien, but this civility may not be an inborn feature of humanity, but must be consciously preserved and cultivated. In this sense, a great deal still remains to be done for Eastern Europe's new political systems.

It is obvious that the preceding factor, people's ability to cope with human differences, has a great deal to do with the political freedoms and human rights people gained with the collapse of communism. In fact, the former could be seen as a sub-factor of the latter. In one sense the difference between these two factors is clear: people's ability to cope with differences is in a sense a matter of negative freedom, that is for those people who are perceived as the 'Other', the question is one of protection from any kind of uncivil behaviour, whereas political freedoms and rights are essentially a matter of freedom for something.

It is also important to note that these freedoms and rights were basically non-existent during the era of communism, and that it was essentially the absence of them that kindled the revolutions of 1989 – it was, in fact, through these freedoms and rights that democracy was defined during the revolutionary heydays. However, after the revolutions, the seemingly unlimited amount of 'freedom for' appeared to be difficult to cope with; people were not used to living in a state of freedom and making real decisions themselves. On a somewhat pessimistic note, one can ask whether people still adhere to these freedoms and rights in the face of the problems they have encountered during the transformation.

It is no easy task to answer these questions, but people's satisfaction with democracy undoubtedly sheds some light on the issue. In most of the countries the general pattern looks fairly similar: the vast majority hailed the fall of communism with an enthusiasm bordering on euphoria. But the euphoria soon gave way to widespread dissatisfaction with the development of democracy, as non-communist regimes proved unable to live up to the expectations of newly enfranchised masses. Yet, the importance of such fluctuations in the support for democracy should not be exaggerated. There is great merit to the so-called Churchill hypothesis launched by Richard Rose and associates, that is that democracy in the end is the least of evils (Rose et al. 1998). Those East Europeans who say they are no longer satisfied with the development of democracy in their respective countries, are not necessarily in favour of any of the non-democratic alternatives, including a return to communist rule. In fact, most of these respondents are dissatisfied democrats in the sense that they are not attracted to non-democratic options. In a similar vein, it may be noted that West European *Eurobarometer* data on the support for democracy also testify to variations over time and space. Some of the countries of Southern Europe actually report levels of support for democracy on a par with some of the more disenchanted countries in Central and Eastern Europe (Berglund and Aarebrot 1997).

It should also be kept in mind that support for democracy may be a function of a number of potential predictors. There are at least two groups of incentives that might motivate respondents to vote either way on the item tapping support for democracy – incentives that pertain to economic expectations and those that pertain to the human rights performance of the regime. The empirical evidence thus far strongly suggests that human rights still loom large in the minds of East Europeans (see Chapter 6). Central and Eastern Europe is apparently a far cry from taking newly gained freedoms for granted. To conclude, the ideal of democracy, including respect for human rights and adherence to political freedoms, is still highly valued by the great majority of people in most post-communist countries, although the actual democratic practices may be heavily criticized.

It is also worth mentioning that human rights violations and political repression are by no means confined to the countries with the most questionable democratic credentials. It is true that some of the most blatant human rights violations and some of the most obvious cases of political repression are reported from Belarus and Yugoslavia – the two countries currently competing for the most negative assessment by the international community – but, as we noted above, there are less than favourable human rights reports from a variety of countries, including the three Baltic countries and the Czech and Slovak republics, for their uneven treatment of ethnic minorities. The freedom of the press and the rights of the political opposition, including environmental activists, are still being curtailed in parts of the region, such as Russia and the Ukraine.

All things considered, the transition from communist rule was somewhat smoother in those parts of the region that had devolved from the German or Austro-Hungarian empires with all which that entailed by way of exposure to the rule of law (see Chapter 6). But this historical record did not stop the

Czechs from introducing harsh laws violating the political rights of former communists; nor did it prevent Croatia and Slovakia from sliding into semi-authoritarian rule under Franjo Tudjman and Vladimir Mečiar respectively.

The level of modernity, people's ability to cope with human differences, and their respect for their new freedoms all determine social relations. Civil society, then, and the political culture it produces, constitute the political and organizational dimension of these relations. Indeed, a democratic attitude is not enough – one must also be able to act according to it. A lively political culture and civil society provide opportunities to solve the problems encountered in the sphere of the other three factors.

In most countries of Central and Eastern Europe, the return to multiparty politics in the late 1980s and early 1990s gave new impetus to the dormant civil society arena. It soon became clear that political parties *alone* do not make for a vibrant civil society in the long run – not even a great number of them, as was often the case in Eastern Europe at the time. On the other hand, civil society cannot be reduced to the number of voluntary associations; stamp collectors' associations and chess clubs are of truly limited political relevance. But it is not just a matter of political relevance. Contemporary Eastern Europe features a variety of extremist groups campaigning on a strongly nationalist, sometimes even xenophobic, platform. Their political relevance is obvious, but it may appear difficult (although by no means impossible) to credit them for strengthening democracy; a social group that acts outside the sphere of politics (within the sphere of violence) is not part of civil society.

All in all, civil society is essentially a matter of pluralism, it is a delicate network of groups and also individuals, articulating some specific interests. Mainstream democratic parties, trade unions, human rights organizations and other interests groups are needed to create this network. Civil society thus breaks up power while aggregating it all at once. Civil society covers most fields of life but it also guarantees that no field of life becomes too dominant; sports clubs and cultural organizations tend to counterbalance each other. Civil society is also constantly changing, and therefore very difficult to grasp analytically. It is this kind of pluralist, comprehensive, and network-like civil society that is not yet in place in Central and Eastern Europe, at least not to the same degree as in most established democracies of the West.

The emergence of this kind of civil society organization is particularly important in those countries where civil society remained practically non-existent until the very end of communism. It is, in other words, of paramount importance throughout the entire region, with the possible exceptions of Poland, Hungary and what used to be Czechoslovakia, the only socialist countries to develop a third sector of significance while the

Marxist–Leninist parties were still in charge. Communist Central Europe served as an occasional hotbed for strong and vocal dissident movements ever since the mid-1950s; and it can now take pride in having a civil society arena with much more substance to it than the countries of Eastern and South Eastern Europe. Indeed, recent examples, such as the Impulse 99 initiative in the Czech Republic, which draws on many of the principles once promoted by the renowned *Charter 77*, testifies to the resilience of communist-era civil society – even at a time when new business opportunities have stimulated people's activity to a much greater extent than political and social problems.

It is also worth mentioning that pluralist democracy, with its emphasis on competition among parties and other civil society organizations is contingent upon the freedom of the media to report and act independently of government authorities. This represents a clean break with standard communist operating procedures, unacceptable to many East European post-communist leaders who dismiss the freedom of the press as being contrary to the 'national interest'. This has been the case especially in Yugoslavia, Croatia, Slovakia under Vladimir Mečiar, and to a lesser extent in other countries. As a rule, governing parties make a point of restraining the media by formal as well as informal means as part and parcel of an overall strategy to curb the influence of civil society on public life.

There are of course various types of civil societies. For the time being, post-communist democracies would seem to face two basic alternatives. They can opt for a West-European-style corporatist arrangement between structured interest groups and the state, or for a US style pluralist model where civil society manifests itself in the form of numerous Non-Governmental Organizations (NGOs) and interest groups. It is an open question as to what will emerge in the long run. A combination of the two models should not be excluded either, considering that corporatist interests, as we have noted above, are still in the process of affirming themselves in Eastern Europe. On the other hand, we must admit in all fairness that there is a certain Western ethnocentric bias to the recommendations offered by many Western political scientists with respect to civil society. The East European, to say nothing of the Russian, model of democracy might turn out to be quite different from that which prevails in the West. By way of example, the East European model might compensate for the lack of NGOs by mobilizing pre-democratic clientilistic networks to a much greater extent than is – and was – customary in the West.

Where Do Post-Communist Democracies Stand?

What kinds of conclusions can we draw on the basis of the overview we have created? What does the overall picture of democracy actually look like in today's Eastern Europe when we approach it in terms of a consolidation perspective based on the factors we have discussed above?

In terms of institutional consolidation, the picture is in fact quite straightforward. First of all, new constitutions have been adopted and seem to be functioning well in most post-communist countries. Hungary is the only country in our universe that still uses an amended communist-era constitution but there are no signs that this constitution somehow functions particularly badly; besides, it may be beneficial in the long run not to adopt a constitution in too much haste.

As regards the political system, the situation is obviously far from ideal. Parties still face serious problems in their identity formation, political systems in many countries have repeatedly been shaken by financial scandals, governments have generally been short-lived, and, perhaps most seriously, the political system has not been able to deliver as much material and social well-being as people have expected. No wonder, then, that a great majority of East Europeans appear highly indifferent or even hostile to the realm of official politics – which does not necessarily mean that they deplore its existence.

As for elite relations, it has proved difficult to provide the reader with a short overview. What appears certain, however, is that these relations, whether political, economic, or intellectual, are often influenced by the communist past, that is the question who were the communists and how did people cooperate with them. The salience of this factor is therefore, first and foremost, a function of time.

Internationally most countries are firmly on the path towards cooperation with the West – with the exception of Yugoslavia and Belarus, and possibly Albania, which has been partially rehabilitated in the eyes of the West following the Kosovo crisis. Integration into the Western institutions, such as the EU and NATO, has indeed been the main policy objective, almost regardless of political orientation. It should also be kept in mind that integration policy may easily create cleavages within and between the post-communist countries. Those countries that were included in the first group of EU-membership candidates have clearly benefited from this, somewhat to the detriment of the others.

All in all, in spite of the problems encountered in the political system, the situation in terms of institutional consolidation seems already more or less stabilized. It may indeed be the case that we should no longer talk about a specific consolidation period in this respect. It is also worth noting that the new institutional arrangements have been tested regularly during the last ten years – striking miners in Romania, the peaceful dissolution of Czechoslovakia are cases in point – and they have usually survived the test. 'Only', and notoriously, in Yugoslavia, Belarus and Albania has the establishment of formal democratic structures failed in many respects.

With regard to the attitudinal and social aspects of democratic consolidation, the picture is much more diverse and more difficult to capture in a few sentences. Firstly, in terms of social cohesion and people's ability to adapt to the requirements of modernity, the problems are no longer primarily economic in nature but rather political and social: increasing inequality undermines the general satisfaction with democracy that came with the transition from communism. Indeed, the struggle against growing inequality is one of the most important political challenges that post-communist countries are currently facing. This is actually a rather paradoxical situation, as these countries are simultaneously trying to rid themselves of the coerced equality of the past.

In terms of people's ability to cope with ethnic and other human differences, much still remains to be done. The tragedy of former Yugoslavia is naturally the most striking example of ethnic hatred in the area, but the plight of the Roma throughout the region suggests that much still needs to be done. This may indeed still be a problem of the transition period: in a situation where the world seems to have become much more uncertain and insecure, scapegoats are needed more than in 'normal' times.

The ability to cope with human differences naturally also reveals a great deal about how people have internalized the new political freedoms and human rights, and how they can cultivate them. The situation is actually rather difficult to interpret: on the one hand we have witnessed a fair number of human rights abuses, but at the same time it seems that human rights are still held in very high esteem – people are generally fairly satisfied with democracy, or at least they do not see any alternatives to it. Indeed, it is the existence of these new freedoms and rights that still defines the notion of democracy.

In terms of civil society, and the political culture that it creates, the situation is far from satisfactory. Whatever civic action there is, it remains rather sporadic, and due to the widespread scepticism towards politics it may not include an explicit political aspect at all. It is not necessarily a question of the number of civic associations – even in such a country as Yugoslavia, there are a number of civil society organizations, though seriously constrained by the ruling regime – but of the absence of a political climate with lobbying and cooperation among interest groups as central components. Yet, the weakness of civil society may be interpreted in a more positive light: as long as democracy functions well, and when it is perceived to be safe, the need to participate in civic activities seems less acute. Perhaps we are still too obsessed with a republican form of politics.

Be that as it may, in terms of people's democratic attitude, and their willingness to act accordingly, we can nevertheless identify many elements that are obviously contingent upon the recent transition to democracy. In this respect, we can, without hesitation, talk about a consolidation period in Central and Eastern Europe.

The final conclusion to be drawn is that, self-evident as it may be, the more developed a country is in terms of institutional consolidation, the better off the country seems to be in terms of attitudinal consolidation as well. In fact, if we were to quantify the eight factors to which we have paid attention, the correlation between institutional and attitudinal consolidation would surely be positive. Not surprisingly, the first group of EU-membership candidates – the Czech Republic, Slovenia, Poland, Hungary and Estonia – have top scores on attitudinal as well as institutional consolidation.

*

Let us finish this chapter with a few general remarks about the prospects of democracy in contemporary Central and Eastern Europe. As we pondered upon the impact of the international environment on democratic consolidation, we deliberately refrained from mentioning one crucial point. If the post-communist democracies continue to rely heavily on financial and intellectual support from the West, they actually risk becoming too dependent on the West. Consequently, they may not trust themselves to a desirable degree when developing their democratic systems. Moreover, international contacts are usually an elite level affair and the dependency on the West may lead to clientelistic or oligarchic democracy with a weak civil society. Oligarchs are not only local; in today's world they are often trans-national.

This poses a challenge to the leaders of Western democracies as well. It is their responsibility to see to it that the policy of integration does not become a factor that actually endangers, or at least slows down, the development of endogenous democratic attitudes in Central and Eastern Europe. They should also be careful that they do not undeservedly, on the grounds of simplified economic indicators, favour some countries at the cost of some others. The establishment of new demarcation lines in Europe, based predominantly on economic values, would seriously endanger the consolidation process in those parts of Eastern Europe that seem to be worst off.

The emphasis that we wish to place on the notion of endogenously emerging democracy – on attitudinal consolidation in other words – implies that the consolidation process in the region should lead to something more than just a copy of Western democracy. The principles and values of democracy need to be adjusted to the specific conditions of East European countries. At the moment, we think there is reason to be optimistic: we feel, rather intuitively though, that more and more people in Eastern Europe are developing into the realistic self-relying sceptics needed in this process of independent adjustment. Attempts to force and implant Western, especially American, values and views on post-communist democracies by economic control and political pressure are therefore doomed to fail.

We also want to argue that the post-communist democracies of the year 2000 are already much more concerned with their capacity to deal with the challenges of the future than with overcoming the legacies of the past. Democracy will thus be judged more and more on its own merits than by way of a comparison with the past. This also means that ideologies will have an ever smaller role – the popularity of politics and politicians will depend on practical deeds to a much greater extent than on ideological declarations. In this respect, there is indeed very little reason to believe that the conditions for continuing success would not be good; and nothing really suggests that this will change in the foreseeable future. At the same time, however, there is little doubt that some countries will need a considerable amount of time – perhaps a generation or two – before we can start talking about 'fully consolidated democracy', before the legacies of the past have been overcome.

Finally, it must be remembered that the process of democratic consolidation in Eastern Europe takes place in an increasingly globalized world. The challenges, and of course also the promises, that East European democracies face may indeed exist and emerge anywhere on the globe. On the other hand, if democracy encounters serious problems elsewhere – if for instance people in the West were to become ever more alienated from the realm of politics – this would have direct consequences for the development of democracy in Eastern Europe. In the following chapter, which sets out to analyse the post-communist party systems, these systems will be analysed within the context of one such 'global' trend, namely societal fragmentation.

NOTES

1. That Linz and Stepan presented these conditions in this very order was, of course, not arbitrary. Civil society is the major generator of political society, which in turn sets the rules of the legal system, the bureaucracy and the economic society.

2. Many Poles had hoped that their new constitution could be adopted in May 1991, that is two hundred years after the Polish Third of May Constitution of 1791, the first modern constitution in Europe (Suchocka 2000).

3. Czechoslovakia and the Czech Republic are unique. The communist takeover in 1948 took the form of a normal change of government. The communists enjoyed widespread electoral support and were able to form a majority government with the support of the social democrats. The new communist rulers therefore saw no need to change the constitution. In fact, the only major amendment to the constitution occurred in the aftermath of the Prague Spring of 1968 when the Husak regime transformed the unitary state into a federal republic. Vaclav Hável could thus be sworn in as the first democratically elected president without any constitutional changes whatsoever.

4. All Eastern European constitutions are available in English on the Internet, some even in more than one translation. We have in most cases used the translations provided in the site http://www.uni-wuerzburg.de/law/.

5. This is not the case when all seats are distributed within one single national constituency as d'Hondt originally envisaged. The beneficial effect for major parties is an artefact of regional subdivisions into many constituencies.

6. The Gini coefficient is equal to '0' in the case of total income equality (everyone has the same earnings) and to '1' in the case of total inequality (one person receives all the earnings). A Gini value between 0.2 and 0.35 is generally thought to represent a relatively equal income distribution.

REFERENCES

Berglund, Sten and Frank Aarebrot (1997), *The Political History of Eastern Europe in the 20th Century: The Struggle Between Democracy and Dictatorship*, Cheltenham, Edward Elgar.

Centeno, Angel Miguel and Tania Rands (1996), 'The World They Have Lost: An Assessment of Change in Eastern Europe', *Social Research,* Vol. 63, No. 2.

Culik, Jan (1999), 'Rising Discontent: The Czech Republic in 1999', *Central Europe Review*, Vol. 1, No. 25 (http://www.ce-review.org/99/25/culik25.*html*).

Dahl, Robert A. (1971), *Polyarchy: Participation and Opposition*, New Haven and London, Yale University Press.

Di Palma, Giuseppe (1990), *To Craft Democracies. An Essay on Democratic Transitions*, Berkeley, Los Angeles and Oxford, University of California Press.

Haerpfer, Christian, Cesary Milosinski and Claire Wallace (1999), 'Old and new Security Issues in Post-Communist Eastern Europe: Results of an 11 Nation Study', *Europe–Asia Studies*, Vol. 51, No. 6.

Hellén, Tomas, Sten Berglund and Frank Aarebrot (1998), 'From Transition to Consolidation', in Sten Berglund, Tomas Hellén and Frank Aarebrot, eds, *The Handbook of Political Change in Eastern Europe*, Cheltenham, Edward Elgar.

Higley, John, Judith Kullberg and Jan Pakulski (1996), 'The Persistence of Post-communist Elites', *Journal of Democracy*, Vol. 7, No. 2.

Kostadinova, Tatiana (2000), 'East European Public Support for NATO Membership: Fears and Aspirations', *Journal of Peace Research,* Vol. 37, No. 2.

Kupferberg, Feiwel (1999), *The Break-up of Communism in East Germany and Eastern Europe,* Hampshire and London, Macmillan.

Linz, Juan and Alfred Stepan (1996), *Problems of Democratic Transition and Consolidation: Southern Europe, South America and Post-Communist Europe*, Baltimore and London, The Johns Hopkins University Press.

National Human Development Report (1999), Commissioned by UNDP, produced by the

Romanian Academy, Bucharest, Romanian Academy Press.

Plasser, Fritz, Peter A. Ulram and Harald Waldrauch (1998), *Democratic Consolidation in East-Central Europe*, Hampshire and London, Macmillan.

Pridham, Geoffrey, ed., (1990), *Securing Democracy: Political Parties and Democratic Consolidation in Southern Europe*, London, Routledge.

Pridham, Geoffrey (1999), 'Democrazation in the Balkan countries. From theory to practice', in Geoffrey Pridham and Tom Gallagher, eds, *Experimenting with Democracy: Regime Change in the Balkans*, London, Routledge.

Przeworski, Adam, Michael Alvarez, Jose Antonio Cheibub and Fernando Limongi (1996), 'What Makes Democracies Endure?', *Journal of Democracy,* Vol. 7, No. 1.

Řeháková, Blanka and Klára Vlachová (1995), 'Subjective Mobility after 1989', *Czech Sociological Review,* Vol. 3, No. 2.

Reljić, Dušan (1998), 'Der Kampf um die Medien in Osteuropa', in Magarditsch Hatschikjan and Franz-Lohtar Altmann, eds, *Eliten im Wandel. Politische Führung, wirtschaftliche Macht und Meinungsbildung im neuen Osteuropa*, Paderborn, Verlag Ferdinand Schöningh.

Report on the Situation of Roma and Sinti in the OSCE Area (2000), OSCE, High Commissioner on National Minorities.

Rose, Richard and Christian Haerpfer (1998), *New Democracies Barometer V. A 12-Nation Survey,* Studies in Public Policy 306, Glasgow, University of Strathclyde.

Rose, Richard, William Mishler and Christian Haerpfer (1998), *Democracy and its Alternatives: Understanding Post-Communist Societies,* Baltimore and London: The Johns Hopkins University Press.

Sartori, Giovanni (1976), *Parties and Party Systems: A Framework for Analysis,* Cambridge, Cambridge University Press.

Schedler, Andreas (1998), 'What is Democratic Consolidation?', *Journal of Democracy,* Vol. 9, No. 2.

Schöpflin, George (1993), *Politics in Eastern Europe, 1945–1992*, Oxford and Cambridge, Blackwell.

Suchocka, Hanna (2000), *The Constitution and Transformation – Selected Questions*, paper presented at the 6th World Congress of the ICCEES, Tampere, Finland, August 2000.

Vogt, Henri (2000), *The Utopia of Post-Communism: The Czech Republic, Eastern Germany and Estonia After 1989*, Doctor of Philosophy Thesis, St. Antony's College, University of Oxford.

Women in Transition (1999), The MONEE Project, Regional Monitoring Report No. 6, UNICEF/ International Child Development Centre, Florence.

3. Societal Fragmentation and Post-Communist Party Politics

This chapter seeks to understand how the current Central and East European party systems relate to, or are dependent on, the general societal fragmentation in these countries. Because of this aim, there are also two rather distinct points of departure in our analysis. In the first part, we will explore the phenomenon of societal fragmentation in post-communist Europe. Two notions are particularly invaluable for this exploration, namely *atomization* and *individualism*, the former having a negative and the latter a positive meaning, although they are also in many respects interdependent. In the second part, we will depict the general pattern of Central and East European party system development over the past ten years, particularly concentrating on the specific problems parties have had to come to terms with during the first post-communist decade.

The third and concluding part, then attempts to create a synthesis of the two preceding ones. The basic argument is that owing to societal fragmentation – particularly the increasing influence of individualism – parties will encounter serious problems in their future development. Above all, they will face a very difficult task as they try to create an identity for themselves. This identity should be simultaneously flexible and firm, flexible enough to satisfy individualized individuals, but still firm enough to make for meaningful distinctions between parties.

Fragmented Societies

In a 1994 article Erik Allardt, the renowned Finnish sociologist, draws attention to four societal trends that according to him characterize contemporary Europe:

1. the weakening of the bonds between class and politics;
2. the fragmentation of society: the decreased importance of

45

comprehensive and long-standing social systems;
3. a special case of fragmentation: the relative decline of the nation state;
4. and finally, as a result of fragmentation, the re-emergence of civil society.

It is a moot question whether these trends are the most relevant ones for depicting European societies today. Such trends as globalization, integration, or, regarding the region of interest to us, simply the task of constructing a new economic and political system are certainly also highly significant. But it may be noted that all four trends named by Allardt have a common denominator, namely fragmentation. We will follow Allardt's line of argument and assume that this phenomenon shaped the 1990s more than anything else.

It is obvious, however, that the reasons for fragmentation in Central and Eastern Europe are somewhat different from those in the West. Two factors appear particularly relevant in this respect: the communist legacy of atomization, and the new kind of individuality and individualism, modelled upon the West, that East Europeans have had to learn. Let us take a closer look at these two factors and their influence on societal fragmentation in post-communist countries.

*

One can argue, albeit engaging in a degree of simplification, that the societies of Central and Eastern Europe became thoroughly *atomized* during the era of communism. Atomization has been a widely discussed concept in the social sciences, but we will refrain from going into details here.[1] Suffice it to say that in our understanding atomization not only refers to minimal interaction between different actors on a particular societal level but also to the estrangement of individuals and social groups *vis-à-vis* the state and the realm of politics. In other words, atomization may include both a horizontal and a vertical component. During the years of communism the latter was often dominant – people's (non)-relations with the political system heavily influenced their relations with each other as well.

It is also noteworthy that atomization is usually a combination of personal deliberate choices and some kind of pressure evolving from the surroundings: a person experiences or judges a certain situation in a manner that leads to atomization; for someone else the same situation would not have caused any problems whatsoever. The notion of 'negative integration' (Rose 1995) illuminates this delicate balance between voluntary and forced atomization: people were bound to reflect upon their relationship with the system even if they did not want to, and through this reflexive process they decided to become negatively integrated as they realized that the ways of the system were not exactly their cup of tea.

In Eastern Europe – as everywhere else – the level of atomization varied a great deal, depending on the ruthlessness of repression, on people's position in society, and on the cultural traditions of different nations, classes, or social groups. In Poland the Catholic Church was always able to resist societal atomization to a greater extent than churches, for instance, in the GDR or Czechoslovakia; the church always towered as an alternative public space for the Poles. Still, the logic was similar everywhere: people voluntarily stuck to their private spheres and ignored the public; they built walls around themselves, and within these walls they could live a more or less happy life. Society thus came to be compartmentalized; it became a *Nischengesellschaft*.[2] The niches may not have been bigger than a single family, although sometimes even that was too big. A 22-year-old university student from Prague put this point well, as she described her life during communism in a 1993 interview:[3]

> We were just living our kind of life – and at that time, you know, in the 80s, it was not as oppressive as for example in the 50s. [...] Still, it was an oppressive regime but then again, if you belonged to the generation that was brought up under this oppression, after some time you built your protective wall and lived your own life. [...] You didn't really care what the cruel world was like behind your wall, which was bad in fact, but that was basically the only way to survive.

The virtual absence of societal dynamism was probably the most obvious consequence of – or perhaps reason for – East European atomization. The notion of 'flattened societies' (Wessels and Klingemann 1994), which refers to the highly similar wage, consumption, and social security levels within communist countries, helps to clarify the complex relation between lacking dynamism and atomization. A waterfall may serve as a useful metaphor: as is well known, the steeper and higher a waterfall is, the more energy it contains. In a flattened society, as in a flat landscape, the waterfalls remain small – ergo, there is very little by way of dynamism in society. Or, indeed, there may be no waterfalls at all, just small lagoons of still water which do not have to mix with each other, hence atomization. On the other hand, this absence of societal energy was in fact functional from the regime's point of view: in an atomized society the emergence of an energetic movement that could challenge the governing regime was rather unlikely.

*

The atomization of the communist era was, above all, a function of two mutually connected factors. One was the *legitimacy of the system*; the other was *fear*. Generally, as the system's legitimacy decreased – particularly in the 1980s owing to economic recession and ever louder demands for basic human rights – people opted consciously for their own private spheres. An overwhelming majority thus became politically very passive, although they usually continued to participate in the ventures of the semi-official and semi-compulsory organizations, for example industrial, peasant, youth, and women's unions. This overall pattern was occasionally disrupted by the well-known revolts against the communist parties, notably in Hungary 1956, Czechoslovakia 1968, and Poland 1980–81, when a great number of people suddenly became politically mobilized, worked together for a common goal, and reformed their relationship with the system. The level of both horizontal and vertical atomization decreased dramatically under such extraordinary conditions. On the other hand, after the crushing of these revolts the need to identify with the system again declined dramatically – and vertical atomization increased accordingly.

It is also worth bearing in mind that from the mid-1970s onwards, a kind of civil society – or, to use the concept of Hungarian philosopher Elemer Hankiss, a 'Second Society' – began to reappear in Eastern Europe (Hankiss 1988). A network of independent civic organizations was born; a network that also counteracted atomization. However, the number of people involved in the activities of the Second Society remained relatively low in most East European countries, and large parts of the population were practically unaware of the existence of these organizations. For example, in Czechoslovakia, the original signatories of *Charter 77*, the most influential civic organization, numbered only 242; even by 1989 the movement had not attracted more than 1886 signatories (Prečan 1990). Even though this may not say much about the real influence of *Charter 77* within the country (there were of course a number of more or less active supporters), it does reveal something about the difficulties involved in undermining atomization in Czechoslovak society. Solidarity in Poland is naturally the major exception to this rule. In a few months after it had been founded in 1979, it had already acquired some 9.5 million dues-paying members (Grzybowski 1991, 61).[4]

It is also worth asking what happened to the ruling communist parties as the legitimacy of the system decreased. We can safely argue that the attitude of the members to their parties became increasingly critical as time passed; the Party was no longer seen as the right means to realize any beautiful ideals of socialism. Indeed, one explanation for the smooth transition of 1989 is that not only ordinary citizens but also many party members, even party cadres, had lost faith in the legitimacy of the governmental supremacy of the Communist Party. The communist parties gradually became instruments for advancing personal aspirations rather than for building a better world. Party membership may not have been indispensable for securing a place in the best schools and universities for one's children but it was certainly not harmful. This self-seeking nature of party membership was, in fact, one form of fragmentation: even within the party people built walls around themselves.

Let us now turn to the second essential factor leading to atomization during the communist era, namely fear. It is evident that a certain amount of fear was absolutely vital for the endurance of the communist systems, as it is, perhaps, for all totalitarian systems. Yet, fear was not so much a phenomenon of everyday life; it rather existed in the realm of what is usually reserved for the political, in the space where individuals formed relationships to the governing system; those who never formed such relationships, probably never experienced the fear, although its existence definitely was no secret. As Mary Fulbrook notes, regarding the GDR, 'the climate of fear was the outer parameter of existence within the total *Überwachungstaat*; it did not have to be a feature of everyday life' (Fulbrook 1997, 55). It was thus wise not to create a relationship with the system at all, for there was always the possibility that fear would have become an inner parameter. It was actually pragmatic to be vertically atomized.

Possibly the most serious and most lasting consequence of fear during the communist era was that it destroyed the possibility of *trust* in society. True, people could trust that they would get a job, and a place for their children in a kindergarten, as well as basic health care – things that they may not have at the moment. In this context, however, trust refers to the elementary confidence between people, on the one hand, and to citizens' belief in their polity, in those who govern them, on the other; this is the kind of trust that provides the basis for the emergence of any common morals. People could not necessarily even trust their close friends; often the family remained the only safe haven (Šiklová 1997). (Of course people usually trusted their friends, a fact that in the former GDR has led to bitter revelations as the *Stasi* archives have gradually revealed their secrets.)

It was not just fear that determined people's relationship to the political order; the system began to appear ever more ridiculous as the gap between promises and gains increased. Attitudes towards politics thus grew profoundly ambivalent with the passage of time. This ambivalence between fear and ridicule could not but engender a profound sense of distrust towards all public institutions – a sense that remains a conspicuous feature in most countries of the region. But it is too often forgotten that this phenomenon can only be understood in the light of the legacy of communism, that is it is not only caused by problems emerging after the transition.[5]

The thesis of communist era atomization is naturally more complex than this. One counter-argument is that during communism people actually had a stronger sense of community than they do now; nowadays popular wisdom has it that people only think about business opportunities and their own self-interests. This brings us to the final point about fear in Central and Eastern

Europe before 1989: paradoxically, fear can also be seen as a force opposing atomization. The following reply of a twenty-seven-year-old Estonian female student illuminates this well; in the autumn of 1997 she was asked: 'Many people claim that as the old system disappeared a certain feeling of community also disappeared. Do you agree?' Her reply:

> [...] only if we take into consideration that communism was a threat to our identity. Our identity was in danger, that was the factor that brought people together. It was fear that connected us, communism didn't create any feelings of community as such.

It remains an open question whether this kind of 'communitarianism' actually resists atomization or not. Or maybe we should simply talk about 'sociability in the midst of atomization'?

*

How, then, has this communist legacy developed under the new circumstances? Ideally, the collapse of the old system should have led to the disappearance of atomization. The essential freedoms – of speech and expression, of demonstrating, voting, and association – that have been introduced should have provided a means to resist vertical as well as horizontal forms of atomization. Alas, reality has not been this rosy. Three, in many ways interrelated, points seem relevant in this respect. First of all, it has become apparent that the profound sense of distrust that communism had established could not be erased from society in the course of a mere decade; instead, ordinary citizens are now afraid of themselves rather than of the 'others' – that is the Party. Re-establishing trust has been all the more difficult while a number of people have ruthlessly sought to benefit from the turbulence in society, and while, as will be seen, mismanagement and even corruption have definitely not been unknown phenomena in most European post-communist polities.

Some rather striking survey evidence testifies to the continued existence of distrust in society. In a Bulgarian survey in November 1998, as many as 85 per cent of respondents said that they could not fully trust other people (*National Human Development Report*, Bulgaria 1999, 66; cf. Mishler and Rose 1998, 13). In the New Democracies Barometer V of 1998, 52 per cent of respondents in eleven Central and East European countries claimed that 'the level of corruption and taking bribes' had increased in comparison with the communist regimes; only 5 per cent believed that it had decreased (Rose and Haerpfer 1998, 58; cf. Chapter 6 in this volume).

Secondly, many people, especially pensioners and middle-aged persons without education, have experienced severe material and existential problems during the past ten years. They have often felt disappointed, cheated and estranged, and, as a result, become even more atomized than before, at least in relation to the political power that they have blamed for their problems. At the same time, there are indications that those who have profited from the transformation are often not willing to share their successes with those who have been less fortunate. All in all, the dramatically increased differences in material standards of living, all the disappointments and unfulfilled expectations that people have experienced over the past ten years, have emerged as new sources of atomization and alienation.

Thirdly, and almost paradoxically, there is also some evidence that the need to adapt to new circumstances as quickly as possible, the need to learn new things, has been so strong that it has also had negative consequences for how people behave towards each other. Above all, it has often been argued that there were more feelings of unity or community among people earlier, more time to spend with friends, more willingness to give a hand if needed – although, as noted above, all this may have been a byproduct of the coercive nature of the system. A young Estonian university teacher reflected upon this in a 1997 interview (Centeno and Rands 1996):

> At the moment people are relatively speaking very much concerned about money, it is actually banal to say so, everybody says so. So when we compare this to the time of the Singing Revolution [1988–89] or even to the Soviet time, nobody was really allowed to have that much money and people were in many senses spiritually freer, they visited one another. [...] There seemed to be more time to sit down, whereas at the moment everybody seems to be in a hurry. If you ring to an old friend who now works in a private company, you always have the feeling that you can't talk for too long, that he is in a hurry, that he's got something more important to do, but I hope this will disappear with the passage of time.

All in all, the level of atomization in society has not necessarily decreased during the post-communist era, although its forms, and the basic logic causing it, have definitely changed. Nevertheless, there is also reason to be optimistic: in so far as atomization is a result of the communist legacy and the rapid transformation, its influence will decrease with the consolidation of the new system. Moreover, and some might say this is not true – the level of atomization may decrease owing to the new individualism that the collapse of communism has engendered. This can probably better be understood in a historical perspective: the atomization of the communist era may have been a result of people's unsuccessful attempts to resist the uniformity that the system imposed on its subjects. People simply built walls around themselves in order to find a space for their individuality, for their individual freedom, for their personal development, but since the dividing line between individualism and atomization is very narrow indeed, they in the end found themselves atomized. This absence of individualism may also be seen as an important reason for the revolutions: the imbalance between the apparent individualism of the West and the forced collectivism of the East could not be sustained indefinitely.[6]

*

Historian Tony Judt has described East European communist-era perceptions of West Europe as follows:

> [...] the place where 'Europe' continued to function as a powerful myth and common project was in Eastern Europe, where dissidents, young people, and even reform-minded communist managers longed to share in the personal, political, and moral benefits of 'Europeanness', to 'return' to a Europe from which they had been cut off by their enforced attachment to a different and distinctly dysfunctional myth, 'socialism' (Judt 1999, 167).

Indeed, there is no doubt that prior to the change of 1989 'Europe', or the Western world in general, provided an attractive ideal for many citizens of the communist countries. Besides, as the material gap between the two systems began to widen in the 1980s, and as more and more information from the West streamed into these countries, the fascination with this mythical other world gradually increased. Two aspects of this 'West' seemed particularly important: one was the freedom(s) people there enjoyed, especially the freedom to travel; and the other the high material standard of living, the possibilities of consumption, that they were blessed with. In practice, of course, these two aspects intermingled.

Yet, most people's attitude towards the West remained profoundly ambivalent, at least with respect to the capitalist economic system. Many ordinary citizens had only a limited idea of daily life on the other side of the iron curtain. The ideological machinery of the communist parties was not totally unsuccessful in blurring the information about the capitalist world to be gauged from the growing presence of Western media. Above all, the prevalence of such problems as unemployment and inequality in the West was emphasized by the communist regimes. With respect to the economic order, therefore, the two main views about the West, both over-simplified, might have been phrased as 'capitalism is a paradise' and 'capitalism just as communism has its internal shortcomings' – the latter being of course the pragmatic formula that helped people to survive under communist rule, a formula that legitimized their political system to at least some degree.

Contrary to common expectations, the relations between Europeans in East and West did not necessarily become much easier after the collapse of communism. Perhaps the most important reason for this was that this 'West' was not of the kind people had expected: Western societies had long ago entered what is often referred to as the post-modern era, whereas the tradition of modernism still prevailed in Eastern Europe.[7] In more concrete terms, the societies of the East proved to be more different from the West than people had realized when they took to the streets in 1989. There were remarkable differences in terms of value orientations, personal skills, forms of entertainment, environmental awareness and technological level. With the collapse of communism, it became possible for the citizens of Eastern Europe to learn more about the Western modes of life, to adapt to the patterns of 'post-modernism'. As it has turned out, this process of adaptation has been easy for some people but extremely difficult for others. The young, the educated, and the urban have been adjusting quickly to post-modern conditions whereas the old, the non-educated and the rural still seem to stick to the patterns of modernism. In fact, the new, post-communist pattern of social stratification has by and large emerged along the lines of this 'cleavage' between post-modernism and modernism.[8]

One central aspect of Western 'post-modernism' is the essential role of 'individualism'. The importance of the individual and individuality has therefore also increased in post-communist Eastern Europe, as people have sought to become more and more 'Western'. It is worth bearing in mind, however, that increased individualism is also a 'natural' consequence of the disappearance of the old system, a system that had sought to protect the individual from cradle to grave.

The new individualism comprises two basic components. One is the idea of *self-governance*, which refers to the possibility to make unconstrained decisions, to take initiatives, to choose freely, to live without a predetermined future; in brief, this is the primary result of the new freedoms that were acquired in 1989. Moreover, and this will no doubt become more and more important, self-governance also involves an element of reflexivity. As access to information is no longer limited in Central and Eastern Europe, people can freely reflect upon the affairs of their societies. The other component consists of the *value orientations* people hold, especially the consumption-based, enjoyment-seeking, self-expressive life-styles they have tried to attain; it is these values in particular that people of the East have tried to adopt from the West.

The two components are analytically distinct but interrelated: in general, it is only through self-governance that a self-expressive life-style becomes possible. It is also noteworthy that the difference between these two components resembles the distinction made by Dieter Fuchs and Hans-Dieter Klingemann. Their point of departure is Europe's continuing process of societal modernization, which also involves individual modernization. The latter counts two components: an increase in personal skills and a change in value orientations (Fuchs and Klingemann 1995). We would contend that the idea of self-governance is clearly more basic in the East European context than the acquisition of new personal skills, which are merely instruments for making independent decisions.

The hypothesis of rising individualism has been a central theme in Western social science at least since the days of Georg Simmel. The validity of this hypothesis has been very difficult to ascertain in a watertight fashion despite great efforts to do so in recent decades. In the former communist countries, this has proved even more difficult on account of the lack of reliable data, particularly from the communist era. Yet a few empirical findings exist that support the thesis in the conditions of post-communist Eastern Europe. On the basis of extensive surveys conducted in Estonia between 1990 and 1995, Lauristin and Vihalemm have argued that such values as technological development, wisdom, and world peace are in decline, whereas such aspirations as attaining a pleasant and comfortable life have been growing in importance. The conclusion made by these two scholars leaves hardly any room for interpretation:

> A significant role in this [individualization] process has been played by a growing influence of the Western entertainment industry, but more important is an increasing consumerism of the transitional society as a whole. After decades of scarcity and depression, the desire to lead a pleasant and comfortable life, and the wish to rid oneself of everyday routine and economic problems seems overwhelming. The younger generations in particular are rapidly integrating into the international youth culture, assuming the individualistic-hedonistic value orientations which prevail there Lauristin and Vihalemm 1997, 254–5).

The words of a 23-year-old female student from Eastern Europe nicely echo this conclusion as she answers the question whether she sees society as individualistic at the moment – her reflection could be from anywhere in today's Eastern Europe:

> This is what I meant [when I talked about] this 'just for fun'. The West, with its freedom and capitalism, with its welfare, simply brings new possibilities for individual, egoistic development. It's easy today to be after pleasure only, nobody will stop you, you just have to make sure you have enough money.

The available evidence does support the thesis of increased individualism under post-communist conditions, but we should be wary of interpreting this as a one-dimensional phenomenon. At the end of the day, the level of 'individualism' is always subject to the overall historical context – if it changes, the pattern of individualistic as opposed to collectivist behaviour also changes. The more collectivist values are easily forgotten when there are no collective needs or threats on the horizon. Again using Estonia as an example, as the return to independence started to appear more or less certain by the year 1990, ordinary Estonians could leave the realm of official politics to parties and politicians proper, as it was now possible and safe to be concerned with one's individual affairs only. But if the situation were to take a turn for the worse and the national existence of Estonians were to be jeopardized, it is very likely that people would become highly collectivist once again. Another example: the decision to join NATO was made with surprisingly little public discussion and criticism in Poland, Hungary and the Czech Republic. It was cast as a question of collective security, as a prerequisite of all individual aspirations.

Be that as it may, individualism, and particularly its self-governance component, is something that people have had to learn after 1989. To make one's own decisions and to take initiatives has not always been easy, but it has required a great deal of mental adaptation and learning. This was also suggested by two young Estonian men in September 1997, as they answered the question what had been the most difficult thing to learn after the breakdown of communism:

I think the most difficult thing to learn has been the relationship to yourself.

I don't know about myself. About people in general I would say that it is the fact that you have to rely on yourself in the end, you have to 'find' things yourself, you have to 'watch' things yourself. You cannot expect that others would do things for you.

Two important aspects of this learning process need to be mentioned. Firstly, individualism – and the freedom that has made it possible – also spells responsibilities. Without the recognition of the responsibilities towards other people, individualism easily turns into horizontal atomization. As indicated above, many feel that this has happened far too often during the past decade. Due to the communist legacy of coerced equality (that is uniformity) and the absence of freedom during that era, freedom is presently perceived as a much more important objective than equality or responsibility towards others; people need to be rewarded for their achievements rather than on the basis of equality. Individual freedom has thus become a central moral principle at the expense of those for whom the transformation has caused severe problems. The weakness of civil society under post-communism can also be understood in this light: activity in a civic organization requires responsibility towards other members of society (cf. Chapter 6).

The other point, closely related to the first one, is that this individualism ought not to be an exclusive category (not at least in the sense of the Western *Zeitgeist* of the 1990s). On the contrary, it should involve inclusion, fusion, dialogue and communication. Alliance, fusion and integration are the catchwords of the day rather than confrontation and opposition; the latter belonged to the era of the black-and-white world, dominated by two rival political systems (Weil 1993). Individualism can thus mean cooperation, and thereby also reduce atomization in society; it can even be conducive to a positive development of civil society, if people decide to express their individuality through civic organizations. In this sense the Central and East European countries still seem to have a long way to go. The structure of public opinion is still permeated by notions of contradiction and opposition – native Baltic people vs. Russians, capitalism vs. communism, past vs. future, NATO vs. neutrality – although to a lesser extent than ten years ago.

Finally, a note of caution is needed with regard to attitudes towards the West among East Europeans and with regard to individualism: variations within and between countries and nationalities are considerable. Latvians and Estonians generally perceive the Russian soul as much more collective-minded than their own. By virtue of their individualism, Estonians, Latvians and Lithuanians always belonged to the 'West' and could not become part of the 'East'. Moreover, it is noteworthy that in the Balkans, the level of 'collectivism', for example in the form of traditional family values and clientelism, may be much higher than in the heartland of Central Europe, which is historically strongly influenced by Protestantism and its brand of individualism. One could therefore assume that in Central European countries such as the Czech Republic or Hungary, it would be easier to adapt to the demands of the new individualism than in, say, Russia or Romania. But even this may be too simplistic: educational, social and generational factors may in the end be more important determinants of the level of individualism than national stereotypes.

*

Let us return, for a moment, to Allardt's classification with which this chapter started, and particularly to the second and third factors listed by him. The second factor addresses itself to the 'absence of long-standing and comprehensive social systems'. The rapid change in Eastern Europe has made it virtually impossible for such systems to emerge, and those that may have existed previously are still undergoing profound transformation. Moreover, particularly owing to the increasingly individualistic life styles and the presence of atomization that we have discussed above, such systems are not very likely to emerge in the foreseeable future.

Allardt's third point, that is the relative decline of the nation state, may take place in Central and Eastern Europe as well. The level of 'post-modernism' or 'modernism' within these societies may also change attitudes towards nationhood. For 'post-modernists', who may acquire an international job, and start reading *The Economist* instead of the local newspaper, the nation state is likely to signify something completely different than it does, say, for small holders. Differing popular opinions about 'country' and 'nation' can also lead to increasing fragmentation of society (cf. Chapter 4).

More generally, these attitudinal differences are prime examples of the *Ungleichzeitigkeit* or non-synchronicity of Central and East European societies: people seem to live in different times, for they have adapted to the new circumstances with varying paces; this 'living-in-different-times' naturally also leads to societal fragmentation. While this feature exists in all societies to some degree, in today's Eastern Europe it may be exceptionally meaningful due to the rapidity and profoundness of the ongoing transformation. In fact, along with atomization and individualism, *Ungleichzeitigkeit* could be seen as the third determinant of East European fragmentation; it strongly interacts with the other two factors and we have therefore refrained from analysing it separately. We have summarized our arguments up to this point in Table 3.1.

Table 3.1: Main determinants of social fragmentation in Eastern Europe

	Before 1989	After 1989	Possible future role
Atomization – basically negative, but during communism also a way of 'surviving' – two forms: 'vertical' in relation to the polity and 'horizontal' between people.	The less legitimacy the system had, the more vertical atomization. Fear led to distrust towards other people and the polity.	Still present in spite of the new freedoms and the end of systemic fear: Distrust still usual, inequality dramatically increased, transformation as such difficult.	Increasing individualism easily turns into atomization if the former cannot assume collective forms. Atomization in relation to the realm of politics will continue unless parties create core identities for themselves.
Individualism – basically positive but turns easily into atomization.	Constrained by the limited individual freedom and coerced uniformity. Attempts at individualism easily led to atomization.	Self-governance. Increased reflexivity. Consumption-based, enjoyment-seeking value orientations. Increasing differences in terms of individualism: non-synchronicity. Models sought from the West.	Will grow in importance, particularly as regards hedonistic value orientations. Civic organizations, for example political parties should provide channels for fulfilling individualism.

One concluding remark still needs to be made. We have deliberately avoided assigning weights to atomization and individualism. The truth is that we do not know which of them – atomization or individualism – dominates at present; nor does it really matter. We do believe that individualism will continue to grow in importance and, to the extent that individualistic actors will be sensitive to responsibility and cooperation in the sense described above, the amount of atomization will at least not significantly increase. However, fences between the two phenomena are so low that it is often difficult to see which is dominant; things may change very rapidly. Moreover, the balance between atomization and individualism is subject to variation as we move from one societal sector to the other; especially in politics 'individualism' often materializes in the form of atomization. Why this is so, is the theme of the next part of the chapter.

Party Politics without Traditions

Probably the harshest post-communist criticism of political parties and party politics in general originates from the pen of celebrated Russian novelist and ex-dissident Alexander Solzhenitsyn. In his view, parties only serve to fragment society; they divide societal harmony – just as the Latin root of the word *partiri,* 'to divide into parts', presupposes. He writes:

> The struggle between parties is not even remotely concerned with the search for truth: what is at stake is party prestige wresting away some executive power. [...] Party rivalry destroys the national will. The principle of party-mindedness necessarily involves the suppression of individuality, and every party reduces and coarsens the personal element. An individual will have views, while a party offers an ideology (Solzhenitsyn 1991, 69–70).

Although one may have serious problems in agreeing with Solzhenitsyn, his critical view appears surprisingly useful as one tries to understand the development of party systems in Central and Eastern Europe since the late 1980s.

The development of party systems may be divided into three major phases. In the first phase in the latter half of the 1980s, a number of new civic movements were founded or, as for example in the case of Poland's *Solidarność* (Solidarity), existing movements were reactivated. These movements were originally not meant to become political parties; their organizational structure therefore remained fairly loose. Towards the end of the 1980s, the popularity of these movements gradually increased, so that they eventually came to be the most important actors in ousting the communist regimes. In view of the revolutionary events of the late 1980s, they were very widely supported indeed: for example in Estonia, several events, notably song festivals, where the Estonian Popular Front, *Rahvarinne,* played a crucial role, attracted hundreds of thousands of participants in a country of approximately one million native Estonians. In Czechoslovakia, at least half the population participated in the general strike on 27 November 1989, which practically sealed the success of the Velvet Revolution in that country, and the leaders of *Občanské fórum* (Civic Forum) soon assumed power. As already mentioned, Solidarity in Poland had some ten million members in a country of 38 million, and in the first semi-free election in June 1989 it gained 99 out of 100 seats in the Upper House of the Parliament. In a word, for the majority of East Europeans these organizations epitomized the 'New Truth', the negation of the Truth that the communist systems had sought to teach their subjects.

In the second phase, partly overlapping the first one, new parties started to emerge with remarkable speed and the civic movements gradually started to crumble. In most countries this phase started only just before the collapse of communist rule or right after it, and by and large ended by the time of the first democratic elections. In the Baltic countries, however, party formation began as early as in 1987, that is several years before the regaining of independence in August 1991. Also in Hungary, which more or less skipped the first phase, the situation was somewhat different. The Hungarian Democratic Forum (HDF), already structured like a party, was founded in the autumn of 1987, and the year 1988 saw the emergence of several political groups that later became parties, such as FIDESZ and the Alliance of Free Democrats (SZDSZ). As political parties were legalized in early 1989, the number of parties skyrocketed (Nyyssönen 1999, 128–9).

All sorts of parties were founded. First, there were parties with a clear connection to a civic movement or parties that even saw themselves as part of a civic movement. In most cases this kind of party formation from within factionalized the original movements and thus paved the way for their break up. Hence, although a party or an electoral alliance carrying the name of a civic movement usually participated in the first democratic election, the success of these parties was rather modest compared with the popularity of the movements just a few months earlier. The Czech lands were the main exception to this rule, as the Civic Forum gained some 50 per cent of the votes in the first election in June 1990, but it effectively split up shortly after these elections. In Romania, too, the organization that had managed to topple the Ceauşescu dictatorship, *Frontul Salvării Naţionale* (the National Salvation Front), gained an overwhelming victory in the 1990 elections, two thirds of the vote. Yet, the leaders of the Front were only half-heartedly reformed communists; and as the communist power apparatus was still partly in place, the Front was able to control most of the media against the fragmented opposition throughout the electoral campaign.

There were also completely independent new parties. There were parties that traditionally exist in most multi-party polities, such as social-democratic, agrarian, conservative and patriotic parties. Some of them, particularly the conservative and agrarian parties, claimed that they were the successors of parties from the inter-war period. And there were all kinds of single-issue parties: women's parties, ecological parties, ethnic parties, radical democratic parties, parties that were founded primarily as jokes. Most parties of this kind remained insignificant under post-communist conditions.

Lastly, there were new parties that were in fact not all that new. The old communist parties did not simply go away but reappeared under a new, usually some sort of socialist, label. Moreover, in Poland, the GDR, Czechoslovakia, and Bulgaria several 'bloc parties', that had cooperated more or less closely with the leading party under communism, now became independent and started to distance themselves, with varying success, from their former rulers (Segert and Machos 1995, 247).[9]

In one respect the appearance of all these parties was not self-evident at all. During the years of communism many dissident voices in Eastern

Europe had altogether discarded the traditional forms of politics, including parties and party politics. They had preached in favour of new kinds of political formations, of the kind that would better match such concepts as 'anti-politics'. But the ideas of these intellectuals did not find much resonance after the change had actually arrived. Most people simply hailed the new parties as a sign of freedom, as an indisputable emblem of new times. Yet, it soon became apparent that the emergence of these different parties and the dissolution of civic movements signified a lamentable transformation from the unanimity of revolutions to the reality – or even banality – of party struggle. It seemed that there was no longer a Truth in society, no unifying enemy, no all-embracing idea of resistance. This became all the more manifest as the euphoria of 1989 gradually faded away with the appearance of the first practical problems and disappointments. The logical consequence of this new party struggle was that a great majority of people appeared to lose their confidence and interest in parties and politics in general.

In the third phase which still continues, party systems have started to consolidate and stabilize although the changes from one electoral period to another remain fairly remarkable by Western standards (party mergers and splits, high electoral volatility). In spite of this people have remained highly indifferent towards parties and other political institutions; party system consolidation has taken place under general indifference and distrust. Parties have thus not gained a position that would even remotely resemble the position, the popularity and legitimacy, of the revolutionary civic movements of the late 1980s. Many parties simply cannot represent one Truth.[10]

Party Fragmentation and the Instability of Party Systems

Let us now take a somewhat more detailed look at the development of post-communist party systems and electoral politics. In order to do this, it is useful to refer to Attila Ágh's (1998, 101–2) recent article. In it, Ágh lists five tendencies that characterized party politics in Central and Eastern Europe in the 1990s:

1. electoral and party fragmentation;
2. high electoral volatility and protest voting – the volatility figures from the first to the second post-communist election in East-Central Europe varied from 28 per cent to well over 50 per cent whereas the Western long-term mean is under 10 per cent (Tóka 1998);
3. the return of the 'post-communist' vote and parties – in Poland, Hungary, and Lithuania the reformed communist parties managed to take office after the second, and in Bulgaria after the third post-communist elections;

4. growing abstention at elections, Slovakia being the most notable exception;[11]
5. declining (low, in any event) confidence in parliaments and parties.

Taken at face value, this list may seem convincing. But the last point of the list seems to be overwhelmingly more important than the others, or one could simply see the first four as practical implications of the fifth. This is also the point that we arrived at above. Let us therefore concentrate on the reasons for the apparent indifference towards parties.

The first reason is the same as in Ágh's list: party fragmentation. Post-communism has simply seen too many parties competing for the support of the electorate.[12] However, this point is already history, particularly considering the number of effective parties, at least in the economically developed parts of Central and Eastern Europe, on which the analysis of this chapter is mainly based (Table 3.2). The primary reason for this has been clever electoral engineering. In most of the first parliamentary elections an electoral threshold was introduced so that even parties with renowned leaders and reasonably well-organized party structures failed to win enough votes to secure parliamentary representation. In Hungary, for example, some 40 parties emerged in the year after the establishment of a multi-party system in 1989, but only seven parties succeeded in winning seats in the first democratic parliament due to the 4 per cent threshold. (Tóka 1998, 240). Poland was a major exception, as there was no threshold clause in the country's first post-communist electoral law. Due to this, as many as 24 parties or groupings were voted into the *Sejm* in the first totally free elections of October 1991. By the next elections, two years later, an electoral threshold had been accepted (and d'Hondt's system applied); as a consequence, the number of parties in the *Sejm* dropped to six (plus the representatives of the German minority). Romania is another case where no threshold was introduced in the first democratic elections, which is why 18 groupings out of over 70 that ran for election were voted into the House of Deputies. Nevertheless, it is somewhat difficult to talk about fragmentation in the Romanian case, since the National Salvation Front took two thirds of the vote.

One could of course argue that with even stricter electoral engineering, less fragmentation could have been possible. Indeed, the fact that most countries opted for proportional representation (PR) – at least for half or more of the seats – was undoubtedly conducive to party political fragmentation. Rejecting PR would probably have been interpreted as being against the principles of political pluralism. Be that as it may, party fragmentation is hardly a primary problem in the most developed post-communist political systems at the moment.

Table 3.2: Post-communist parliamentary elections in East Central Europe (lower houses)[a]

Country	Elections held: month/ year	No of parties with seats	Turnout % (1st round)	Threshold % (parties/ coalitions)	Remarks
Estonia	9/92	9	67	*5	* concerns national-level
	3/95	7	69	*5	compensation mandates
	3/99	7	57	*5	
Latvia	6/93	8	90	4	
	10/95	9	72	5	
	10/98	6	72	5	
Lithua-nia	11/92	11	**75	4	*9 parties gained a seat only in single-mandate districts
	11/96	*14	53	5/7	
	(10/00)			5/7	**average of two rounds
Poland	10/91	24	43	None	* '1' = German minority
	9/93	*6+1	52	5/8/**7	** threshold for nationally allocated mandates
	9/97	*5+1	48	5/8/**7	
Czech Republic	*6/90	4	97	5	* figures for the Federal Assembly of Czechoslovakia
	*6/92	6	85	5	
	6/96	6	76	5/**7-11	** depending on the number of parties in the coalition
	6/98	5	74	5/**7-11	
Slovakia	*6/90	5	99	5	* figures for the Federal Assembly of Czechoslovakia
	*6/92	5	84	5	
	10/94	9	76	5	** parties must prove they have at least 10,000 members
	9/98	6	84	**5	
Hungary	5/90	7	65	*4	* concerns national-level compensation mandates
	4/94	7	69	*5	
	5/98	5	57	*5	
Slovenia	4/90	*8+1	83	**	* '1' = national minorities
	12/92	*8+1	86	**	** lists numerically entitled to at least 3 seats out of 90 on national level eligible to remainder seats
	10/96	*7+1	73	**	
Romania	5/90	18	86	None	* '1' = minority deputies
	9/92	7	76	3	** maximum; depends on the No. of parties within coalition
	11/96	*6+1	76	3/**8	
Bulgaria	6/90	4	89	4	
	10/91	3	84	4	
	12/94	5	75	4	
	4/97	5	62	4	

a: The ten countries included in the table are those with the best democratic record among the post-communist countries (see 'Introduction' in Berglund, Hellén and Aarebrot 1998). The order of the countries is from north to south. *Source*: Berglund, Hellén and Aarebrot (1998).

As Table 3.2 shows, there is still a fair number of parties represented in the parliaments, but not that many more than, say, in the Nordic countries. Moreover, the number of effective parties is usually significantly lower than the number of parties in the parliament.

Table 3.3: Post-communist parliamentary elections – Albania and countries devolved from former Yugoslavia and the Soviet Union

Country	Elections held	Parties/coalitions with seats [a]	Turnout % (first rounds)
Albania	1991	3	97
	1992	5	91
	1996	5	89
	1997	3	73
Armenia	1995 [b]	5	56
	1999	6	52
Belarus [c]	1995 [d]	2	65
Bosnia	1990	9	N/A
	1996	5	83
	1998	5	70
Croatia	1992	7	76
	1995	5	69
	1997	6	71
	2000	5	77
Georgia	1992	13	81/75[e]
	1995	3	68
	1999	5	68
Kazakhstan	1994	6	74
	1995	6	81
	1999	5	63[f]
Macedonia	1994	6	77
	1998	6	73
Moldova	1994	4	79
	1998	4	87
Russia	1993	9	50
	1995	5	65
	1999	7	62
Ukraine	1994	5	75
	1998	9	70
Yugoslavia	1992	5	56/58 [g]
	1993	4	67
	1996	4	63

a: We have generally not counted the number of parties within coalitions. In the elections of Armenia, Belarus, Georgia, Kazakhstan, Russia, and the Ukraine a significant number of non-party candidates have usually been elected, above all from single-member districts. Figures are thus closer to the number of effective parties rather than to the number of all parties/ groupings represented in the parliament.

b: Nine parties, including the leading opposition party ARF, were barred from participation.

c: 1990. Despite opposition calls for an early legislative poll, the pre-independence Supreme Council elected in April 1990 ran its five-year term.

d: Figures on the elections in 14 and 28 May 1995; 141 seats remained vacant out of 260, by-elections in November and December 1995, 62 seats remained vacant.

e: Single/multi-member districts;

f: Second round;

g: Serbia/Montenegro

In the politically less developed countries, notably in the South and East, there may be more substance to party fragmentation. As evidenced by Table 3.3, the number of parties or coalitions elected to parliament has remained at a moderate level, but party systems in these countries tend to be more fragile than in Central Europe. Coalitions may include half a dozen parties or more. In many countries a significant number of non-party MPs have been elected from single-member constituencies. Armenia, Belarus, and Russia are good cases in the latter context.

A clearly more important factor that has caused difficulties for parties in the eyes of the electorate is the instability of the party systems and thereby the entire political systems. Party mergers and splits have been commonplace. (This has partly been a result of electoral engineering.) Individual voters have had serious problems in making sense of all these changes. The most remarkable example in this respect is probably Poland, where the Polish Peasant Party was the sole party with an unchanged party label contesting both the elections of 1993 and 1997. In Latvia the changes from the elections of 1993 to those of 1995 were almost as extraordinary: only two out of eight parties continued under the same name in the latter parliament. This instability naturally also goes a long way towards accounting for the high volatility in the elections. It is in fact difficult to ascertain whether people have changed their party preference from one election to the next due to dissatisfaction with their previous choice, or because this party had ceased to exist at least in its original form. Conversely, of course, parties may have been forced to merge or split because of high volatility.

The instability of the party systems has had a negative impact on executive power as well. It has made it more difficult to form effective and long-standing government coalitions. Moreover, party mergers and splits have often resulted in strained relations between the political leaders of the parties before and after the split or merger. The Czech Republic is a good case in point. Dr. Václav Klaus survived as Prime Minister for five years from 1992 to 1997.[13] In late 1997, however, Klaus was forced to resign after a scandal concerning the finances of his party, Civic Democratic Party (ODS), and a caretaker government took over. Soon after this, ODS split into two, as a number of 'separatists' founded a new party, the Free Democrats. The relationship between Klaus' remnant ODS and the Free Democrats have been explosive ever since. Hence after the elections in June 1998, as the right-wing parties were unable to form a coalition because of these personal clashes, the ODS and the social democrats made the so-called Opposition Agreement according to which the ODS will not vote against Milos Zeman's social democratic minority government, even though formally in opposition. As a result, the ODS often tips the scales without being responsible for the decisions made.

The above example serves as a useful bridge to the next three factors on our list; they are related to the internal 'behaviour' of the parties and their leaders. First, the citizens of several post-communist countries have witnessed morally unsatisfactory deeds by their politicians; corruption, even bribery, mismanagement in any event. In Estonia, scandals having to do with economic affairs paved the way for the retirement of three post-communist governments in the course of just five years (1992–97). The former Slovak Prime Minister Vladimir Mečiar is probably the most notorious personification of such questionable deeds, at least in Western eyes, although his popularity among the voters of his own country did not seem to suffer as much as one would have expected.

Secondly, it is evident that parties have failed to recruit young people in any significant numbers; the phenomenon has also been referred to as the 'senilization of parties' (Ágh 1998, 107). For many young people, however, it may not be the senilization of parties in itself that is the most serious problem, but rather the fact that they widely believe that the members of the old guard, still active in parties, were probably not entirely innocent during the communist era; in any event their general appearance is not too different from those who had governed the country under communism. One can also find empirical evidence for this popular wisdom. On the basis of late-1993 surveys in Russia, Ukraine, Hungary, the Czech Republic, and Slovakia Wyman et al., for example, conclude the following:

> [W]ho were the party members? In some respects the patterns are familiar: party members were twice as likely to be male and twice as likely to be over 30. One more striking finding of our survey is that in each of our countries they are also overwhelmingly former members of the communist party. In other words, it is largely the same people active in politics now as were active in the communist period (Wyman et al. 1995, 538–9).

There is no reason to believe that this would have changed in the latter half of the 1990s, although the proportion of communist-era old guard will naturally decrease with the passage of time. Nevertheless, it is interesting to see how some parties, clearly suffering from senilization, have been trying to raise the profile of young leaders/candidates, particularly females, within their parties. A good case in point is the Czech Social Democratic Party where Petra Buzková has been given the role of the new fresh face. The German PDS – a party that has been surprisingly successful among young people – has also promoted several young women to the highest party rank.

Thirdly, and closely connected to the second point, it is hard to see that the organizational structure of East European parties would be sufficiently flexible or elastic to cope with the rapidly changing circumstances. Instead parties tend to be top-down constructions reminiscent of truncated pyramids; particularly in the Balkan countries clientelistic patterns often override formal structures and decision-making procedures; and, as the senilization thesis implies, the basis for leadership recruitment has been far too narrow. Moreover, contacts between parties and other civic organizations are still often insufficient, and parties have also had many difficulties while building up local networks, partly owing to all the factors listed above. Those communist successor parties whose local sections were not entirely destroyed in the aftermath of 1989, are possible exceptions to this rule. The most prominent examples may be the Russian Communist Party and the German PDS that both owe their popularity to strong surviving local networks.

*

All the points that we have listed so far, fragmentation, instability, and 'internal' problems, have had a profound impact on the identity formation of parties – no doubt the essential issue for parties' future existence and development. There are, however, several other and even more direct factors that also influence identity formation.

First, parties are simply so young that their identity cannot yet be consolidated or firm (mergers and splits have definitely not made them older!). This is particularly relevant in view of the fact that, at least in the West, it is socialization into a party at a young age that secures allegiance. Under communism this kind of political socialization was naturally impossible; political socialization took place primarily on the terms of the ruling system, not in terms of the individual's free choice among different parties. We would, however, expect young East Europeans who came of age in the 1990s, to be more inclined to identify with the new parties than the older generations. This in turn would be a completely different situation from that in the West where the young are generally more critical towards parties, less attracted to them, than the middle-aged and the old (Biorcio and Mannheimer 1995, 222). It seems, however, that increasing individualism effectively undermines political socialization. As we mentioned earlier, it is the young who appear to be the most individualistic and therefore possibly the most indifferent towards parties. It is also noteworthy that young people who have always had a democratic party system may easily take it for granted – unlike older people for whom the existence of multi-party politics still remains invaluable.

Secondly, there are hardly any significant parties that have, in Giovanni Sartori's words, a 'historically derived identity' (Rivera 1996). Historical cleavages may nevertheless exist in these societies. Rural–urban and religious–secular cleavages, which are part of the cleavage structures of most countries at the moment (Hellén, Berglund, Aarebrot 1998, 373), have clear connections to the pre-authoritarian era. But the parties representing these historical cleavages have, by and large, not been able to assume the rules, traditions or organizational structures of the pre-war parties; in this sense these party formations are entirely new. There are also parties that assumed historical names (without any outspoken ideological legacy) after 1989, but the significance of these parties has been rather limited; and even if they have won substantial popular support, as for example in the case of *Isamaaliit* ('Fatherland Union') in Estonia, it is highly questionable whether this has been because of the historical connection or for other reasons.

One central historically derived identity could be that of social democracy – an ideology to which most communist successor parties have laid claim. The electoral success of these parties has varied a great deal, but in countries where they managed to return to power in the second free elections, it is doubtful indeed whether this return had anything to do with social democracy. A much more likely explanation is that people were simply disappointed as the dreams and expectations of 1989 had not become fulfilled as soon as they had hoped.[14] Indeed, it is reasonably safe to argue that the former communists are still despised by a great number of East Europeans, and that any connections to socialism or to the left in general are not particularly *à la mode*.

The social democrats of the Czech Republic, at the moment the strongest social democratic party in the entire region that also holds reins of government, provide us with a somewhat different example. It is not a communist successor party; and it can therefore in principle be seen as a true representative of historical social democracy, so influential in the country in the inter-war period. Yet, one ought to bear in mind that in the first elections in 1990 no social democrats were elected, in 1992 they gained only some 7 per cent of the vote, whereas in the 1996 elections the percentage was already over 26.[15] To conclude, the social democratic traditions were recreated only during the 1990s; they had virtually disappeared during the long years of communism.

The third argument is probably the most essential given the thrust of this chapter. It is readily apparent that most influential parties in the West have already become what Otto Kirchheimer referred to as catch-all parties at the expense of their original identity as parties of mass integration (Kirchheimer 1966; Mair 1998, 37). In other words, they are in principle meant to improve the fortunes of all people, not of one particular class or group. This catch-all identity is a result of the declining role of ideologies, on the one hand, and the emergence of an ever larger middle-class, on the other. But in spite of this, parties in the West still have a certain core identity that essentially determines their behaviour. For example, Catholic parties would not challenge the role of the Church in society, and the Green parties are still not willing to defend the use of nuclear energy. All in all, connections between parties and their constituencies have been weakening, but this is by no means an unequivocal trend.

In the fragmented East European societies as we have tried to describe them, creating links between parties and their constituents is a difficult task indeed. There are no or only a few clearly defined social classes to which a party could anchor its support; and in cases where such classes have been discernible, they have proved to be far too small to guarantee any substantial electoral support.[16] In other words, and this is also the first point in Allardt's classification with which we started off this chapter, *the fragmentation of society has created a situation in which socio-demographic group interests tend to remain very vague; societal cleavages do exist, but their influence is, as a rule, constrained by the overall fragmentation of societies.* Membership of a specific social group has thus not been the decisive factor determining party choices, but other factors – especially the relation to the communist past – have been more crucial.[17]

One possible conclusion of this is that cleavage structures in these societies should actually become more and more crystallized, and there should be more conflicts over political issues – in this respect the catch-all nature that the majority of Central and East European parties have opted for may need some modification. Translating this into the language of cruel pragmatism, it might be useful for parties to create permanent division lines in society; parties could, as it were, undermine fragmentation by fostering deeper fragmentation while building bigger 'cells'.

Our final point regarding people's indifference towards parties is again clearly different from the ones above. It is the question of instrumentality: can people expect to gain something by being party sympathizers or even members? In other words, is there reason to believe that one can use a party for creating a better society/community (participatory democracy), or, alternatively, for creating a nice career for oneself (instrumental democracy)? East Europeans, eager to build a better society, might very well find other instruments than political ones in pursuit of their goals. Similarly, party membership is not necessarily beneficial for career opportunities at the moment; the world of business offers much more seductive prospects for the future, prospects that are well compatible with the enjoyment-seeking value orientations we have alluded to earlier. However, it is worth noting that if our hypothesis of rising individualism holds true, it is more than likely that the relative role of instrumental as opposed to participatory democracy will increase in the future. This has also been the case in Western democracies. As idealistic as it may sound, parties should become means for people's individualistic self-expression.

This brings us back to the question of the overall position of parties within society. It is clear that the communist parties profoundly discredited the very name 'political party'. Solzhenitsyn has by no means been the only exponent of the view that parties can only offer ideologies in post-communist Eastern Europe; it is unreasonable to expect this legacy to be forgotten in the course of a mere decade. Moreover, parties find themselves in a vicious circle at the moment: since the position of parties is relatively weak, people are not interested in them, and since people are not interested in parties, they continue to be weak. Here again, it is interesting to draw a parallel to Western Europe. Peter Mair argues that the importance of parties in people's lives has been decreasing, and parties have tried to compensate for this loss by tightening their grip on the state (Mair 1998). Whether this argument survives close scrutiny is of course debatable, but the point here is that in Eastern Europe this may not be a wished-for direction of development, due to the traumas created by the close relations between the Communist Party and the State. An optimal strategy for parties might be to create an impression of themselves as, above all, civil society actors (cf. Allardt's fourth point) – as mere links between the state and the people; parties should dissociate themselves from the state apparatus as such.

*

We have identified four reasons for the problems that post-communist political parties have been facing during the past ten years of transformation. First, we have addressed the fragmentation as well as the instability of party systems. Secondly, we have explored various internal problems of the parties. Thirdly, we have described problems of identity formation within parties. And last but not least, we have touched upon problems connected with the instrumental use of parties.[18] In general terms, the low turnout, hypothesized by Attila Ágh, is not confirmed by the data presented in Tables 3.2 and 3.3. Turnout in parliamentary elections has been declining only slowly, and in some countries not at all.[19] Moreover, if one compares East European turnout figures with those of Western Europe, the differences appear to be rather modest. Poland is the notable exception, with turnout figures only around 50 per cent, but then again, even these figures are not significantly lower than those of the US elections in the 1990s. It is also worth noting that in some cases the turnout in the first elections was exceptionally high, so high that it is hardly surprising that voter turnout has since been falling. It is certainly difficult to improve upon Czechoslovakia's 98 per cent turnout in the June election of 1990.

Several ways of accounting for these relatively high figures easily come to mind. It has definitely been important for some voters to vote against the communists to prevent them from returning to power. In this sense, the post-communist societies are still much more ideological than the countries of the West. It is also reasonable to assume that elections in general and the act of voting in particular still have more by way of 'excitement' attached to them than they do in established democracies. The most likely explanation in our view, however, is that it is parties rather than democracy that have been discredited. The fact that one can vote, even the fact that parties, however ridiculous and unskilful, exist in the first place, are considered inseparable and valuable elements of democracy. In other words, the idea of democracy as such, the idea of free elections as such, the idea of a parliamentary system as such – all these have not been discredited but, rather, still held in high regard.

This is the legacy of the change that cannot be forgotten: the majority of the populations, in spite of all the economic problems and unexpected events during the past ten years, are more satisfied than dissatisfied with the changes that have taken place. This means that, as long as the legacy of the change, of a *positive* change, prevails, the position of parties in these societies may actually remain a secondary question. But as this legacy gradually fades away, it will become more and more important that people perceive parties as reliable channels for making their demands and aspirations known to the decision-making machinery.

Conclusion: Parties and Politics in Fragmented Societies

It is now time to return to our initial question of how political parties can function in the fragmented Central and East European societies. In other words, how can political parties, grounded, by definition, on collective action, survive in societies that are, if our thesis holds true, seeking to become more and more individualistic and that are still in many ways atomized? Significantly, this question not only applies to post-communist countries but it is highly relevant for most present-day democracies: individualism is undoubtedly one of the greatest challenges to democracy in Europe at present.

Before trying to provide some tentative answers to this question, let us briefly repeat what we argued above. In the first section, we saw how fragmentation in many ways prevails in contemporary East European societies. It is a result of three main factors: first, vertical and horizontal atomization which is, above all, a legacy of communism, reinforced under post-communism due to disillusionment about the new era (for example the growing inequality) and particularly the realm of official politics and parties; secondly, individualism – encompassing the components of self-governance and enjoyment-seeking value orientations – that became possible in a new manner after the collapse of the old order and largely adopted from the West; and thirdly, partly as a result of the two other factors, the non-synchronicity of the patterns of life among different societal groupings – some people have adapted to the new circumstances more easily and quickly than others. In the second section, we tried to display those difficulties that the new parties and party systems have encountered over the past ten years. The result was a rather long list of problems. What is important, however, is that all these problems have not been able to undermine the fundamental support for the idea of democracy – in this respect the legacy of a positive transformation is still strong.

More specifically, we concluded that the identity formation of parties has been difficult in post-communist societies. It has proved truly problematic to create reliable core identities that would appeal to a substantial part of the electorate. There are several reasons for this but, as we have tried to argue, it is precisely the fragmentation of society that appears to be the most important of them. Furthermore, we also mentioned that it is very likely that instrumental as opposed to participatory party politics will become more and more important in the future, partly as a result of increasing individualism. What we have not contemplated thus far, however, are the actual consequences of this state of affairs, particularly whether it is actually harmful. We therefore have to pose two new and rather essential questions. First, what developmental direction should parties in Central and Eastern Europe take and what are the available options? Secondly, what do we actually expect of democracy, how should it be defined, and what is the role of political parties in it?

As a preliminary answer to the first question, a few points seem worth mentioning. In terms of politics, we would like to argue that collectively oriented identity politics and institutional politics will have to make room for more *individualistic politics*. This means that parties are bound to remain relatively loose coalitions, and their identities must be flexible; individuals must be able to join and leave them freely, maybe to a degree comparable with a supermarket. More importantly, the identity formation of parties must be based on the affirmation of this flexibility. It follows from this that parties must consciously pursue issue-oriented rather than ideology-oriented politics and policies; it is not the overall ideological standpoints that will be decisive but the nature of the decisions that will be made one by one, case by case.

The established democracies of the West might offer usable models in this respect. The following anecdote from Finland is highly illuminating: In the elections to the European Parliament in autumn of 1998, a young Left Alliance MEP candidate had as his electoral campaign manager a young Coalition (Conservative) Party activist; the two close-to-extreme ends of the political spectrum cooperated. The explanation for this was simply that in terms of European policy the Coalition Party member had deemed that the left-wing friend was closer to her views than any of the candidates of her own party. In spite of this, she did not have any intention of changing her party affiliation – in her view domestic policy was a completely different matter (*Helsingin Sanomat*, 18 May 1999). This may be a rather extreme example, but it is indeed not difficult to see similar tendencies elsewhere in today's Western politics: parties have become more flexible in recent years; there is nothing strange about social democrats and conservatives sitting in the same government; it is often difficult to distinguish between 'left' and 'right'. What is important is that these examples only become possible if there is a great deal of mutual trust between different parties and their individual members. The point is thus that *maybe only trust between political parties can lead to trust between parties and their electorate*. But, as we have stated, trust is something that cannot be built overnight, especially not in the realm of party politics. The negative communist legacy, that is atomization, is still strong in this sense.

The most essential problem remains though: although boundaries between parties cannot be particularly high, they must nonetheless be firm. How can we create a party identity that is flexible and firm at the same time? 'More trust' may be an answer to this as well: if people trust that whatever a party does, it does it well or to the best of its knowledge, without falling into horse trading too easily, an identity for the party will certainly emerge. Creating a kind of non-identity might offer another solution. The Western Green parties serve as good examples in this respect, also because they are newcomers in politics. As is well known, these parties originally discussed whether they should become parties in the first place, since that might restrict their identity as free-floating idealists. This original ideology is still clearly visible: they still want to let, literally, all flowers flourish. The identity of these parties is then clearly formed through the deeds and ideas of a very heterogeneous group of supporters; the identity is that of not having a precise identity, or that the same party can contain, say, pragmatists and idealists. Many Central and East European parties may have to function like this in the future.

The second question regarding the 'fitting' notion of democracy is, of course, even larger and more difficult to answer. Let us nevertheless raise a few points. First of all, even if party systems throughout the region continue to be somewhat unstable and volatile, and party identities remain vague, this may not necessarily undermine democracy. Quite the contrary. In the final analysis, democracy is meant to allow individuals to speak their mind and to attain support for their views, including the possibility of changing opinions and acting according to these changes. In other words, a situation where party systems are deeply frozen and where a majority of voters simply vote for a party because they have always done so – as they have in the West for a very long time – is not necessarily conducive to a lively, debating, and creative democracy. The problem is, of course, what the right level of instability and vagueness of identity should be.

Finally, there is the question of increasing individualism and the possibilities of democracy. Individualism today implies that people have multiple identities, they move from one cultural context to another, without really attaching themselves to any of these contexts. Moreover, individualism also means continuous learning and reflectivity – otherwise one would not survive in different cultural contexts. In Eastern Europe the fact that people have had to learn so many new things, and through this process attain new realism, may also have led to a better understanding of different cultural conditions – this increased awareness of other cultures is definitely conducive to increased tolerance. This in turn may spell veneration of the principle of plurality, the principle that can be conducive to the emergence or strengthening of civil society, the principle that hopefully defines the future of European democracy. Then it may not be that important at all whether or not political parties can create a core identity for themselves or not.

NOTES

1. For an excellent short introduction to the theme of atomization, see Gellner 1996, ch. 18. Gellner notes that 'the irony of "real socialism" was that the socialist fusion of productive, political and ideological hierarchies with the ideocratic monopoly of association, aided by modern administration and communication networks, really led, not to a newly restored social man, but to something closer to total atomization than perhaps any previous society had known' (Gellner 1996, 134).

2. Günter Gaus, who coined the term *Nischengesellschaft*, defined a niche under GDR conditions as follows: 'It is the preferred place for people over there, the place in which the politicians, planners, propagandists, the collective, the great goal, the cultural legacy – in which all of these depart so that a good man, with his family and among friends, can water his potted flowers, wash his car, play Skat, have conversations, celebrate holidays' (Quoted in Maier 1997, 29).

3. The interview passages used in this chapter are derived from the theme interviews Henri Vogt conducted for his doctoral thesis among randomly selected university students in the Czech Republic (1993), Estonia (1997) and Eastern Germany (1996). The thesis, entitled *The Utopia of Post-Communism,* was finished in 2000.

4. It is noteworthy that during the communist era relations between those who were politically active, the dissidents and intellectuals, and those who remained politically passive were by no means unproblematic. Most importantly, as Raymond Tamás (1999, 182) remarks, 'dissidence challenged the moral stance of those who were silently opposed to the communist regime but did not dare to do anything about it'.

5. At least in Central Europe, one should also take into account an even older tradition, that is the mood of profound scepticism towards political power, adapted as a result of the bitter historical experiences of these countries. This has been formulated by Mihaly Vajda as follows: 'Deep down, there is always something much more simple, more palpable, more lifelike than any abstraction: Let me be, leave me alone, don't try to tell me how to live' (Quoted in Jørgensen 1992, 42).

6. Robert Skidelsky has tried to understand the post-communist world, as he says, in terms of a single organizing idea, which is called the rise and fall of collectivism. In Skidelsky's view, collectivism is something promoted from above, that is by the state; it is not a natural feature of human culture. As he maintains 'the possibility of collectivism resulted directly from the enhanced organizational and economic capacity of the modern state. It is this feature which distinguishes collectivism from all previous interference by rulers with the lives of their subjects' (Skidelsky 1995, 17; cf Gurevich 1995, 4).

7. Perhaps somewhat paradoxically, the 'modernity' of Eastern Europe naturally implies that these countries became much more 'Western' during the 40 years of communism. They became, to a certain extent, middle-class societies similar to the societies in the West – a factor that is without doubt highly conducive to a positive development of democracy in the future (Berglund and Aarebrot 1997, 165).

8. This cleavage (cf. for example the notion of two-thirds society) also exists in the established Western democracies, but its emergence has been much smoother, and the cleavage probably therefore not as striking. On the other hand, it is worthwhile to consider the thoughts of the late Christopher Lasch as he talked about the 'Revolt of the Elites'. According to Lasch, a hyper-postmodern elite, only a small percentage of the entire population, has come to dominate the Western societies – they are educated in the best universities, they eat in the best ethnic restaurants, and their point of identification is by no means national but the same kind of elites all over the world. They are thus not willing or capable of caring about those people who do not belong to their group (Lasch 1995).

9. Dieter Segert and Chilla Machos (1995, 242) have distinguished between three different types of post-communist parties: 1) those that emerged from the ashes of the ruling communist parties or their bloc parties (*Nachfolgeparteien*); 2) those that were closely linked to the more or less clandestine opposition of the communist system (*Oppositionsbewegungen*); 3) and those with roots in the pre-socialist era.

10. According to Ernest Gellner (1996), it is the absence of a moral order – the absence of Truth which actually defines a civil society. In this sense a fragmented society and a civil society have a lot in common, or, better said, a civil society requires a certain degree of fragmentation.

11. In the elections of 1998, which seemed to be crucial for the future of Slovakia and particularly for its relations with the rest of Europe, the turnout rose from 76 per cent to 84 per cent; in other words, when politics appears crucial enough people are still willing to participate and at least cast their vote.

12. It is also worth noting that in spite of the high numbers of parties, only a tiny minority of people has ever belonged to them; in most countries the percentage of party members remained under ten per cent even in the initial stages of party formation. This again testifies to the profoundness of atomization in communist societies, and to how quickly people became disillusioned after the euphoria of 1989. Membership figures have remained very low throughout the 1990s (Bauman 1994).

13. The Czech Republic was in fact the only country in the entire region where the governing coalition of the early days of democracy remained in power for more than one parliamentary period.

14. Adam Michnik, renowned Polish writer and political activist, has written a very illuminating essay on this return, calling it restoration. To him it is a logical backlash of the revolution: 'A restoration promises the return of the good old days. The mark of restoration is its sterility. Sterility of government, lack of ideas, lack of courage, intellectual ossification, cynicism, and opportunism. Revolution had grandeur, hope, and danger. It was an epoch of liberation, risk, great dreams, and lowly passions. The restoration is the calm of a dead pond, a marketplace of petty intrigues, and the ugliness of the bribe' (Michnik 1999, 248).

15. The history of the social democrats in Slovenia is reminiscent of the Czech case: they do not have ties to the former ruling communist party; in 1992, they only scored 3.3 per cent of the vote but four years later their share of the votes was already 16.1 per cent.

16. This is naturally a completely different situation from the one that prevailed in Western Europe as party formation started there in the late 1800s and early 1900s; people had only one dominant identity, be that class, ethnicity, or position on the urban–rural axis. In Eastern Europe cleavages are much more heterogeneous and usually cross-cutting. In the words of Whitefield and Evans (1998, 237), 'electorates in post-communist societies are fractured in multiple ways rather than neatly polarized. Rather than a single axis of opposition between classes, sectors, or ages over distribution or between ethnic groups over rights, we find instead numerous social and ideological cleavages within any society'.

17. András Kovács (1996) has provided useful empirical evidence for this hypothesis. The question he posed was why the social democrats, that is the former communists, had returned to power in Hungary in 1994. His data showed that trust in the socialists, or a lack of trust in them, is not primarily motivated by socio-demographic group interests, but rather by differing attitudes toward the old and new political and economic systems (Kovács 1996, 523).

18. The third and fourth sets of problems are similar to those of Roberto Biorcio and Renato Mannheimer (1995) as they analyse the relationship between citizens and parties through the two primary axes of instrumentality and identification.

19. Compared with the preceding elections, the turnout tended to be much higher in those elections that had a substantial amount of protest voting and that brought the communists back to power.

REFERENCES

Ágh, Attila (1998), *The Politics of Central Europe*, London, SAGE Publications.

Allardt, Erik (1994), 'Makrosociala förändringar och politik i dagens Europa', *Sosiologia*, Vol. 31, No. 1.

Bauman, Zygmunt (1994), 'After the patronage state: a model in search of class interests', in Christopher G. A. Bryant and Edmund Mokrzycki, eds, *The New Great Transformation? Change and Continuity in East Central Europe*, London and New York, Routledge.

Berglund, Sten and Frank H. Aarebrot (1997), *The Political History of Eastern Europe in the 20th Century: The Struggle Between Democracy and Dictatorship*, Cheltenham, Edward Elgar.

Berglund, Sten, Tomas Hellén and Frank H. Aarebrot, eds, (1998), *The Handbook of Political Change in Eastern Europe*, Cheltenham, Edward Elgar.

Biorcio, Roberto and Renato Mannheimer (1995), 'Relationships Between Citizens and Political Parties', in Hans-Dieter Klingemann and Dieter Fuchs, eds, *Citizens and the State*, Beliefs in Government Vol. 1, Oxford, Oxford University Press.

Centeno, Angel Miguel and Tania Rands (1996), 'The World They Have Lost: An Assessment of Change in Eastern Europe', *Social Research*, Vol. 63, No. 2.

Fuchs, Dieter and Hans-Dieter Klingemann (1995), 'Citizens and the State: A Changing Relationship?' in Klingemann, Hans-Dieter and Dieter Fuchs, eds, *Citizen and the State*, Beliefs in Government Vol. 1, Oxford, Oxford University Press.

Fulbrook, Mary (1997), *Anatomy of a Dictatorship*, Oxford, Oxford University Press.

Gaus, Günter (1986), *Wo Deutschland Liegt. Eine Ortbestimmung,* Munich: Deutscher Taschenbuch-Verlag.

Gellner, Ernest (1996), *Conditions of Liberty. Civil Society and its Rivals*, London, Penguin.

Grzybowski, Marian (1991), 'The Transition of the Polish Party System', in Sten Berglund and Jan Åke Dellenbrant, eds, *The New Democracies in Eastern Europe. Party Systems and Political Cleavages*, Aldershot, Edward Elgar.

Gurevich, Aaron (1995), *The Origins of European Individualism*, Oxford, UK and Cambridge, USA, Blackwell.

Hankiss, Elemer (1988), 'The "Second Society": Is There an Alternative Social Model Emerging in Contemporary Hungary?', *Social Research*, Vol. 55, No. 1–2.

Hellén, Tomas, Sten Berglund and Frank Aarebrot (1998), 'From Transition to Consolidation', in Sten Berglund, Tomas Hellén and Frank H. Aarebrot, eds, *The Handbook of Political Change in Eastern Europe*, Cheltenham, Edward Elgar.

Helsingin Sanomat, 1999, May 18.

Jørgensen, Knud Erik (1992), 'The End of Anti-politics in Central Europe', in Paul G. Lewis, ed., *Democracy and Civil Society in Central Europe*, New York, St. Martin's Press.

Judt, Tony (1999), 'Nineteen Eighty-nine: The End of Which European Era', in Vladimir

Tismaneanu, ed., *The Revolutions of 1989*, London and New York, Routledge.

Kirchheimer, Otto (1966), 'The Transformation of West European Party Systems', in Joseph LaPalombara and Myron Weiner, eds, *Political Parties and Political Development*, Princeton, Princeton University Press.

Kovács, András (1996), 'Did the Losers Win? An Analysis of Electoral Behaviour in Hungary in 1994', *Social Research*, Vol. 63, No. 2.

Lagerspetz, Mikko and Henri Vogt (1998) 'Estonia', in Sten Berglund, Tomas Hellén and Frank H. Aarebrot, eds, *The Handbook of Political Change in Eastern Europe*, Cheltenham, Edward Elgar.

Lasch, Christopher (1995), *The Revolt of the Elites and the Betrayal of Democracy*, New York, Norton.

Lauristin, Marju and Peeter Vihalemm, eds (1997), *Return to the Western World: cultural and political perspectives on the Estonian post-communist transition*, Tartu, Tartu University Press.

Maier, Charles S. (1997), *Dissolution: The Crisis of Communism and the End of East Germany*, Princeton, Princeton University Press.

Mair, Peter (1998), *Party System Change: Approaches and Interpretations*, Oxford, Clarendon.

Michnik, Adam (1999), 'The Velvet Restoration', in Vladimir Tismaneanu, ed., *The Revolutions of 1989*, London and New York, Routledge.

Mishler, William and Richard Rose (1998), 'Trust in Untrustworthy Institutions: Culture and Institutional Performance in Post-Communist Societies', Studies in public policy 310, Glasgow, Centre for the Study of Public Policy, University of Strathclyde.

National Human Development Report, Bulgaria 1999, Volume II: Bulgarian People's Aspirations, Sofia, UNDP.

Nyyssönen, Heino (1999), *The Presence of the Past in Politics. '1956' after 1956 in Hungary*, Jyväskylä, SoPhi.

Prečan, Vilem, ed. (1990), 'Charta 77, 1977–1989. Od morální k demokratické revoluci', Dokumentace, Čs. středisko nezávislé literatury, Scheinfeld-Schwarzenberg a ARCHA-Bratislava.

Rivera, Sharon Werning (1996), 'Historical Cleavages or Transition Mode. Influences on the Emerging Party Systems in Poland, Hungary and Czechoslovakia', *Party Politics*, Vol. 2, No. 2.

Rose, Richard (1995), 'Mobilizing Demobilized Voters in Post-communist Societies', *Party Politics*, Vol. 1, No. 4.

Rose, Richard and Christian Haerpfer (1998), *New Democracies Barometer V: A 12 Nation Survey*, Studies in Public Policy 306, Glasgow, University of Strathclyde.

Segert, Dieter and Csilla Machos (1995), *Parteien in Osteuropa: Kontext und Akteure*, Opladen, Westdeutsche Verlag.

Šiklová, Jiřina (1997), 'Feminism and the Roots of Apathy in the Czech Republic', *Social Research*, Vol. 64, No. 2.

Simmel Georg (1957), *Das Individuum und die Freiheit*, Berlin, Verlag Klaus Wagenbach.

Skidelsky, Robert (1995), *The World after Communism: A Polemic for our Times*, Basingstoke, Macmillan.

Solzhenitsyn, Alexander (1991), *Rebuilding Russia*, London, Harper Collins.

Tamás, Raymond (1999), 'The Legacy of Dissent', in Vladimir Tismaneanu, ed., *The Revolutions of 1989*, London and New York, Routledge.

Tóka, Gábor (1998), 'Hungary', in Sten Berglund, Tomas Hellén and Frank H. Aarebrot, eds, *The Handbook of Political Change in Eastern Europe*, Cheltenham, Edward Elgar.

Vajda, Mihaly (1988), East-Central European Perspectives, in John Keane, ed., *Civil Society and the State: New European Perspectives*, London, Verso.

Vogt, Henri (2000), *The Utopia of Post-Communism: The Czech Republic, Eastern Germany and Estonia After 1989*, Doctor of Philosophy Thesis, St. Antony's College, University of Oxford.

Weil, Frederick D., ed. (1993), *Democratization in Eastern and Western Europe*, Greenwich, Connecticut and London, Jai.

Wessels, Bernhard and Hans-Dieter Klingemann (1994), 'Democratic Transformation and the Prerequisites of Democratic Opposition in East and Central Europe', Berlin, Wissenschaftzentrum Berlin für Sozialforschung.

Whitefield, Stephen and Geoffrey Evans (1998), 'Electoral Politics in Eastern Europe: Social and Ideological Influences on Partisanship in Post-Communist Societies', in John Higley, Jan Pakulski and Włodzimierz Wesołowski, eds, *Post-Communist Elites and Democracy in Eastern Europe*, London, Macmillan.

Wyman, Matthew, Stephen White, Bill Miller and Paul Heywood (1995), 'The Place of "Party" in Post-Communist Europe', *Party Politics*, Vol. 1., No. 4.

4. Democratization and Nationalism

Old Nations and New Democracies

In general terms, it would be impossible to argue that national sentiments and ethnic identity have not had an impact on the new democracies of Central and Eastern Europe. The peaceful dissolution of former Czechoslovakia, the not so peaceful disintegration of former Yugoslavia, and the momentous disruption of the territorial structure of the former Soviet Union can hardly be ignored. Events such as the wars in Bosnia and Kosovo and rebellions in Chechnya, Ossetia, Abkazia and Nagorno-Karabakh have not served to increase political stability in Russia, Georgia, Armenia and Azerbaijan. Grievances among Hungarian minorities in Slovakia, Romania and Voivodina and the difficult integration of Russians in Estonia, Latvia, Moldova and Kazakhstan are matters of concern to observers of democratic development. Nevertheless, this chapter will deal with the question of national challenges to democracy in more specific terms. Our main question reads: to what extent does nationalism in fact have a negative impact upon satisfaction with democratic development among the citizens of Central and Eastern Europe? The answer to this more specific question is less obvious.

Nationalism and Democracy for the People or by the People? Two Classical Models

The relationship between democracy and nationalism in contemporary Europe is indeed complex (Alter 1994; Kellas 1998; Gellner 1997; Kedourie 1993; Smith 1991; Tamir 1993). Very different relationships exist between the two notions from one set of cases to another (Altermark, Andersen and Knutsen 2000). Bosnia, Kosovo and Yugoslavia are recent reminders that strong nationalism may indeed be detrimental to democratic development. But cases as diverse as Britain's Ulster problem and Russia's war in Chechnya suggest that provincial national crises may coexist with substantial satisfaction with democratic development among the citizens of 'core-nations'. In some countries, such as the Czech Republic and Switzerland, democratic governance may be seen as part and parcel of the national idea. Thus, the existence of national diversity does not necessarily imply low satisfaction with democratic development (Barnes and Simon 1998).

In classical theory democracy and national identity have been linked at the very inception of democratic government. The French and American revolutions abolished monarchy as a form of government and it became necessary to replace dynastic heritage with popular sovereignty. America's revolution included anti-monarchic and anti-British sentiments as the reverse of the democratic coin. Similarly, by removing the King institutionally as well as personally, the French revolutionaries substituted him for the notion of a General Will of the people – defining this collective, theoretical 'ruler' as *la Nation*. The rather simplistic thesis, which emanated from the two classical democratic revolutions, about national identity as a *sine qua non* for democratic development – and vice versa – is cast in doubt every day when we survey developments in contemporary Europe.

The ideas of territorial claims and/or cohesion are certainly at least as strongly related to national sentiments as is democratic governance. In pre-revolutionary America, the Crown was the only common factor constitutionally linking the 13 colonies, and the Kingdom of France was defined as a territory primarily in terms of dynastic claims. In Europe today territorial claims are no longer the prerogative of the rulers. These claims have become 'democratized' at least since the 1848 revolutions, inspired by the *Sturm und Drang* of national romanticism. Sometimes popular territorial claims are in harmony with the interests of the elites ruling the territorial polity – and sometimes they are most definitely not. Theoretically, democratically elected leaders are therefore as likely to find themselves at odds with popular notions of territorial claims, as are any other leaders.

In juxtaposing territoriality, national identity and democratization, two major observations can be made. First the three factors do not form a consistent causal pattern indicative of a 'united field theory' of democratic state- and nation-building. Rather, they form an opportunity space where just about any combination of harmony or conflict is possible. Secondly, notions of democracy, territory and nation are not stable over time. Popular sentiments as well as the aspirations of political elites are in a constant flux. When area specialists search for culturally 'objective' roots for historical territorial claims, they are more often wrong – and in some cases serve as the 'useful idiots' of nationalist politicians – to paraphrase Vladimir Lenin. Historical claims are, more often than not, rhetorical rather than substantial.

But despite these observations much of the contemporary discussion about nationalism and democracy fluctuates between two visions, or rather two *ideal types* of visions. First, there is the nation-state idea that the 'ethnos' of a state is identical to its inhabitants. Admittedly, if we compare the contemporary states of Central and Eastern Europe with their counterparts during the inter-war period, in almost all cases the proportion of the ethnic core has increased significantly. This process was further enhanced during the 1990s with the dissolution of the Czechoslovak and Yugoslav multi-ethnic polities. In fact, the relative increase of Russian speakers in Estonia and Latvia during the Soviet occupation is the only exception to this trend.

The other vision is that of an integrated Europe where all ethnic groups will be minorities, although cynics might note that extreme right-wing nationalism is a growing force within the core of the European Union, from Belgium and France to Austria. But for contemporary Central and East Europeans the idea of an integrated Europe may well serve to counteract the nation-state ideal.

*

The notion that democratization and the development of a national identity are two sides of the same coin stems from the two classical ideal types of nationality, commonly referred to as the *French* and the *German* models (Özkirimli 2000). These two models are rooted in early interpretations of the events of the Great French Revolution of 1789 and the 1848 revolutions in the German principalities.

The French model is basically an elitist notion of replacing the dynastic definition of the territory of France with an equally centralized concept of republican rule based on the General Will of the people – *la Nation*. Thus, when the French masses changed status from royal subjects to citizens, they remained subjects in terms of their duties and obligations to the state. But the new citizenship status also granted them participatory rights. It is a moot question to what extent the revolutionary leadership bestowed these rights upon the citizens only in order to promote democracy. It is rather more tempting to interpret popular participation as the only way of legitimizing the new leadership. Defining the territorial integrity of France remained the task of the elites in Paris. In terms of legitimacy the metaphysical 'Natural Rights of Men' replaced the metaphysics of 'Crown and Altar'. But irrespective of the motives for democratization, the revolutionary regime became totally dependent on *la Nation* to provide the rationale for ruling. Democratization and a national definition of territorial integrity became intertwined (Hobsbawm 1990).

Table 4.1: The French model

Level	Pre-Modern Rule	Process	National Concept
Government	Monarchical, dynastic definition of authority and territory.	Substituting the dynasty for the General Will of the territorial population.	*La Nation.*
Governed	Royal Subjects.	The development of citizenship.	The resident citizens remain the subject of *la Nation*, but are also granted participatory rights in order to legitimize *la Nation*.

The ideal type referred to as the German model is almost antithetical to the French, at least as regards the theoretical 'site' of the definition of territorial integrity and cohesion. When the German revolutionaries met in Frankfurt in 1848 to draft a German constitution, their basic notion was that the definition of a German territory rested in a linguistic, that is a culturally defined, community of peoples – *Volksgemeinschaft*. Whereas the essence of the French model is continuity in terms of territoriality, the German linguistic definition of the nation brought the nationalist revolutionaries in direct conflict with the territorial definition of the German principalities. It should be noted that this popular or *völkisch* notion of territoriality was never actually implemented. When the learned delegates of the Frankfurt parliament finally completed their German constitution in the aftermath of the revolutions of 1848, and offered the German Crown to the King of Prussia, he rejected their German state as 'a Crown of Clay' insisting that he would only become Emperor when offered 'a Crown of Gold'. In other words, to the King of Prussia the consent of the Princes was more important than the support of an elusive language community of peoples. In fact, the unification of Italy is probably closer to the model than Germany. We will therefore refer to this ideal type as the *tribal* model.

Table 4.2: The tribal or 'German' model

Level	Pre-Revolutionary Rule	Process	National Concept
Government	Territorial fragmentation legitimized by the principalities.	State-building = Unification.	The Unified State becomes a Nation-State by definition.
Governed	Territorial definition based on German speakers as a linguistic community.	The revolution as an attempt to organize the community politically.	The people (*Volk*) become subjects of the State, since they have always been members of the Nation.

In the tribal model territory is defined in terms of common cultural traits within a given population (Smith 1991). Existing borders, states and their princes are in theory of no consequence; only culturally defined boundaries really matter. Instead of introducing democratic principles in order to legitimize the regime, the tribal or ethnic model may call for regime change in order to promote the building of a nation-state with 'natural' culturally based borders. Aspiring ethno-nationalist elites equate the state-building project with a process of unification. A successfully unified state thus becomes a nation-state by definition. On the mass level the process may be described as a grand educational project designed to mobilize the ethnic community into political action. It is imperative that people accept their role as subjects of the national whole – and in theory they should do so gladly since they have 'always' been members of the nation. The nation precedes the state. Democratic procedures may serve to enhance these processes, but they are not quite as endemic and logically necessary as in the case of the French model.

The Dualistic and *Tabula Rasa* Models

The concepts 'nation as *raison d'état'* or 'nation as a linguistic community' are too narrow to be useful for understanding the early democratic development in Central and Eastern Europe. As the new states of Central and Eastern Europe emerged between 1848 and 1918, the political forces within them striving for democracy and nationhood were faced with a wide set of options for defining nationality. Towards the beginning of the 20th century civil rights, parliamentary government and at least manhood suffrage had become more or less universal democratic norms, whereas the 18th century American revolutionaries had been slave owners and their French counterparts had reduced their 'democratic' demands to calls for regular assembly meetings on the budget.

Nationhood gradually acquired a modern and secular basis. Sources of inspiration as diverse as Herder and Darwin contributed towards extending the definition of national community beyond linguistic attributes to embrace species, ethnicity and race. Collectors of national epics, folk songs and popular customs also helped to strengthen the feeling of community – in some cases, but not always, in favour of the existing states (Prizel 1998). Modern historiography worked in the same general direction by producing 'suitable' interpretations of the past. All in all, the number of ingredients in the national stew increased and different cooks were free to make their own recipes. Race, the survival of the fittest, tribe, religion, historical heritage, folkways and customs became available as new elements for alternative definitions of nationhood.

In the light of this multiplicity of different elements, two major points must be made, particularly if one wants to understand the historical development of Central and Eastern Europe:

- First, it is not pre-ordained that a territorial definition must be based *either* on dynastic rule *or* on a sense of cultural community. It is definitely conceivable for dynastic rulers *as well as* ethnic communities to develop, albeit disparate, notions of nationality while sharing at least substantial parts of the same territory.

- Secondly, pre-modern territoriality is by no means a necessary condition for predicting the existence of contemporary European states. Indeed, in the 20th century, several states have been defined territorially in the vacuum of the military or political defeat of their former imperial rulers. Under these circumstances it is also possible to envisage different cultural concepts competing for a role in defining the 'nation' of such new territorial states, since no previous indigenous state has ever laid claim to any notions of cultural identity.

As regards the first point, it actually reflects the national politics of Germany throughout the 19th century. The dream of a predominantly Protestant German Empire with Prussia as the dominant region, advocated by the Hohenzollern dynasty, coexisted and competed with the original idea of the Frankfurt Parliament of a Pan Germanic Empire (of all German speaking peoples). Bismarck tilted the balance in favour of a Prussian-led Protestant Empire in 1870, but his victory was only temporary, and the struggle between different national concepts remained a central theme and an unresolved contradiction at least until 1945 (Alter 1994).

To avoid confusion we refer to this model as the *dualistic model*. It calls for the monarchy to embrace a national idea and to strive towards becoming a national monarchy instead of a power solely based on religiously sanctioned dynastic succession. In addition, the national definitions propagated by heads of state and their political supporters tend to be modified to fit the existing territory or to support an extension of that territory. Thus, by defining the nation in linguistic rather than religious terms, the King of the Netherlands and the Dutch Conservatives could defend a larger territorial expansion in 1815. An alternative, Protestant Netherlands would have been smaller than the original kingdom. Similarly, the German Emperor and Bismarck defined the German nation not only in linguistic terms, but also in terms of Evangelical-Lutheran Christianity in order to exclude the possibility of Habsburg infringements.

National monarchies do not preclude the formation of nationally motivated popular movements in opposition to the state. The content of the national definition used by such movements will be different from the definition employed by the state. To the dissidents, the national ideal, once defined ideologically, takes precedence over territorial integrity. Such movements are as likely to be movements for unification of existing state territories as proponents of autonomy or separatism. Disparate definitions can coexist in a dualistic manner. Thus, the Pan-Germanic movement, originally based on the notion of a language community and later including ideas of race and medieval imperial dreams, remained a force in the lands of the German Hohenzollern and the Austrian Habsburg dynasties. Eventually, the movement, in the extreme form of National Socialism, was given the opportunity to fulfil this dream and to create such a state.

The existence of dual or multiple sets of national definitions will almost inevitably lead to polarization among political elites. Conservative and Monarchical forces face National Liberals. To the extent that the territorial structure is disputed, politics often take the form of a zero sum game, making important institutional compromises difficult – if not impossible. Under democratic government voters are constantly exposed to conflicting loyalties between supporting 'national' state institutions *versus* internalizing their 'national', ethnic identity. Lack of consensus makes heavy polarization along this cleavage a definite possibility. Under these circumstances, democratic consolidation is not facilitated.

Table 4.3: The dualistic model

Level	Pre-Modern Rule	Process	Contested National Concept
Government	Monarchical, dynastic definition of authority and territory.	Elite polarization between national-liberal proponents of ethnic nationhood and conservative-monarchical proponents of statehood.	No unified or unchallenged definition of a nation-state. Competing paradigms exist simultaneously. Under democratic regimes competing political elites will seek to form cleavages across these paradigms.
Governed	Territorial definition based on cultural communality.	The people are exposed to conflicting loyalties between state institutions and ethnic identity.	Elite competition in non-democratic regimes. A tendency towards lack of national consensus. Under democratic regimes a strong polarization along these cleavages is a distinct possibility.

Statehood is not necessarily championed by vested interests. Many of the new Central and East European countries that came into being in the wake of the First World War, either had no past as independent states or emerged in a void created by the combined military defeats of the four dominant empires of the region (Berglund and Aarebrot 1997). Popular national movements had existed before and parts of the intelligentsia had devoted themselves to the collection of national memorabilia, but the new status of territorial sovereignty was less the result of systematic plans on the part of would-be political elites and more a consequence of windows of opportunity opening up in the aftermath of major events elsewhere. The revolution in Petrograd was more important for the formation of the new Baltic states than the schemes of politicians dreaming of statehood in Tallinn, Riga and Vilnius. The notion of a Czechoslovak state was declared in Pittsburgh, Pennsylvania, at a conference dominated by Slovak-American trade unionists (Krejcí and Machon 1996). Prior to the Great War, the political leaders in Prague, Masaryk and Beneš, had dreamt about a future Czech state and were in fact working towards maximizing Czech autonomy within the Austro-Hungarian dual monarchy. They certainly had no plans for the kind of Czechoslovakia that President Wilson helped bring about at Versailles. But when events in Petrograd and Versailles created windows of opportunity, political elites in Riga and Prague of course seized those opportunities.

The *tabula rasa* model refers to those cases where state-building did not occur prior to external events conducive to the formation of a new territorial entity. In terms of cultural identity some mobilization and clarification had previously occurred in the form of national movements and projects. Several optional definitions of nationhood were available to the masses and the leadership of these states. By the end of the First World War, the number of different recipes was quite extensive.

Table 4.4: The Tabula Rasa *model*

Level	Pre-Modern Rule	Process	Constructing a National Concept
Government	No state has existed.	The structuring of, and competition among, potential state-building elites taking advantage of the same 'window of opportunity'.	No unified or unchallenged *authorized* definition of the nation-state. Competing paradigms may exist simultaneously. Under democratic regimes such coexisting paradigms may form cleavages.
Governed	Several optional definitions of cultural community are available.	Simultaneous processes of political mobilization and competing projects for ethnic consciousness.	Consensus about national independence does not entail consensus about the content of national ideas. Lack of earlier statehood makes democracy attractive as a legitimizing force. Democratic consolidation is to some extent dependent on non-interference from external actors, while national consolidation to the detriment of democratization may result from interference.

These new states lacked a unified or authorized definition of the nation state at the outset. It became the task of the new leaders to arrive at compromises about the definition of statehood. This was particularly important in terms of defining the basis for national independence, but consensus about national independence did not necessarily entail consensus about the content of national ideas in general. The absence of earlier statehood and state traditions made democracy itself attractive as a legitimizing force. A former province of an autocratic historical empire could easily define itself as a new, national, democratic, modern state – the very antithesis of their former provincial status.

But the use of democracy as a legitimizing force presupposes protection from external pressures or non-interference by external actors. When such pressures were increasingly felt with the rise of the new totalitarian states with imperial aspirations, Nazi-Germany and the Soviet Union, during the 1930s, the leaders of the new nations were faced with a Hobson's Choice, pitting national unity against 'disorderly democracy'. Unfortunately, more often than not, national unity was deemed more important than democracy. By contrast, in the uni-polar world of the 1990s, a weakened Russia has not been able to exert similar pressure upon the neighbouring states. It is therefore possible that national identity and democratic consolidation go hand in hand.

The four models of national development discussed above serve to differentiate between different patterns of nation-building, but the rhetoric of nationalism is more unified than these patterns suggest. In the wake of the First World War all the new states of Central and Eastern Europe were looked upon as national democracies whereas in reality they varied structurally from ethnically homogenous Hungary to 'nation-states' such as Czechoslovakia and Yugoslavia – in reality mini-empires with a nation-state ideology. The dismantling of the latter two states in the 1990s may have reduced this variation to some extent, but contradictions between national rhetoric and the structural basis of national consolidation still exist. The Russian Federation is faced with such a contradiction (Prizel 1998). The Russian rhetoric when defending the confrontation with Chechnya is very much in line with what we have referred to as the French model. The Kremlin readily accepts that Chechens are different from Russians, but they must remain incorporated into the Russian Federation since they are citizens of the territory of that federation. In contrast, when the Russian government defends its support of Milosevic's rump-Yugoslavia, the arguments are cast in terms of the German or tribal model that Serbs and Russians are Slavic brothers united in the Orthodox faith. But were this logic to be employed by minorities in Russia, it would be considered threatening to the very existence of the Russian Federation itself. Just imagine what would happen if Tatars were to come out strongly in favour of their ethnic and religious brethren in Chechnya.

For the purposes of this chapter, the four models presented above are only interesting for their ability to increase our understanding of nationalist challenges to democracy. In Table 4.5 we have summarized the models in terms of their theoretical consequences for the policies towards minorities, and their consequences for how such minorities will trust or reject a democracy dominated by the ethnic core-group of the country. It is possible to deduce malign as well as benign consequences. The French model is conducive to the enactment of inclusive citizenship laws; and so is the *tabula rasa* model when the new nation is left to develop democracy without external interference. Basically, all residents are primarily citizens and hence their ethnicity is of no relevance to their rights. There is little reason to expect minorities to be less satisfied with democracy than the majority under these circumstances. Conversely, in countries employing the tribal model or the *tabula rasa* model (when the new nation is subject to external pressure), the 'ethnos' legitimizes the 'demos'. In terms of political rights, this situation is more problematic for ethnic minorities. They are given the message that the citizens of the 'core-ethnos' are politically more relevant than they are themselves. This is not exactly a mobilizing message and we would expect this situation to be detrimental to their identification with the democratization process promoted by the majority.

Table 4.5: Models of nationhood and their consequences for support for democracy among ethnic minorities

Model		Consequences for minorities	Expected differences in minorities' trust in democratic development
French Model		Ethnically inclusive – residents are citizens	Minorities are at least as satisfied with democratic development as the majority
Tribal Model		Ethnically exclusive – the 'ethnos' is the basis of true citizenship	Minorities tend to be less satisfied with democratic development than the majority
Dualistic Model		One concept of nation may be exclusive; an alternative concept may be inclusive. Thus, 'a Russian citizen' vs. 'a Soviet citizen'	Satisfaction with democratic development will vary among minority groups depending on their alignment with competing concepts and the incumbency of elites adhering to alternative concepts
Tabula Rasa Model	*New nation subjected to pressure from external powers*	Under international pressure, the concept of national survival and unity takes precedence over democratic norms to the advantage of the core 'ethnos'; ethnic exclusiveness is the result	Minorities will tend to be less satisfied with democratic development, especially minorities who share 'ethnos' with the core population of an external power exerting pressure upon the nation
	New nation developing on its own accord	In the absence of international pressure the new nation can be inclusive	Minorities may be at least as satisfied with democratic development as the majority

The *tabula rasa* model is circumstantial. Under this model residency is possible as a basis for full citizenship in the absence of external threats, but when outside adversaries put the pressure on, belonging to the core-nation becomes all the more important. The dualistic model is also circumstantial but less predictable. Countries close to this model harbour ethnic and residential ideals all at once. Different notions of nationhood create deep political cleavages, and citizens belonging to ethnic minorities may find themselves strongly affected by changing political alignments. Satisfaction with democratic development among different minority groups is thus contingent upon the vicissitudes of day-to-day politics.

In employing models we render an impression that structures exist and that national sentiments are predictable. The Central and East European territorial space has mainly been divided by historical processes beyond the control of the peoples of the region. The relationship between territory and identity has therefore been a matter of adapting to political circumstance; it has seldom been a matter of principle. Belief in democracy under different notions of nationhood may be entirely coincidental. We will try to investigate more closely the relationships between nationalism and satisfaction with democratic development below. Only then will it be possible to understand whether or not the different models of nationhood have an impact on the ability of the different Central and East European states to cope with the challenges to democratic development.

Nationalities and Satisfaction with Democracy

With enclaves and exclaves of national minorities, the nation-states of contemporary Central and Eastern Europe are far from perfect. It is difficult to say to what extent identity and territory interact and influence the level of satisfaction with democracy among ethnic core groups. And it is even more hazardous to speculate on how these core groups compare to their ethnic brothers and sisters living in diaspora in neighbouring countries. In an attempt to answer these and related queries, we have merged the data from the Central and East European Barometers (CEEB 2–8, 1991–97). The data sets were pooled in order to achieve a significant number of respondents from important national minorities. For each country we have calculated the percentage of the respondents who are very or fairly satisfied with the development of democracy within the ethnic core-populations and among the more important national minorities within the countries.[1]

In Table 4.6 we present the results for the Baltic countries and Poland.[2] The general impression is that ethnic Estonians, Latvians, Lithuanians and Poles are generally more satisfied with democracy than the national minorities within these countries. The CEEB material enables us to study the Russian, Belorussian, Ukrainian and Polish minorities throughout the region. Satisfaction with democracy among the core-ethnic groups varies from 30 per cent in Latvia to 40 per cent in Estonia; the corresponding figures for the Russian, Belorussian and Ukrainian minorities in these countries vary from 15 per cent to 28 per cent. The Polish minorities in Latvia and Lithuania are somewhat more satisfied, 26.1 and 28.8 per cent respectively. These variations may be attributed to the extent to which the very existence of the minorities has been a bone of contention in the domestic political struggles of the 1990s. Thus, a mere fifth or less of Russians and Belorussians in Estonia and Latvia – two countries where their citizenship rights had been at issue throughout the 1990s – were satisfied with democracy. By contrast, as many as 28 per cent of Russians and Poles in Lithuania – with its considerably more liberal citizenship laws (Hushagen 2000) – were satisfied with democracy.

Even though less satisfied with democracy than the core-populations of the Baltic states, the Russians, Belorussians and Ukrainians[3] of Estonia, Latvia and Lithuania are considerably more satisfied than the core-populations of Russia, Belorussia and the Ukraine (Duvold 2000; Södergren 2000). Table 4.7 indicates that satisfaction with democracy among the three latter nationalities varies from nine per cent in Russia to 17.3 per cent in the Ukraine – considerably less than among Russians, Belorussians and Ukrainians in the Baltic states.

Table 4.6: Satisfaction with democracy among nationalities in the Baltic countries and Poland

Country	Core Nation	Russian	Belorussian	Ukrainian	Polish	Lithuanian
Estonia	40.1% 4401	21.9% 2016	15.7% 121	26.7% 157		
Latvia	30.2% 3934	20.0% 2219	17.5% 189	16.0% 144	26.1% 157	20.9% 91
Lithuania	35.3% 5779	28.0% 543	20.9% 43		28.8% 407	
Poland	37.0% 5855					

Looking at Ukrainians in Russia and Russians in the Ukraine we find that these minorities are even less satisfied with democracy than are the Russian and Ukrainian core-populations. The Ukrainian minority in Belarus is an exception; as many as 28.6 per cent of Ukrainians in Belarus are satisfied with democracy which is more than twice the satisfaction registered for Russians, Poles and Belorussians themselves. The Ukrainians in Belarus are in fact more supportive of democracy than Ukrainians in the Ukraine. In general terms, satisfaction with democratic development seems to be weaker in most CIS countries than in the rest of Central and Eastern Europe.

Table 4.7: Satisfaction with democracy among nationalities in Russia, Belarus and the Ukraine

Country	Core Nation	Russian	Ukrainian	Polish	Tatar	Muslim
Russia All	9.0% 3532		3.0% 100		9.7% 124	7.8% 64
Russia Euro	14.4% 1893		6.5% 61			
Belarus	13.0% 3221	12.4% 604	28.6% 112	12.1% 198		
Ukraine	17.3% 4422	14.8% 1241				

Table 4.8 provides data on the satisfaction with democratic development in the countries of former Czechoslovakia.[4] Before the separation of the Czech Republic and Slovakia, Czechs were considerably more satisfied with democracy than the Slovak, Moravian and Hungarian minorities. After the separation, satisfaction with democracy among Czechs and Moravians within the Czech Republic has increased further to 39.9 and 37.8 per cent respectively (Olson 1997). When the Slovaks became the core-nation of the new Slovakia, their satisfaction with democracy also increased. But this increase from 17.9 to 21 per cent is marginal compared to the case of the Czech Republic. In fact, satisfaction with democracy is higher among Slovaks in the Czech Republic than among Slovaks in their homeland. Czechs and Hungarians in Slovakia are particularly dissatisfied with the development of democracy which is hardly surprising considering the nationalist overtones that were introduced into Slovak politics by former Prime Minister Vladimir Mečiar.

Table 4.8: Satisfaction with democracy among nationalities in Czechoslovakia, the Czech Republic and Slovakia

Country	Core Nation	Slovak	Moravian	Czech	Hungarian
Czechoslovakia	34.1% 1989	17.9% 990	19.6% 138		12.5% 72
Czech Republic	39.9% 5377	27.9% 111	37.8.% 262		
Slovakia	21.0% 5056			14.3% 77	10.8% 409

The four countries presented in Table 4.9 are similar in the sense that their core-populations account for a very large proportion of the total population. Together with Poland they are thus proximal to the 'ideal nation-state model'. Two of them, Hungary and Slovenia, are among the most economically advanced countries of the entire region. The other two, Romania and Bulgaria, have a history of independent statehood that predates the First World War, albeit with substantive border changes since then. In Hungary, satisfaction with democracy is low compared to the other three countries but this applies to the Hungarians themselves as well as to the barely measurable Croat and Gypsy minorities. Satisfaction with democracy in Hungary thus has little by way of ethnic differentiation attached to it; and the relatively low level of satisfaction across ethnic groups may be interpreted as a sign of realism within a relatively mature democracy. Hungary experienced a soft transition from reform communism to pluralist democracy, and it is reasonable to expect the process of rising expectations to take its toll on the general level of democratic satisfaction.[5]

Indigenous Slovenians in Slovenia display a relatively high level of satisfaction with democracy, 35.7 per cent. The small Serb and Muslim minorities in Slovenia are actually more satisfied with the development of democracy than ethnic Slovenians. The Croat minority is slightly more satisfied with democracy than the Slovenians themselves but less satisfied than Croats in Croatia (see Table 4.9). The Serbs, Croats and Muslims of Slovenia testify to the peaceful and democratic potential of South Eastern Europe. The Slovene leaders promote liberal democracy and the voters are strongly in favour of European integration and EU membership. These policies are very different from the backward looking policies of the Croatian, Bosnian, and particularly, the Serb leadership.

Nationalism has loomed large in the Romania of the 1990s.[6] Here we see the same pattern as in Estonia, Latvia and Slovakia. The Hungarian and Gypsy minorities – whose very existence in the country has been a bone of contention in Romanian politics – are less satisfied with the state of democracy in Romania than the ethnic core population. But Hungarians in Romania are more satisfied with democracy than Hungarians in Hungary. We would be inclined to interpret this somewhat paradoxical outcome as an indication of the maturity of Hungarian democracy rather than as an expression of happiness among Hungarians in Romania.[7] In Bulgaria[8], as in Hungary, satisfaction with democracy is generally low, and this assessment is shared by ethnic Bulgarians and ethnic and religious minorities such as Muslims and Turks. In general, the Gypsies are the least satisfied with democracy throughout the region.[9]

Table 4.9: Satisfaction with democracy among nationalities in Hungary, Slovenia, Romania and Bulgaria

Country	Core Nation	Hungarian	Croat	Serb	Gypsies	Muslim	Turks
Hungary	22.2% 6608		20.0% 70		19.2% 104		
Slovenia	35.7% 5105		36.2% 126	46.1% 115		55.9% 43	
Romania	35.5% 6043	28.1% 469			16.9% 36		
Bulgaria	18.6% 6611				12.6% 302	18.4% 38	22.0% 459

Turning to the countries of former Yugoslavia[10] the level of satisfaction with democracy seems to be surprisingly high compared with the more developed countries of Central and Eastern Europe. The Yugoslav data indicate a satisfaction level among Serbs of 38.9 per cent. This is very high, indeed, considering the structure of the regime. But the high level of satisfaction with democracy in Yugoslavia may at least to some extent be dismissed as a by-product of the successful efforts by the Belgrade regime at national mobilization for military purposes throughout most of the period covered by the CEEB. It is also worth keeping in mind that the Serb minority in Slovenia is more satisfied with democracy than the Serbs of Yugoslavia.

Croatia is an ethnically rather homogenous state with 43 per cent satisfaction with democratic development among the Croat core-population. But this high score among Croats may also be strongly related to national mobilization, in this case by President Franjo Tudjman, during our period of investigation. Macedonian respondents are also quite satisfied with democracy in their country – 45.6 per cent. Muslims, Gypsies and Turks are even more satisfied with democracy in Macedonia than the Macedonian core. The Serbs and the Albanians, on the other hand, are considerably less satisfied with democracy than the Macedonians. This ties in neatly with the pattern already identified in Estonia, Latvia and Slovakia, where ethnic minorities have been very much the focus of nationalist politics. In Macedonia, in particular the Albanian minority forms the basis of one of the most important political cleavages. Albania's[11] high satisfaction with democracy is probably more associated with the hope for a democratic future than with experience with democracy as a form of government. It is hardly surprising that the barely measurable Greek minority is less satisfied with democracy than the Albanians.

Table 4.10: Satisfaction with democracy among nationalities in Yugoslavia, Croatia, Macedonia and Albania

Country	Core Nation	Albanian	Muslim	Gypsies	Serb	Greek	Turk	Serbo-Croat
Yugoslavia	38.9% 739		50.0% 64					
Croatia	43.0% 1882							
Macedonia	45.6% 3691	20.9% 839	54.8% 62	53.9% 107	33.3% 107		48.9% 92	42.9% 42
Albania	49.8% 5992					27.8% 72		

There is a great deal of ethnic variation among the countries on the Southern fringes of the former Soviet Union – Moldova[12], Kazakhstan[13], Georgia and Armenia[14]. Moldova is a country divided into a cis-Dnestr region fully controlled by the Moldovan government and a trans-Dnestr region where governmental authority is challenged by the presence of the Russian Army. It is noteworthy that satisfaction with democracy among Moldovans is quite high, but it is also evident that a Russian minority supported by their 'own' Army is even more satisfied with Moldovan democracy. Other minority groups are less satisfied than both Russians and Moldovans. The Kazakhs of Kazakhstan are considerably more satisfied with democracy than the Russian and Ukrainian minorities, whose satisfaction with democracy is roughly on the same level as the satisfaction within the core-nationalities of their home countries. Minorities not belonging to the Slavic speaking core-populations of the former Soviet Union, Germans, Tatars and Uzbeks are generally speaking as satisfied with democracy as are the Kazakhs.

Table 4.11: Satisfaction with democracy among nationalities in Moldova, Kazakhstan, Georgia and Armenia. Minorities from the CIS countries and Romanians

Country	Core Nation	Russian	Ukrainian	Armenian	Azerbaijan	Georgian	Romanian
Moldova	32.5% 2331	41.7% 230	28.7% 216			12.0% 50	25.0% 64
Kazakhstan	24.5% 1171	9.3% 1187	9.0% 178				
Georgia	44.3% 3870	27.6% 348	31.7% 60	31.6% 351	37.4% 139		
Armenia	13.8% 4769						

In the Caucasus, Georgia and Armenia[15] display quite different profiles. Armenia is ethnically homogenous, but the general satisfaction with democracy is quite low. The Georgian core-population has a relatively high level of satisfaction with democracy and the national minorities in that country, though less satisfied than the Georgians, still have a higher level of satisfaction with democracy than their ethnic brothers and sisters in neighbouring Armenia. Similar comments apply to the Armenian minority in Georgia. The Russian minority is the least satisfied with Georgian democracy, but their level of satisfaction is higher than that of Russians in Russia.

Table 4.12: Satisfaction with democracy among nationalities in Moldova, Kazakhstan, Georgia and Armenia (other minorities)

Country	Core Nation	Greek	German	Bulgarian	Tatar	Uzbek	Jewish
Moldova	32.5% 2331			18.5% 54			
Kazakhstan	24.5% 1171		23.9% 113		17.3% 81	21.2% 66	
Georgia	44.3% 3870	31.0% 71					23.2% 56
Armenia	13.8% 4769						

In general, a distinction should be made between countries where ethnic relations have been instrumental in forming political cleavages in the 1990s and countries where such cleavage-formation has not been dominant despite the existence of ethnic minorities. Table 4.13 is designed to compare these two groups of countries. We have calculated the difference in satisfaction with democracy between specific minority groups and the ethnic core-populations. In Estonia, Latvia, Slovakia, Romania, Macedonia, Kazakhstan, Georgia and Moldova the relationship between the dominant ethnic group and at least some of the minorities has played an important role in the formation of the regimes, the party-systems or at least in the formulation of policies towards citizenship.

Table 4.13: Satisfaction with democracy – difference between minorities and core-populations in countries where ethnic cleavages occur and in countries where such cleavages are not dominant

Classification	Country	National Minority	Satisfaction with democracy: Difference between ethnic minority and core-population
Countries where policies towards national minorities is a dominant cleavage	Estonia	Russians	-18.2
	Latvia	Russians	-10.2
	Slovakia	Hungarians	-10.2
	Romania	Hungarians	-7.4
		Gypsies	-18.6
	Macedonia	Albanians	-24.7
	Kazakhstan	Russians	-15.2
	Georgia	Russians	-16.7
	Moldova	Romanians	-7.5
		Russians	+9.7
Countries where policies towards national minorities is *not* a dominant cleavage	Lithuania	Russians	-7.5
		Poles	-6.7
	European Russia	Ukrainians	-7.9
	Belarus	Russian	-0.6
		Ukrainians	+15.6
	The Ukraine	Russians	-2.5
	Czech Republic	Moravians	-2.1
		Slovaks	-12.0
	Hungary	Croats	-2.2
		Gypsies	-3.0
	Slovenia	Croats	+0.5
		Serbs	+10.4

In countries classified as having a dominant ethnic cleavage, all the minority groups except Russians in Moldova are less satisfied with democracy than core-populations in their respective countries, ranging from a difference of 7.4 per cent between the Hungarian minority and the Romanian core-population of Romania to a difference of 24.7 per cent between the Albanian minority and the Macedonian core-population of

Macedonia. The Russians of Moldova are 9.2 per cent more satisfied with democracy than the core group of ethnic Moldovans, but it is debatable whether the Russians are happy with Moldavian democracy as such or with the presence of Russian Army units on the Eastern banks of the Dnestr.

The other set of countries includes Lithuania, European Russia, Belarus, the Ukraine, the Czech Republic, Hungary and Slovenia. In these countries minority groups exist, but ethnic politics has not been a dominant basis for cleavage formation in general. For this group of countries, the difference in democratic satisfaction between minority groups and core-populations is considerably smaller than in the former group of countries. Ukrainians and ethnic Russians in European Russia display the largest difference in terms of democratic satisfaction – 7.9 per cent. All other differences are smaller and in some cases, Ukrainians in Belarus, and Croats and Serbs in Slovenia, the minority groups are even more satisfied with democracy than the core-populations.

The existence of ethnic minorities in a country almost always entails at least some historical conflicts or grievances between minorities and the majority. But, as demonstrated by the table, the very existence of minorities is not itself a sufficient condition for dissatisfaction with democratic development among minorities throughout the region. It takes a political agenda conducive to the formation of cleavages along ethnic lines and the creation of institutional structures – such as citizenship laws and chauvinistic political parties – that serve as reminders of past conflicts to politicize the ethnic minorities (Smith 1999).

But nationalism in Central and Eastern Europe today is not only limited to the structures of the past as reflected in the political attitudes of national minority groups throughout the region. We would argue that the character of the national question changed during the 1990s, from the inward looking euphoria of newly-won national independence and democratic prospects, notably among the core-populations, to more realistic orientations towards the world of inter-regional cooperation and the global economy into which the Central and Eastern European polities seek integration. The rather simplistic view that democratic and especially economic development would materialize more or less automatically with national independence and democratic consolidation has been replaced by a growing realization that the Central and East European countries must actively pursue policies towards international integration in order to receive their fair share of the European pie. It may therefore be more relevant to look at the orientations among voters towards these processes than to examine nationhood as a remnant of past conflicts and settlements.[16]

National versus International Orientation

The orientation among Central and East Europeans towards the inter-national community is not only a matter of geography. In our opinion it is also a matter of orientation either towards the future or the past. CEEB 6 contains a question where the respondents were asked to mention countries or areas of particular importance to the future of their own country. This was an open-ended question and we have classified the respondents' answers and ordered them according to the following four categories:

1. We have interpreted the response 'Russia' in terms of adherence to the past legacy of the Soviet Union. This may not be entirely correct, as it is conceivable that some respondents simply see Russia as an important future partner. This particularly applies to countries within the Commonwealth of Independent States.
2. Answers referring to respondents' own country, other Central and East European countries or Central and Eastern Europe as a whole, we have classified as an expression of a national or regional orientation. This response is considered more parochial than the last two categories.
3. Responses including names of West European countries, the European Union or 'Europe', we have considered to be indicative of an orientation towards European integration.
4. Respondents indicating names of countries beyond Europe reflect a more global orientation and are considered to be the most cosmopolitan.

Figure 4.1 provides a summary of the geographical orientation among respondents in Central and Eastern Europe as of 1995 (CEEB 6) in terms of the proportion favouring European integration. The three countries whose citizens clearly favour European integration most strongly are Slovenia, the Czech Republic and Poland. This is hardly surprising considering that they all belong to the first tier of applicant members to the EU. Similarly, the bottom of the list comprises six countries that are all members of the CIS, and hence their citizens, maybe realistically, consider Russia to be a more important future partner than the EU. A relatively low degree of enthusiasm for European integration is also found among Yugoslav respondents. This is to be expected given the confrontational position of that country towards the Western powers which was already evident at the time of the survey in 1995. Conversely, three of Yugoslavia's adversaries in the Balkan conflict, Albania, Macedonia and Croatia display a very high level of European orientation supplemented by a very strong orientation towards countries outside Europe, notably the United States of America.

A majority or more of the voters in the EU applicant countries come out in favour of European integration – a position adopted by 25 per cent or less

of the voters in the CIS countries. The relatively strong Russian orientation
in the Baltic states is not only an artefact of the large Russian speaking
minorities; it is also a by-product of the resilience of past legacies which go
a long way towards accounting for the Bulgarian and Lithuanian cases.

*Figure 4.1: Profile of geographic orientation among respondents in Central
and Eastern Europe (CEEB6, 1995)*

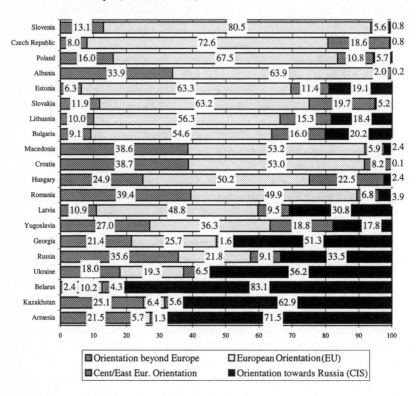

Do these differences in geopolitical orientation constitute a challenge to
democracy in Central and Eastern Europe? In an attempt to answer this
question, we have taken a close look at the satisfaction with democratic
development among respondents with different geopolitical orientation
within each country. Each cell of Table 4.14 indicates the percentage of the
respondents who are either very satisfied or fairly satisfied with the
development of democracy in their respective countries.

Three observations can be made. First, respondents oriented towards
European integration tend to be more satisfied with democratic development
than respondents who are oriented more specifically towards countries in
Central and East Europe, including their own. This is true for

all countries with valid data. Secondly, in four countries, Albania, Croatia, Slovenia and Romania satisfaction with democracy drops rather monotonically from relatively high values among people oriented beyond Europe towards lower support for democracy among the more nostalgic respondents looking towards Russia and the CIS countries.

Table 4.14: Satisfaction with democratic development by geopolitical orientation in 19 Central and East European countries (CEEB 6, 1995)

	Orientation beyond Europe	European orientation (EU)	Cent./East Eur. Orientation	Orientation towards Russia (CIS)
Albania	73.18 (39)	57.28 (536)	NA (9)	3.70 (27)
Poland	44.29 (14)	56.87 (524)	53.08 (130)	44.58 (83)
Georgia	48.94 (23)	56.25 (240)	31.13 (106)	40.55 (365)
Czech Republic	46.07 (8)	54.24 (601)	32.00 (200)	NA (7)
Macedonia	31.80 (43)	46.52 (417)	NA (7)	NA (13)
Croatia	57.14 (36)	44.61 (482)	36.21 (58)	NA (1)
Estonia	36.17 (4)	42.48 (612)	33.94 (109)	25.00 (172)
Romania	41.13 (35)	40.67 (445)	28.92 (83)	21.51 (93)
Kazakhstan	25.00 (27)	38.81 (62)	22.64 (53)	13.03 (503)
Slovenia	41.21 (16)	38.29 (773)	30.23 (86)	NA (8)
Armenia	20.14 (13)	34.38 (32)	25.00 (32)	18.12 (767)
Latvia	28.57 (8)	34.05 (555)	27.78 (72)	20.38 (265)
Lithuania	28.00 (7)	29.01 (486)	22.78 (79)	19.44 (144)
Slovakia	25.68 (14)	28.28 (534)	26.24 (221)	33.80 (71)
Hungary	19.31 (14)	23.24 (469)	15.86 (227)	12.00 (25)
Ukraine	19.40 (13)	19.63 (214)	15.69 (102)	13.03 (660)
Bulgaria	17.02 (9)	18.46 (363)	12.77 (141)	8.94 (246)
Belarus	18.87 (5)	11.11 (126)	8.33 (48)	13.43 (685)
Russia	5.49 (32)	8.65 (185)	4.88 (82)	6.47 (417)

This trend is indicative of a Western and modernizing bias. It is significant that two of the four countries, Croatia and Slovenia, have experienced the turbulence of the dissolution of old Yugoslavia, while the other two, Albania and Romania, were burdened with extraordinarily primitive and sultanistic communist regimes. For the rest of the countries the general picture is less obvious. In most of them, satisfaction with democracy is highest among respondents who are oriented towards European integration rather than among those with a global perspective. It should be noted that most of these countries have applied for membership in the EU after 1995. Nevertheless, satisfaction with democracy is highest among European-integrationists also in Georgia and Kazakhstan. Belarus stands out as an interesting exception. The large group of citizens with an orientation towards Russia is quite satisfied with democracy. This group is also more satisfied with Lukashenko's brand of democracy than are the Belorussians who favour European integration or who link their country's future to their Central and East European neighbours. Admittedly, the very few globally oriented Belorussians express the highest satisfaction with democracy. Whatever we may call the regime in Minsk, it is looked upon rather favourably among those who orient themselves towards Russia.

In order to get a clearer picture of the relationship between satisfaction with democracy and geographical orientation, we reduced the number of orientations into two, named after the two types of nationalism that have marked Russian politics ever since Peter the Great (Parland 1993). Those Russians who, like Leo Tolstoi, went to live among simple folks in the countryside, grew patriarchal beards, and who sought the roots of the nation in the traditions of the Russian village – *mir* – were called *narodniki*. Others, following the example of Peter the Great, dreamt of Russian imperial greatness through modernization and expansion. These were called *zapadniki*. This distinction has survived to the present day (Sandle 1999). There are parallel lines from Peter the Great to Gorbachev and from Tolstoi to Solzhenitsyn. We have been tempted to employ these terms in classifying the geopolitical orientations that may be gauged from CEEB 6. In our view, modern 'Narodniki' are those who consider their country's future to be linked up with their own country, Mother Russia or one of their Central or East European neighbours. Conversely, modern 'Zapadniki' look towards the EU, NATO and European integration in general or name specific West European countries or countries outside Europe. In Table 4.15 we have used this twofold classification for a comparison of the level of satisfaction with democratic development among 'Zapadniki' and 'Narodniki'.

To what extent could this cleavage be considered a challenge to the consolidation of democracy throughout the region in the 1990s? *One criterion* is the extent to which satisfaction with democracy is higher among 'Zapadniki' than among 'Narodniki'. We have ranked the countries according to this difference.

In the three countries at the bottom of the table, Russia, Belarus and Slovakia, 'Zapadniki' and 'Narodniki' seem to be equally satisfied or dissatisfied with democracy. This is hardly surprising for those familiar with the regimes of Bratislava and Minsk in 1995 when the survey was conducted. Mečiar's and Lukashenko's governments were exceptional in their lack of interest in Western integration, and 'Narodniki' therefore had no more reason to be satisfied with democracy than 'Zapadniki'.

Table 4.15: Satisfaction with democratic development among 'Zapadniki' and 'Narodniki' and the difference between the two groups in 19 Central and East European countries (CEEB 6, 1995)

	'Zapadniki'		'Narodniki'		Difference
Albania	64.06		11.11		52.95
		935		36	
Czech Republic	53.19		30.92		22.27
		690		207	
Romania	40.88		25.00		15.88
		800		176	
Croatia	50.00		35.59		14.41
		846		59	
Georgia	52.63		38.43		14.20
		475		471	
Estonia	42.03		28.47		13.56
		659		281	
Latvia	33.33		21.96		11.37
		639		337	
Macedonia	39.01		30.00		9.01
		851		20	
Lithuania	28.88		20.63		8.25
		561		223	
Slovenia	38.81		30.85		7.95
		938		94	
Bulgaria	18.16		10.34		7.83
		457		387	
Hungary	22.31		15.48		6.84
		614		252	
Kazakhstan	26.04		19.78		6.25
		338		556	
Ukraine	19.54		13.39		6.15
		348		762	
Poland	54.22		49.77		4.45
		664		213	
Armenia	22.81		18.40		4.41
		171		799	
Russia	6.63		6.21		0.42
		513		499	
Belarus	13.41		13.10		0.31
		179		733	
Slovakia	27.71		28.08		-0.37
		682		292	

The Russian situation is more difficult to interpret. Gorbachev's successor Yeltsin had a more ambiguous profile than Gorbachev with respect to geopolitical orientation. Yeltsin's participation in the G8 meetings was clearly 'Zapadnik' policy, but Russia's solidarity with its Serb brethren was equally 'Narodnik'. Nevertheless, the main policies of the leadership of the Russian Federation have been modernization and integration (Prizel 1998). But the main opposition group, the Communist Party, has tried to exploit the 'Narodnik' dimension particularly in its appeal to elderly voters. Contemporary Russia is actually very close to our dualistic model. Geopolitical orientation remains a bone of contention and it has little or no impact on satisfaction with democracy.

In the rest of the countries of the region there is a significant and universal tendency towards higher satisfaction with democracy among 'Zapadniki'. The difference between the two groups of respondents may be large as in Albania, where the 'Zapadniki' are 53 percentage points more satisfied with democracy than the 'Narodniki', or on the small side as in Poland and Armenia (four percentage points), but the impact of geopolitical orientations remains indisputable. The more dissatisfied the 'Narodniki' are and the greater the difference to 'Zapadniki', the stronger the challenge to democracy is likely to be. But the seriousness of the challenge is not merely a function of the gap between the two groups of respondents. The size of the two groups must also be taken into account. In the Albanian case there would seem to be little cause for alarm despite the huge attitudinal discrepancy between the two groups. The Albanian 'Narodniki' may indeed represent a kind of nationalism not conducive to democracy, but in the final analysis they are too few to make a difference. In the Czech case, however, a difference of 22 per cent between the two groups may spell problems for the consolidation of democracy considering that one third of the Czechs come out as 'Narodniki'.

In Figure 4.2, the countries have been placed in a scatter diagram according to these two criteria. Countries with a potential nationalist challenge should be located in the upper right quadrant of the diagram where large differences between 'Zapadniki' and 'Narodniki' go hand in hand with the presence of a sizable 'Narodniki' minority. This particular quadrant turns out to be empty. Countries with large differences between 'Zapadniki' and 'Narodniki' tend to have relatively small 'Narodniki' minorities. In sum therefore, the challenge is not overwhelming. The countries closest to the upper right quadrant are the Czech Republic, Estonia, Latvia and Georgia.

We are thus well advised not to read too much into a mere difference in terms of satisfaction with democracy. At the very most it represents a potential challenge. To understand how national orientations and sentiments may be challenging to the new democracies of Central and Eastern Europe, it will be necessary to take a closer look at all factors previously discussed. Only by doing this will it be possible to obtain an impression of how combinations of the factors might turn into real threats.

Figure 4.2: Relative size of 'Narodniki' group and the difference between 'Zapadnik' and 'Narodnik' satisfaction with democratic development in 19 Central and East European countries (CEEB 6, 1995)

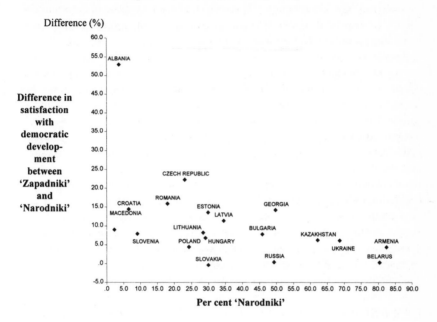

Models of Nation-States, Ethnic Legacies of the Past and Contemporary Orientation

A meaningful analysis of the nationalist challenge to democracy requires that we understand how different factors interact by reinforcing the importance of territorial identity in Central and Eastern Europe. In this chapter we have concentrated on three elements:

1. The development of national concepts during the formation of the modern nation-states in the 20th century throughout the region. This has been summarized into four different models of nation building and statehood.
2. Ethnic minorities as legacies of past imperial structures and as vehicles for present-day ethnic identities.
3. Differences in geopolitical orientation emphasizing the contrast between super-national integration and orientation towards modern world markets versus ideas of self-sufficiency and orientation towards the Central and East European area and, to some extent, the legacy of the Soviet past.

Using these three elements or factors, it is easy to identify different groups of countries, but the implications of such an exercise for satisfaction with democracy are not always readily apparent. The relationship between the three factors on the one hand, and satisfaction with democracy on the other hand, is at best tenuous. We must therefore evaluate to what extent combinations of the factors serve to increase the potential for challenges to democratic development.

One obvious approach is to investigate if differences in satisfaction with democracy between ethnic minorities and ethnic core-populations coincide with similar differences between West-oriented respondents and their more conservative countrymen. In Table 4.16 below we have summarized the position of countries from Figure 4.2 and used italics to indicate if ethnic minority groups are significantly less satisfied with democratic development than the core-populations, as indicated in Table 4.13 above.

The respondents from four countries, Estonia, Latvia, Georgia and the Czech Republic, have 'Narodnik' minorities larger than 20 per cent who are more than ten per cent less satisfied with democracy than the 'Zapadnik' majority. But in Estonia, Latvia and Georgia this potential challenge to democracy is exacerbated by the existence of a significant ethnic cleavage. In Macedonia and Romania such an ethnic cleavage also exists, but only small minorities in these countries share inward-looking sentiments.

Table 4.16: Relative size of 'Narodniki' group and the difference between 'Zapadnik' and 'Narodnik' satisfaction with democratic development, with significant differences between national minorities and ethnic core-populations expressed in italics (CEEB 6, 1995)

	No difference	Moderate difference 4–10%	Large difference More than 10%
More than 20% 'Narodniki'	Slovakia Belarus Russia	*Kazakhstan* Armenia Poland The Ukraine Hungary Bulgaria Lithuania	*Latvia* *Estonia* *Georgia* The Czech Republic
Less than 20% 'Narodniki'		*Macedonia* Slovenia	*Romania* Croatia Albania

In Slovakia and Kazakhstan substantial 'Narodniki' populations differ little, if any, from their Western-oriented counterparts in their assessment of democracy. Yet ethnic cleavages *do* make a difference with respect to how satisfied people are with the development of a democratic form of government. In the rest of the countries neither ethnicity nor geopolitical orientation seems to be important for how the new freedom and pluralism are evaluated by the citizens. A reasonable conclusion is therefore that democracy in Estonia, Latvia and possibly Georgia and Kazakhstan face potential challenges on both fronts. This by no means precludes a stable future development, but it does call for more statecraft on the part of the leadership than among leaders elsewhere.

But leadership is also constrained by the historical conception of nationhood, discussed earlier in terms of our four models. The models are not constant but may vary in one country from one time-period to another. In Table 4.17 we have classified the countries according to the predominant view among the leadership at three points in time – at the inception of modern statehood some time before 1920, around the time of the first founding election after 1989 and the situation today as we perceive it. None of these views are perfect reflections of the models, but we have treated them in terms of their proximity to the four ideal cases. We have then summarized our earlier discussion about the satisfaction with democratic developments among different groups. On the basis of model proximity and differentiation between groups in terms of satisfaction, we have sought to classify the countries according to the severity of the nationalist challenge to democracy – be it actual or potential. The Baltic states, the former Warsaw-pact countries, Albania and the new states devolved from former Yugoslavia are listed roughly from north to south. We have then listed Russia and the rest of the states devolved from the former Soviet Union.

Our discussion of the countries in the table highlights the fact that most of the Central and East European democracies have been faced with at least potential nationalist challenges since the demise of communism. But there is a difference between a potential and an actual challenge, and we have classified the countries accordingly:

Class 1 contains countries where it would be dubious to argue that even potential nationalist challenges to democracy exist. This group comprises a set of ethnically very homogenous countries. Some of them, that is Lithuania, Poland, Slovenia, Hungary and Bulgaria, are strongly oriented towards Western integration. In Albania this process has hardly got under way. Armenia, the sixth country in this group, is drawn into a national conflict with neighbouring Azerbaijan, but is internally without any significant nationalist challenge. All in all, the prospect for EU membership, the reliance on NATO support for Albania and the safety of Russian protection for Armenia combined with ethnic homogeneity serve to make nationalism of minor importance as a challenge in these countries.

Table 4.17: A conceptual map of nationalist challenges to democratic development in Central and Eastern Europe

Country	Model proximity			Satisfaction with the development of democracy in the mid 1990s	Comments on the nationalist challenges to democratic development
	At the inception of modern statehood, 1920 and before	*At the founding election after 1989*	*Around 2000*		
Estonia	Close to the *tabula rasa* model: Initially the country opted for a movement towards the French model with liberal suffrage and some cultural rights for minorities, but when under pressure in the 1930s, more autocratic regimes moved towards the tribal model.	Strong elements of **the tribal model**: Suffrage included ethnic expatriates of the core 'ethnos' and excluded many residents who belonged to ethnic minorities; ethnicity an important political cleavage.	Movement towards **the French model**, as a combined result of human rights concerns from OSCE over disenfranchised residents, and a consensus among the national political elites over harmonization of laws for EU membership.	Lower (10%+) satisfaction with the development of democracy among ethnic minorities and 'Narodniki'.	A **potentially serious** nationalist challenge, modified by; (a) the desire for European integration, and (b) decreased pressures from Russia. *Class 2*
Latvia					
Lithuania		Closest to **the French model** with suffrage for all residents, but with elements of the tribal model; notably suffrage for expatriates of the core 'ethnos'. Ethnicity is only a minor cleavage.	No significant change.	Marginally lower (6–9%) satisfaction with the development of democracy among ethnic minorities and 'Narodniki'. These groups are relatively small.	**Weak** nationalist challenge. *Class 1*
Poland	Close to the *tabula rasa* model: Initially formally adopting the French model with liberal suffrage and some cultural rights for minorities, when under pressure in the 1930s, a more autocratic regime moved towards the tribal model. More ethnically diversified in the inter-war period.	Close to **the French model** formally, but the country is very homogenous in ethnic terms. Some elements of tribal rhetoric during the early electoral campaigns.	No significant change, practises liberal suffrage, membership in NATO and EU application have stifled further attempts at nationalist rhetoric.	Marginally lower (4%) satisfaction with the development of democracy among 'Narodniki'. No measurable minorities in the CEEB and more than 20% 'Narodniki'.	**Weak** nationalist challenge. Attempts at nationalist rhetoric have led to only limited electoral success. *Class 1*
Hungary	Originally, after 1867, close to **the tribal model** – Magyarization policies. Very limited inter-war democratic period. Dominated by an authoritarian regime adhering to the tribal model, but slightly more liberal than most similar regimes in the region.			Marginally lower (2–7%) satisfaction with the development of democracy among ethnic minorities and 'Narodniki'. Relatively small ethnic minorities, more than 20% 'Narodniki'.	

Table 4.17: continued

Country	Model proximity			Satisfaction with the development of democracy in the mid 1990s	Comments on the nationalist challenges to democratic development
	At the inception of modern statehood, 1920 and before	At the founding election after 1989	Around 2000		
The Czech Republic	Czechoslovakia was originally close to **the** *tabula rasa* **model**: The ruling elites were mainly recruited from the Czech 'ethnos', but varying degrees of exclusivity and inclusivity were practised towards other ethnic groups. Constitutionally the country adopted the French Model, but tribal model elements existed in the form of political cleavages.	A growing disparity between Czech and Slovak elites. The Czech preference for **the French model** contrasted with the Slovak understanding of the situation based on **the tribal model**. No national compromise was found and Czechoslovakia disintegrated. The national challenge was overwhelming.	**The French model** dominant.	The Slovak minority remains 12% less satisfied with democratic development than Czechs. The Moravians are only marginally less satisfied than Czechs (2.1%). More than 20% 'Narodniki' are 22% less satisfied than 'Zapadniki'.	A **potential nationalist** challenge is **strongly modified** (a) by NATO membership and the desire for EU membership, and (b) by the lack of deep ethnic cleavages. *Class 2*
Slovakia			The tribal model strong after separation; currently moving towards **the French model**.	The Hungarian minority remains 10% less satisfied with democratic development, but 'Narodniki' are as satisfied as 'Zapadniki'.	Recently, a **potentially strong** nationalist challenge has been modified by the renewed interest in European integration, but a considerable cleavage persists. *Class 2*
Slovenia	Yugoslavia, the old kingdom as well as the communist regime, was a curious **mixture of the dualistic and** **the** *tabula rasa* **models**. Elite dissent persisted over the definition of the core 'ethnos', and elite consensus failed to emerge even under the extreme external pressure of the German occupation.	Very short initial period close to the tabula rasa model, moved very fast to **the French model** as almost all elites reached consensus on desire for European integration.	No significant change.	The barely measurable ethnic minorities are *more* satisfied with the development of democracy than the core 'ethnos'. 10% 'Narodniki' are marginally (8%) less satisfied.	No nationalist challenge. *Class 1*

Table 4.17: continued

Country	Model proximity			Satisfaction with the development of democracy in the mid 1990s	Comments on the nationalist challenges to democratic development
	At the inception of modern statehood, 1920 and before	At the founding election after 1989	Around 2000		
Croatia		Franjo Tudjman's regime defined the nation primarily in terms of **the tribal model**. Insignificant minorities.	Recent government change has put less emphasis on tribal rhetoric, but the process of resettling former residents of ethnic minorities, notably Serbs, is slow.	No measurable ethnic minorities, but more than 20% 'Narodniki' were 14% less satisfied with democratic development.	The nationalist challenge **plays a role**, despite no significant ethnic cleavages, but ethnic rhetoric remains a strong mobilizing tool. Modernizing and integrationist 'Zapadniki' express stronger satisfaction and is a modifying element. *Class 2*
Serbia	Yugoslavia, the old kingdom as well as the communist regime, was a curious **mixture of the dualistic and the *tabula rasa* models**. Elite dissent persisted over the definition of the core 'ethnos', and elite consensus failed to emerge even under the extreme external pressure of the German occupation.	Close to **the tribal model**.	The Serb 'ethnos' has strengthened its position.	No CEEB data.	**The nationalist challenge is very important.** *Class 5*
Bosnia-Herzegovina		In formal terms the Federation is based on the French model. Republica Srbska is based on the tribal model. In reality **the tribal model** was dominant among political elites in all ethnic groups: Croats, Muslims and Serbs.	Little change.	No CEEB data.	The nationalist challenge is **totally dominant**, and only international troops maintain territorial integrity. *Class 4*
Macedonia		Initially close to **the *tabula rasa* model**, subject to external pressures from many sides including Greece and Serbia.	Similar, but the Macedonian and Albanian political elites are both moving towards **the tribal model**, with different notions of core 'ethnos'.	The large Albanian minority is 25% less satisfied with democracy than are the Macedonians. All other ethnic minorities are as satisfied as the core ethnos. There are very few 'Narodniki'.	**A definite nationalist challenge** to democracy exists in the form of an Albanian cleavage. Greek intervention has largely served to block European integration as an option. *Class 4*

Table 4.17: continued

Country	Model proximity			Satisfaction with the development of democracy in the mid 1990s	Comments on the nationalist challenges to democratic development
	At the inception of modern statehood, 1920 and before	At the founding election after 1989	Around 2000		
Albania	Ethnicity, linguistically defined by ruling elites, has defined the nation in terms of **the tribal model**, to counteract a more divisive definition in religious terms. Under the communist regime, the special Albanian definition of socialism almost had an ethnic content, 'the lighthouse of socialism in Europe'.	The homogenous ethnic composition of Albania enabled early more or less democratically elected governments to pursue active integrative policies towards world markets. When the lack of a professional financial infrastructure caused economic collapse, this came to dominate cleavage formation in Albania. Models of national identity seemed **redundant**.	With increasing ethnic tensions in Kosovo, culminating in crisis and war, **the tribal model** may have become more relevant.	No measurable ethnic minorities in the CEEB material. A very small 'Narodnik' minority is very dissatisfied with democratic development (11% satisfied) compared with an overwhelming 'Zapadnik' majority (64% satisfied).	Nationalist rhetoric may have mobilizing potential, but the ethnic challenge is **weak**. *Class 1*
Romania	Developed largely according to **the tribal model**. This was further enhanced by a communist regime that considered Romanian socialism a special case.	In the initial stages of the Romanian revolution there were elements pointing towards the French model (for example unrest among Hungarians in Timisoara), but the new regime was consolidated proximal to **the tribal model**, with rising popular mobilization directed against Hungarians and Gypsies.	A movement towards **the French model** combined with an increased emphasis on membership in the EU and a consequent normalization of the relationship to Hungary.	The Hungarian minority is somewhat less satisfied with democratic development than the Romanian 'ethnos' (7%); and the Gypsies even more (19%). 'Narodniki' are 15% less satisfied than the 'Zapadnik' majority.	**A potentially serious nationalist challenge**, modified by the desire for European integration. *Class 2*
Bulgaria	Developed largely according to **the tribal model**. During the last years under communism, the old regime attempted to gain popularity by enacting anti-Turkish laws.	Moving towards **the French model.**	The same, but strengthened by desire for European integration.	Muslim and Turkish minorities are as satisfied with the development of democracy as are the Bulgarians. A large 'Narodnik' minority is moderately (8%) less satisfied.	**A relatively weak nationalist challenge** further modified by the desire for European integration. A moderate potential for nostalgia exists. *Class 1*

Table 4.17: continued

Country	Model proximity			Satisfaction with the development of democracy in the mid 1990s	Comments on the nationalist challenges to democratic development
	At the inception of modern statehood, 1920 and before	At the founding election after 1989	Around 2000		
Russia	Tsarist Russia and the Soviet Union were close to **the dualistic model**: between defining Slavic speakers as core nations and including all peoples under the Empire or Socialism. This dualism was never really resolved, governments have tended to fluctuate between them depending upon occasions and circumstances.	Yeltsin's regime was also to some extent **dualistic**, moving towards the French model constitutionally, but clinging to the tribal model in dealing with Chechens and Serbs.	The dualism has continued under Putin.	The ambiguity of the dualist model might be working to Russia's advantage. There is no significant difference in satisfaction with democratic development between 'Narodniki' and 'Zapadniki'. The only measurable minority in European Russia, the Ukrainians, are 8% less satisfied than the Russians. The cost of dualism may be ambiguity and a low general level of satisfaction with democratic development.	Despite the war in Chechnya, in the final analysis, Russian democracy faces **only limited nationalist challenges** in terms of impact on satisfaction with democracy. *Class 3*
Ukraine		Inherited **dualism** in the form of ambiguity between orientation to CIS and orientation towards increasing independence. Expatriate Russians tend to mobilise in favour of CIS orientation.	A territorial split between the more independence oriented Western Ukraine and a more CIS oriented Eastern Ukraine. The former, and the present government, may be leaning towards **the tribal model**, exacerbated by the territorial controversy over the Crimea.	There is only a marginal difference in satisfaction with democratic development of 2% between the Russian minority and the Ukrainian core 'ethnos'. 'Narodniki' are merely 7% less satisfied than 'Zapadniki'.	The ambiguity of dualism exists, but there is **little in terms of manifest nationalist challenges** to democratic development in the CEEB data. *Class 3*
Belarus			In moving ever closer to the CIS and Russia, the Belorussian government has renounced the tribal model as an option and embraced the regime specific **dualism** of the old Soviet Union.	There is no difference in satisfaction with democratic development between the Russian minority and the Belorussian core 'ethnos'. 'Narodniki' and 'Zapadniki' are equally satisfied.	

Table 4.17: continued

Country	Model proximity			Satisfaction with the development of democracy in the mid 1990s	Comments on the nationalist challenges to democratic development
	At the inception of modern statehood, 1920 and before	At the founding election after 1989	Around 2000		
Moldova	Tsarist Russia and the Soviet Union were close to **the dualistic model**: between defining Slavic speakers as core nations and including all peoples under the Empire or Socialism. This dualism was never really resolved; governments have tended to fluctuate between them depending upon occasions and circumstances.	Early in the democratization process the new Moldovan leaders identified with their Romanian ethnic origins – **the tribal model**. East of the Dnestr Slavic speakers identified with Russia – supported by a Russian army.	A tendency towards Moldovan independence and at least an increase in support for **the French model** among Moldovan leaders to the detriment of the tribal model.	Respondents identifying as Romanians are 8% less satisfied with democratic development, compared to those who identify as Moldovans. The Russian minority are 9% *more* satisfied than Moldovans.	Nationalism **is a potential challenge**; Russian and Romanian identifiers are at opposite ends in terms of satisfaction, the Moldovans in the middle. As long as a majority identifies as Moldovans the challenge is defused. *Class 4*
Georgia		The first nationalist government defined Georgia according to **the tribal model**. This government faced ethnic rebellions in Abkhazia and Ossetia.	The present government has more or less voluntarily returned to **the dualistic model**, combining CIS membership with national claims.	The Russian minority is 17% less satisfied with democracy than Georgians. There are as many 'Narodniki' as 'Zapadniki' and the latter are 14% less satisfied.	**A substantial nationalist challenge**, currently kept under control by the dualism and ambiguity of the Shevardnatze presidency. *Class 3*
Armenia		Close to **the tribal model**, further enhanced by the war with Azerbaijan over the ethnic Armenian enclave of Nagorno-Karabakh.	The same basic model, but a lower level of conflict.	A 'Narodnik' majority is 4% less satisfied with democratic development than 'Zapadniki'. No measurable ethnic minorities in the CEEB material.	**Hardly any internal challenge** to democracy. External pressures exist in the form of fears of Azerbaijan and Turkey and a benign view of Russia as protector. *Class 1*
Kazakhstan		Early anti-Russian demonstrations could have instigated an adoption of the tribal model, but the regime has successfully balanced **the dualistic model**.	Continued **dualism** Moving the capital to the Kazakh heartland is in accordance with the tribal model, but inclusive citizenship laws are more in tune with the French model.	A 'Narodnik' majority is 6% less satisfied with democratic development than the 'Zapadniki'. Russians are 15% less satisfied with democratic development than Kazakhs.	A **moderately strong potential nationalist challenge** to democracy, modified by liberal citizenship laws and the ambiguity of dualism model. *Class 3*

Class 2 counts countries where a potential nationalist challenge to democracy exists today and where the challenge was even more manifest around the time of the first post-1989 election. In this class we find Estonia, Latvia, the Czech Republic, Slovakia, Romania and Croatia. Estonian and Latvian democratically elected leaders definitely perceived a nationalist challenge from expatriates and Russian speakers in the early 1990s. Their own enactment of restrictive citizenship laws also contributed to this conflict. Post-communist Czechoslovakia was faced with a nationalist challenge so strong that the democratically elected leaders of the Czech and Slovak republics found no other solution than the territorial division of the state. In Romania popular sentiments in the form of extreme right-wing nationalism directed against Hungarians and Gypsies were definitely a challenge. Croatian politics has been marked by nationalist mobilization against their Serb adversaries until very recently. But in all these countries the challenge of nationalism weakened towards the turn of the century. As prospects for European integration loom ever larger in the popular mind and ethnic animosities of the past wane, it has become easier for the leaders of these countries to call for super-national cooperation.

Class 3 consists exclusively of former Soviet republics. It includes Russia itself, the Ukraine, Belarus, Kazakhstan and Georgia. Like the countries of class 2, this group also faced nationalist challenges to their budding democracies in the early 1990s. Russian moderates were faced with the dual challenge of rising right-wing extremism and a nostalgic and strong communist party. The Ukraine was torn between independence-minded citizens in Western Ukraine and voters in Eastern Ukraine favouring strong links to Russia. Similar cleavages emerged in Belarus. In Kazakhstan ethnic unrest directed against Russians occurred even at the time of Gorbachev's *perestroika*. The Georgian nationalist government of Gamsakhurdia succeeded in alienating ethnic minority groups to the point of rebellion. A distinctive feature of the countries in this group is that the nationalist challenges have largely been defused not by elite consensus on international integration, but by virtue of the structure inherited in the dualistic model. In all the countries, with the possible exception of Belarus, the leaders seem to have been relatively successful in striking a balance between CIS membership and autonomous identity. This dualism has a long tradition all the way back to Imperial Russia, and it excludes the possibility of ever reaching consensus about the definition of nationhood. National identity itself remains contentious. Defusing the nationalist challenge through ambiguity rather than through reliance on external possibilities as in class 2 countries, has a price attached to it: the general level of satisfaction with the development of democracy is lower among class 3 countries.

Class 4 includes countries where the nationalist challenge is a real fact of life. This group consists of Macedonia, Bosnia-Herzegovina and Moldova. The two former countries were established in the aftermath of the recent wars in the Balkans. The three different leaderships of Bosnia-Herzegovina have been sworn into office on the basis of internationally supervised elections, marred by nationalist rhetoric and ethnic strife. In Macedonia the conflict between Albanians and Macedonians increased when the country found itself serving as a base area for NATO mobilization and a receptacle for Albanian refugees during the Kosovo conflict. Western powers and the ambiguous nature of the peace accords only seem to strengthen the nationalist grievances in the countries of the former Yugoslav Federation. For Macedonia the situation is further exacerbated by Greek hostility against making Macedonia part of the European process of integration. The situation in Moldova is similar, but with the Russians playing the role of NATO. The presence of the Russian Army on the Eastern banks of the Dnestr, creating a free haven for the Russian minority, would seem to have aggravated nationalism on both sides. There are nevertheless some indications that the national challenge in Moldova is being defused. People increasingly identify themselves as Moldovans to the detriment of irredentist Romanian sentiments. The Russians would seem to prefer Moldovan nationalism to Romanian irredentism, and the present government tries to exploit this possibility.

Class 5 consists of only one country, Serbia. Faced with nationalism as an external as well as an internal challenge, nationalism must be described as the dominant influence on Serb politics in general. During the 1990s, as the former Yugoslavia disintegrated piece by piece, the federalist identity of rump-Yugoslavia became less and less relevant. The strength of the nationalist challenge is epitomized by the growing conflict between Serbia and Montenegro, two provinces sharing the same alphabet, language and religion. In the wake of the Kosovo conflict the cleavage between a Montenegrin leadership oriented towards market reform and the economically old-fashioned Serb leadership is being rapidly transformed into a conflict between a Montenegrin 'ethnos' and Serbs. The hegemony of the national challenge is so strong that it transmutes other cleavages to fit into its image. Thus, democracy may be looked upon as a challenge to nationalism rather than the other way around.

*

Maybe the most interesting result of this exercise is the observation of two modes of operation that may serve to modify potentially strong nationalist challenges. First, the combination of the French model or at least a reduction in the importance of 'ethnos' combined with a growing belief in the benefits of European integration, typical for Central Europe. Secondly, the skilful use of the dualistic model to reduce the potential for nationalist mobilization albeit at the expense of the general level of support for democratic development, a path taken by many CIS countries. Generally speaking, the countries of classes 1, 2 and 3 do not really face manifest challenges, but effective leadership has been necessary to achieve stability in the countries in classes 2 and 3.

We have seen that leadership is a function of the dominant model for nation-building applied as the new states of Central and Eastern Europe emerged. We have indicated above that two of the models, the *tribal* and the *tabula rasa* models, require elite consensus for democracy to take hold. The other two models, the *French* and the *dualistic* models, pave the way for permanent compromises based on territoriality and a dualistic understanding of the role of government respectively. In countries as diverse as Estonia, Latvia and Kazakhstan elite consensus and the weakening of external pressures have enabled leaders to pursue policies to counteract potential challenges. If the opposite were the case, as it sadly was during the inter-war period, it is easy to envisage a leadership struggling to wipe out the 'treacherous' activities by ethnic minorities or 'cosmopolitans', thus alienating further from the democratic process those citizens who hold views different from those of the leadership. The absence of such negative pressures in contemporary Europe and the presence of a pervasive wish for European integration among leaders and citizens alike, create an atmosphere conducive to democratic development even in countries where there is a potential for ethnic or geopolitical dissent.

A general overview of the situation throughout Central and Eastern Europe does not support the notion that forces of nationalism overtly challenge contemporary democracy. Rather, we have primarily pointed to nationalism as a potential challenge throughout the region. It is fairly safe to conclude that as the first decade of Central and East European democracy has drawn to a close, the differences between ethnic minorities and core-populations, between 'Narodniki' and 'Zapadniki', still exist. But at this time, consensus-building and super-national integration seem to take precedence. In comparing the quite legitimate concern for nationalism, shared by many observers in the early 1990s, with the importance attached to European integration towards the end of this decade, we might even argue that the desire for membership in the EU has served to restrain politicians from using national differences as a mobilizing tool. In a sense, EU membership has 'put a lid on nationalism'. When Milosevic's nationalist rhetoric stands out as a sore thumb in contemporary Europe, it is certainly not because his message is new, but rather because similar rhetoric in other countries has been curtailed. For somebody who experienced the fall of the Berlin Wall and the dissolution of the Soviet Union it is rather amazing to ascertain how fast most of the Central and East European countries seem to have turned their back on the nostalgia of past nation-states in order to embrace international integration. The nation-building efforts necessary to resuscitate their newly won independence have not been adverse to their desire for integration into Western Europe. All in all, democratic development has resisted the nationalist challenge one decade after the democratic autumn of 1989.

NOTES

1. The question asked in the CEEB is as follows: 'On the whole, are you very satisfied, fairly satisfied, not very satisfied or not at all satisfied with the development of democracy in your country?'

2. For a closer description of democratic consolidation in these countries, see Michta (1997), Lagerspetz and Vogt (1998), Smith-Sivertsen (1998), Žeruolis (1998), and Daatland and Svege (2000).

3. The post-communist democratization processes of these countries are analysed by Hahn (1997), Mihalisko (1997), Prizel (1997), Remington (1997), and Urban and Gel'man (1997).

4. The dissolution of Czechoslovakia and the democratic consolidation processes in the Czech Republic and Slovakia have been analysed by among others: Mansfeldová (1998), and Wolchik (1997).

5. For democratic consolidation in Hungary and Slovenia, see documentation and analyses by Tóka (1998), Tökés (1997), and Zajc (1998).

6. Recent analyses of democratization in Romania are found in Pilon (1992) and Tismaneanu (1997).

7. The development of political cleavages in Romania is described by Crowther (1998).

8. The development of parties and cleavages has been analysed by Karasimeonov (1998), and Bell (1997).

9. It should be noted that the relative size of the Gypsy sample is considerably smaller than the relative size of the Gypsy population. It would therefore be reasonable to assume that the Gypsies interviewed by CEEB might be biased against the socially most marginal Gypsies.

10. The democratization processes in the countries devolved from former Yugoslavia have been described by Burg (1997), Cohen (1997), Miller (1997), Perry (1997), and Ramet (1997).

11. For democratic development in Albania, see Pano (1997).

12. Moldavian democratization is discussed by Crowther (1997).

13. See Olcott (1997).

14. See Dudwick (1997).

15. Post-communist democratization has been described by Dudwick (1997), and Slider (1997).

16. For a critical assessment of this analytical framework, see Cohen (1999).

REFERENCES

Alter, Peter (1994), *Nationalism*, London, Edward Arnold.

Altermark, Natalja, Frode Overland Andersen and Terje Knutsen (2000), 'Theories of Transition and a Defenition of Consolidation', in Frank H. Aarebrot and Terje Knutsen, eds, *Politics and Citizenship on the Eastern Baltic Seaboard*, Kristiansand S, Høyskoleforlaget.

Barnes, Samuel H. and János Simon (1998), 'The Postcommunist Citizen', in Samuel H. Barnes, Hans-Dieter Klingemann and Janos Simon, eds, *New European Studies*, Vol. 1, Budapest, Erasmus Foundation.

Bell, John D. (1997), 'Democratization and Participation in "Postcommunist" Bulgaria' in Karen Dawisha and Bruce Parrot, eds, *Politics, Power and the Struggle for Democracy in South-East Europe*, Vol. 2, *Democratization and Authoritarianism in Postcommunist Societies*, Cambridge University Press, Cambridge.

Berglund, Sten and Frank H. Aarebrot (1997), *The Political History of Eastern Europe in the 20th Century: The Struggle Between Democracy and Dictatorship*, Cheltenham, Edward Elgar.

Burg, Steven L. (1997), 'Bosnia Herzegovina: A Case of Failed Democratization', in Karen Dawisha and Bruce Parrott, eds, *Politics, Power and the Struggle for Democracy in South-East Europe*, Vol. 2, *Democratization and Authoritarianism in Postcommunist Societies*, Cambridge, Cambridge University Press.

Cohen, Lenard J. (1997), 'Embattled Democracy: Postcommunist Croatia in Transition', in Karen Dawisha and Bruce Parrott, eds, *Politics, Power and the Struggle for Democracy in South-East Europe*, Vol. 2, *Democratization and Authoritarianism in Postcommunist Societies*, Cambridge, Cambridge University Press.

Cohen, Shari J. (1999), *Politics Without a Past: The Absence of History in Post-Communist Nationalism*, Duke University Press.

Crowther, William (1997), 'The Politics of Democratization in Postcommunist Moldova', in Karen Dawisha and Bruce Parrott, eds, *Democratic Changes and Authoritarian Reactions in Russia, Ukraine, Belarus, and Moldova*, Vol. 3, *Democratization and Authoritarianism in Postcommunist Societies*, Cambridge, Cambridge University Press.

Crowther, William (1998), 'Romania', in Sten Berglund, Tomas Hellén, and Frank H. Aarebrot, eds, *The Handbook of Political Change in Eastern Europe*, Cheltenham, Edward Elgar.

Daatland, Christer C. and Hans Petter Svege (2000), 'The Russian-Speakers in Estonia', in Frank H. Aarebrot and Terje Knutsen, eds, *Politics and Citizenship on the Eastern Baltic Seaboard*, Kristiansand, Høyskoleforlaget.

Dudwick, Nora (1997), 'Political Transformations in Postcommunist Armenia: Images and Realities', in Karen Dawisha and Bruce Parrott, eds, *Conflict, Cleavage, and Change in Central Asia and the Caucasus*, Vol. 4, *Democratization and Authoritarianism in Postcommunist Societies*, Cambridge, Cambridge University Press.

Duvold, Kjetil (2000), 'From Homo Sovieticus to Balts: Colonisers, Migrant Workers or a new Diaspora?', in Frank H. Aarebrot and Terje Knutsen, eds, *Politics and Citizenship on the Eastern Baltic Seaboard*, Kristiansand S, Høyskoleforlaget.

Gellner, Ernest (1997), *Nationalism*, London, Weidenfeld & Nicolson.

Grzybowski, Marian (1998), 'Poland', in Sten Berglund, Tomas Hellén, and Frank H. Aarebrot, eds, *The Handbook of Political Change in Eastern Europe*, Cheltenham, Edward Elgar.

Hahn, Jeffrey W. (1997), 'Democratization and Political Participation in Russia's Regions', in Karen Dawisha and Bruce Parrott, eds, *Democratic Changes and Authoritarian Reactions in Russia, Ukraine, Belarus, and Moldova*, Vol. 3, *Democratization and Authoritarianism in Postcommunist Societies*, Cambridge, Cambridge University Press.

Hobsbawm, Eric J. (1990), *Nations and Nationalism Since 1780: Programme, Myth, Reality*, Cambridge, Cambridge University Press.

Hushagen, Anne (2000), 'The Minority Situation in Lithuania', in Frank H. Aarebrot and Terje Knutsen, eds, *Politics and Citizenship on the Eastern Baltic Seaboard*, Kristiansand S, Høyskoleforlaget.

Karasimeonov, Georgi (1998), 'Bulgaria', in Sten Berglund, Tomas Hellén, and Frank H. Aarebrot, eds, *The Handbook of Political Change in Eastern Europe*, Cheltenham, Edward Elgar.

Kedourie, Elie (1993), *Nationalism*, Oxford, Blackwell.

Kellas, James G. (1998), *The Politics of Nationalism and Ethnicity*, Basingstoke, Macmillan.

Krejčí, Jaroslav and Pavel Machon (1996), *Czechoslovakia, 1918–1992: A Laboratory for Social Change*, Basingstoke, Macmillan Press.

Lagerspetz, Mikko and Henri Vogt (1998), 'Estonia', in Sten Berglund, Tomas Hellén, and Frank H. Aarebrot, eds, *The Handbook of Political Change in Eastern Europe*, Cheltenham, Edward Elgar.

Mansfeldová, Zdenka (1998), 'The Czech and Slovak Republics', in Sten Berglund, Tomas Hellén, and Frank H. Aarebrot, eds, *The Handbook of Political Change in Eastern Europe*, Cheltenham, Edward Elgar.

Michta, Andrew A. (1997), 'Democratic Consolidation in Poland after 1989', in Karen Dawisha and Bruce Parrott, eds, *Democratization and Authoritarianism in Post-Communist Societies: 1. The Consolidation of Democracy in East-Central Europe*, Cambridge, Cambridge University Press.

Mihalisko, Kathleen J. (1997), 'Belarus: Retreat to Authoritarism', in Karen Dawisha and Bruce Parrott, eds, *Democratic Changes and Authoritarian Reactions in Russia, Ukraine, Belarus, and Moldova*, Vol. 3, *Democratization and Authoritarianism in Postcommunist Societies*, Cambridge, Cambridge University Press.

Miller, Nicholas J. (1997), 'A Failed Transition: The Case of Serbia', in Karen Dawisha and Bruce Parrott, eds, *Politics, Power and the Struggle for Democracy in South-East Europe*, Vol. 2, *Democratization and Authoritarianism in Postcommunist Societies*, Cambridge, Cambridge University Press.

Olcott, Martha Brill (1997), 'Democratization and the Growth of Political Participation in Kazakstan', in Karen Dawisha and Bruce Parrott, eds, *Conflict, Cleavage, and Change in Central Asia and the Caucasus*, Vol. 4, *Democratization and Authoritarianism in Postcommunist Societies*, Cambridge, Cambridge University Press.

Olson, Davis M. (1997), 'Democratization and Political Participation: The Experience of the Czech Republic', in Karen Dawisha and Bruce Parrott, eds, *Democratization and Authoritarianism in Post-Communist Societies: 1. The Consolidation of Democracy in East-Central Europe*, Cambridge, Cambridge University Press.

Özkirimli, Umut (2000), *Theories of Nationalism: A Critical Introduction*, Basingstoke, Hampshire and New York, Macmillan and St. Martin's Press.

Pano, Nicholas (1997), 'The Process of Democratization in Albania', in Karen Dawisha and Bruce Parrott, eds, *Politics, Power and the Struggle for Democracy in South-East Europe*, Vol. 2, *Democratization and Authoritarianism in Postcommunist Societies*, Cambridge, Cambridge University Press.

Parland, Thomas (1993), *The Rejection in Russia of Totalitarian Socialism and Liberal Democracy: A Study of the Russian New Right*, Helsinki, Finnish Society of Sciences and Letters.

Perry, Duncan N. (1997), 'The Republic of Macedonia: Finding its Way', in Karen Dawisha and Bruce Parrott, eds, *Politics, Power and the Struggle for Democracy in South-East Europe*, Vol. 2, *Democratization and Authoritarianism in Postcommunist Societies*, Cambridge, Cambridge University Press.

Pilon, Juliana Geran (1992), *The Bloody Flag: Post-Communist Nationalism in Eastern Europe: Spotlight on Romania*, New Brunswick, Transaction Publishers.

Prizel, Ilya (1997), 'Ukraine Between Proto-Democracy and 'Soft' Authoritarianism', in Karen Dawisha and Bruce Parrott, eds, *Democratic Changes and Authoritarian Reactions in Russia, Ukraine, Belarus, and Moldova*, Vol. 3, *Democratization and Authoritarianism in Postcommunist Societies*, Cambridge, Cambridge University Press.

Prizel, Ilya (1998), *National Identity and Foreign Policy: Nationalism and Leadership in Poland, Russia and Ukraine*, Cambridge, Cambridge University Press.

Ramet, Sabrina Petra (1997), 'Democratization in Slovenia – the Second Stage', in Karen Dawisha and Bruce Parrott, eds, *Politics, Power and the Struggle for Democracy in South-East Europe*, Vol. 2, *Democratization and Authoritarianism in Postcommunist Societies*, Cambridge, Cambridge University Press.

Remington, Thomas F. (1997), 'Democratization and the New Political Order in Russia', in Karen Dawisha and Bruce Parrott, eds, *Democratic Changes and Authoritarian Reactions in Russia,*

Ukraine, Belarus, and Moldova, Vol. 3, *Democratization and Authoritarianism in Postcommunist Societies*, Cambridge, Cambridge University Press.

Sandle, Mark (1999), 'Searching for a National Identity: Intellectual Debates in Post-Soviet Russia', in C. Williams and T.D. Sfikas, eds, *Nationalism in Russia, the CIS and the Baltic States*, Aldershot, Ashgate.

Slider, Darryll (1997), 'Democratization in Georgia', in Karen Dawisha and Bruce Parrott, eds, *Conflict, Cleavage, and Change in Central Asia and the Caucasus*, Vol. 4, *Democratization and Authoritarianism in Postcommunist Societies*, Cambridge, Cambridge University Press.

Smith, Anthony D. (1991), *National Identity*, London, Penguin.

Smith, Graham (1999), *The Post-Soviet States: Mapping the Politics of Transition*, London, Arnold.

Smith-Sivertsen, Hermann (1998), 'Latvia', in Sten Berglund, Tomas Hellén, and Frank H. Aarebrot, eds, *The Handbook of Political Change in Eastern Europe*, Cheltenham, Edward Elgar.

Sødergren, Heidi (2000) 'The Latvian Nationalising State and the Question of Citizenship', in Frank H. Aarebrot and Terje Knutsen, eds, *Politics and Citizenship on the Eastern Baltic Seaboard*, Kristiansand S, Høyskoleforlaget.

Tamir, Yael (1993), *Liberal Nationalism*, Princeton, Princeton University Press.

Tismaneanu, Vladimir (1997), 'Romanian Exceptionalism? Democracy, Ethnocracy and Uncertain Pluralism in Post-Ceauşescu Romania', in Karen Dawisha and Bruce Parrott, eds, *Politics, Power and the Struggle for Democracy in South-East Europe*, Vol. 2, *Democratization and Authoritarianism in Postcommunist Societies*, Cambridge, Cambridge University Press.

Tóka, Gábor (1998), 'Hungary', in Sten Berglund, Tomas Hellén, and Frank H. Aarebrot, eds, *The Handbook of Political Change in Eastern Europe*, Cheltenham, Edward Elgar.

Tökés, Rudolf L. (1997), 'Party Politics and Political Participation in Postcommunist Hungary, in Karen Dawisha and Bruce Parrott, eds, *Democratization and Authoritarianism in Post-Communist Societies: 1. The Consolidation of Democracy in East-Central Europe*, Cambridge, Cambridge University Press.

Urban, Michael and Vladimir Gel'man (1997), 'The Development of Political Parties in Russia', in Karen Dawisha and Bruce Parrott, eds, *Democratic Changes and Authoritarian Reactions in Russia, Ukraine, Belarus, and Moldova*, Vol. 3, *Democratization and Authoritarianism in Postcommunist Societies*, Cambridge, Cambridge University Press.

Wolchik, Sharon L. (1997), 'Democratization and Political Participation in Slovakia', in Karen Dawisha and Bruce Parrott, eds, *Democratization and Authoritarianism in Post-Communist Societies: 1. The Consolidation of Democracy in East-Central Europe*, Cambridge, Cambridge University Press.

Zajc, Drago (1998), 'Slovenia', in Sten Berglund, Tomas Hellén, and Frank H. Aarebrot, eds, *The Handbook of Political Change in Eastern Europe*, Cheltenham, Edward Elgar.

Žeruolis, Darius (1998), 'Lithuania', in Sten Berglund, Tomas Hellén, and Frank H. Aarebrot, eds, *The Handbook of Political Change in Eastern Europe*, Cheltenham, Edward Elgar.

5. The Challenge of Human Rights

The rule of law is often cast as a prerequisite of democracy. It constitutes the backbone of the civil liberties and political rights that add substance to the democratic form of government; it provides the platform for private as well as public contractual obligations, and it serves as a guarantee against corruption, arbitrariness and human rights abuse. It is a crucial but highly complex theoretical concept, and like most such concepts it does not lend itself to straightforward measurement. Yet it is imperative that we generate yardsticks by which we can classify countries with respect to the rule of law. Does the rule of law prevail or does it not; and to the extent that it is found to prevail, how do the individual countries compare as regards their achievements within this domain?

The three indices – the political rights, civil liberties and freedom ratings – produced by *Freedomhouse* may be seen as an attempt to provide the public and the academic community with the tools required to compare countries with respect to their civil and human rights records, all of which are crucial for the rule of law. The instruments may be blunt, but the outcome of a decade of measurements would nevertheless seem to corroborate the conventional wisdom about the new democracies in Central and Eastern Europe. The Central European countries of Poland, Hungary, the Czech Republic and Slovenia get top ratings on all counts; the three Baltic republics – Estonia, Latvia and Lithuania – follow suit with scores only marginally different from those of the Central European countries, while the Balkan countries and the CIS (*Commonwealth of Independent States*) member states do less well. Bulgaria and Romania remain squarely among the 'free' states of Eastern Europe, though less convincingly so than the Baltic states and the countries of Central Europe. The successor states of the Yugoslav Federation, the Slovak Republic and the CIS member states perform much worse. With the exception of Slovenia – a former member of the Yugoslav Federation – they are at best listed as 'partly free' or 'not free at all'. It may be noted that the entire Commonwealth of Independent States, including Russia, the Ukraine and Belarus, does not include a single 'free' state (Table 5.1).

Table 5.1: Freedom ratings of post-communist countries 1996–97 on a scale from 1 (most free) to 7 (least free), and CEEB 1996 human rights ratings on a scale from 1 (most positive) to 4 (most negative). The freedom rating is a composite judgment based on survey results.[1]

Country	Political Rights	Civil Liberties	Freedom rating F = Free PF = Partly Free NF = Not Free	Attitudes towards human rights situation (country rating)
	1996–97	1996–97	1996–97	CEEB 7
Estonia	1	2	F	2
Latvia	2	2	F	3
Lithuania	1	2	F	4
Poland	1	2	F	2
Hungary	1	2	F	2
Czech Republic	1	2	F	2
Slovenia	1	2	F	2
Slovakia	2	4	PF	3
Romania	2	3	F	3
Bulgaria	2	3	F	2
Croatia	4	4	PF	1
Yugoslavia	6	6	NF	1
Bosnia-Herzegovina	5	5	PF	–
Macedonia	4	3	PF	2
Albania	4	4	PF	1
Russia	3	4	PF	4
Ukraine	3	4	PF	4
Belarus	6	6	NF	3
Moldova	3	4	PF	–
Georgia	4	4	PF	3
Armenia	5	4	PF	3
Azerbaijan	6	5	NF	–
Kazakhstan	6	5	NF	3
Turkmenistan	7	7	NF	–
Tajikistan	7	7	NF	–
Uzbekistan	7	6	NF	–
Kyrgyz Republic	4	4	PF	–

Source: http://www.freedomhouse.org/

The last column of the table – the re-coded data from the *Central and Eastern Eurobarometer*-surveys (CEEB) – is not part of the standard output of *Freedomhouse*. The item we have singled out for attention – the respondent's assessment of the human rights situation in his/her home country – comes close to tapping the rule of law dimension of interest to *Freedomhouse* (Beetham 1999, 34–5). The question put to the respondents reads: 'How much respect is there for individual human rights nowadays in (your country)? Do you feel there is a lot of respect for individual human rights, some respect, not much respect or no respect at all?' In the table the countries have been listed on a scale from 1 to 4 on the basis of the strength of the positive or negative assessments of the human rights situation. A country like Albania, where almost 75 per cent of the respondents feel there is a lot or some respect for human rights, is given a 1; and countries like Russia and Lithuania, where less than 20 per cent express such confidence in their respective governments, are given a 4.

The two sets of measures turn out to be strongly inter-correlated. The human rights index roughly follows the pattern reported by *Freedomhouse*, at least when it comes to Central Europe (Poland, Hungary, the Czech Republic, Slovenia and Slovakia), two of the Baltic states (Estonia and Latvia) and the bulk of the Balkan states and CIS countries, including Bulgaria, Romania, Russia and the Ukraine. But there are also some deviant cases, most notably Croatia, Yugoslavia, Macedonia and Albania. The surprisingly high levels of satisfaction with the respect for human rights in these countries in no way correspond to the actual situation, as reported and understood by *Freedomhouse*. Similar comments apply to Lithuania, which ranks on a par with Russia and the Ukraine on the human rights index on account of the unexpectedly high level of dissatisfaction with the human rights record of its government.

*

The pros and cons of the various indices may be discussed at some length; and various hypotheses may be put forward to account for the discrepancies between the human rights index and the three *Freedomhouse* ratings. We have an interest not only in this kind of system level indicators but also in mass political behaviour. We, therefore, have little choice but to opt for the human rights data gathered on behalf of the European Commission. This is not a bad choice, though. The standard CEEB human rights item taps important parts of what is generally referred to as the rule of law or *Rechtstaatlichkeit*; and to the extent that the data are biased, they are plagued by a systematic bias which may easily be taken into account, if we feel that citizens of some specific countries may not be relied upon to assess the human rights situation in their respective countries properly.

The Thrust of the Investigation

The focus of this chapter will be on the human rights situation in Central and Eastern Europe as perceived by representative samples of citizens from the full range of countries covered by the CEEB surveys. The analysis breaks down into two main sections.

In the following section, an attempt will be made to identify the major correlates of satisfaction versus dissatisfaction with the human rights situation in the respondents' respective home countries. In the process, two alternative hypotheses will be put to a test. The first hypothesis says that 'losers' are particularly prone to articulate dissatisfaction with the human rights situation in their respective home countries. They have been left behind on the bumpy road from plan to market economy; they have a number of grievances about the capacity of the political system to deliver the material or immaterial goods they feel entitled to, including the protection of their human rights, and they fail to see the difference between the injustices of the past and those of the present. The second hypothesis casts dissatisfaction with the human rights situation as a phenomenon of the 'winners', that is the emerging middle classes of Eastern Europe. They are well-off, well educated and strategically located in the economic transition process, and as such more likely than others to monitor the human rights situation at home with critical eyes. The first hypothesis may incidentally account for the widespread dissatisfaction with human rights in Bulgaria and the latter for the unexpectedly low level of dissatisfaction with human rights among Albanians.

In the subsequent section, the focus is no longer on the human rights situation as such, but on the impact of human rights on the development of democracy, once again as perceived by the citizens of Central and Eastern Europe. Democratic governments are expected not only to protect the human rights of its citizens but also to provide for their material well-being. Development of democracy will, therefore, be cast as a function of the government's human rights and economic records (Klingemann and Hofferbert 1998). The communist regimes of Central and Eastern Europe had promoted economic progress rather than human rights. By the late 1980s, it had become readily apparent that the planned economies of Central and Eastern Europe simply were irreparably behind the mature market economies of Western Europe, North America and Asia, but as a rule it was not economic grievances that made the citizens of Eastern Europe take to the streets in 1989–90 and call for civil liberties, political rights and an end to communist repression. It is probably fair to say that the new democratic regimes of Central and Eastern Europe spelled improvement of the human rights situation throughout the entire region, including South Eastern Europe. Romania of the early 1990s may have been less than an ideal democracy, but it was nevertheless a far better and a much safer place for the political opposition than Romania of the late 1980s when Nicolae Ceauşescu ran the country as his personal fiefdom; and few, if any, are better qualified to appreciate the difference than – in this case – Romanians themselves. We would, therefore, expect the human rights dimension to be a crucial factor at the outset of the transition process but to lose importance as freedom is gradually being taken for granted.

Questioning the Human Rights Record of Post-Communist Regimes

A few short months after the breakdown of communism, East Europeans found themselves exposed to opinion pollsters, prodding for answers to questions that simply were not put under communism. The respondents normally did not hesitate to articulate their opinions, including the kind of critical opinions that had to be suppressed under communism. Some East Europeans had come out publicly against the human rights record of the ruling communist regimes while they were still in command, but such dissent had stiff penalties attached to it. And most East Europeans would probably have thought more than once before offering a negative answer to a CEEB style human rights prod prior to the transition from communism.

Map 5.1: 'No respect for human rights at all'. Over-time averages Percentages[2] *(CEEB 2–8, 1991–97)*

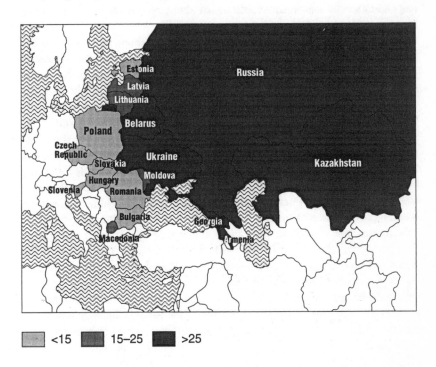

<15   15–25   >25

The fear just is not there any more; and there is certainly no shortage of critical comments about the post-communist regimes in the CEEB surveys. The level of distrust in the government's willingness and ability to respect human rights in fact reaches alarming proportions at times. In Armenia, Russia, the Ukraine and Georgia an average of more than 40 per cent (*sic!*)

of the respondents say they think the government has no respect for human rights at all. With over-time averages hovering around 30 per cent, Belarus and Kazakhstan do better, but not well enough to be considered part and parcel of any of the other two distinct clusters of countries that may be identified – a group of countries with low and another group of countries with moderate levels of distrust in the fairness of the government (Map 5.1). The former includes the countries of Central Europe – the Czech and Slovak republics, Hungary, Slovenia and Poland – as well as Estonia, Bulgaria and Romania, all of which have over-time averages of less than 15 per cent. The latter features Latvia and Lithuania along with Macedonia and Moldova, all with over-time averages of more than 15 and less than 25 per cent.

It is no coincidence that discontent with the government's human rights record is more widespread in countries with shaky economic performance and rapidly rising crime rates than elsewhere. 'Economic hardship' and 'crime and violence' were in fact the two top reasons listed by those respondents who came out sceptical of the government's human rights record (read: not much and no respect at all), when prodded for their underlying motives by the architects of CEEB 3, while 'freedom' and the 'ability to travel' hold top priority among those respondents who expressed confidence in the government's respect for human rights (read: a lot and some respect) at the same point in time (Appendix 5.1). With the possible exception of 'economic hardship', these are arguments of obvious relevance to the international discourse on the rule of law and *Rechtstaatlichkeit*.

The human rights item is closely intertwined with a few of the other standard attitude items in the CEEB barometer, including satisfaction with the development of democracy to which we will return in the following section. But the impact on human rights of the standard set of socio-economic variables, including age, occupation and education, seems to be scant, at least when measured without controlling for country (Table 5.2).

Table 5.2: Human rights and some of its correlates (Pearson's r)

CEEB 7 (all countries)	Respect for Human Rights
Satisfaction with the development of democracy	.49
Satisfaction with development in general	.40
Financial situation next twelve months (anticipated)	.33
Financial situation last twelve months (evaluated)	.32
Attitudes towards the creation of a free market economy	.29
Occupation	.06
Age	.05
Urban/rural residence	−.05
Education	−.00

Source: CEEB 7.

Table 5.3 (below) provides a closer look at the socioeconomic dynamics behind East European citizens' response to the issue of human rights. It sets out to test what was previously referred to as the 'loser'/'winner' hypotheses. It does so by focusing on those respondents who react to the human rights item by expressing an all-out distrust in the good faith and intentions of a government which they claim 'has no respect for human rights at all'. The impact of the 'loser'/'winner' dimension is tapped by four separate, standard CEEB items – education, rural versus urban residence, age and type of work (qualified, semi-qualified and not qualified) – of obvious relevance in this context.

Some comments about each of these indicators may be in order. Education was one of the largely successful pet projects of the now defunct communist regimes of Central and Eastern Europe. By 1989–90 the region actually featured a higher level of education than ever before (Berglund and Aarebrot 1997). Education clearly does not spell instant success anywhere, and particularly not in countries undergoing rapid political and economic change, but it remains an asset as part of the social capital on which the individual citizens may draw. The rural/urban dimension was also profoundly affected by half a decade or more of Soviet style communism in Eastern Europe. Small-scale private farming had to give way to large-scale co-operative or state-owned agrarian-industrial complexes in a deliberate attempt by the communist regime to make agricultural production modern and efficient. The wave of collectivization that swept through Eastern Europe in the late 1940s and early 1950s also served other purposes of crucial importance to the communist regimes. Private farming was wiped out; the peasantry was transformed into an agrarian working class, and the agrarian parties that had survived the transition to communist rule were deprived of their independent power base. The breakdown of communism in the late 1980s and early 1990s has admittedly introduced a dynamic element into rural Eastern Europe, but – all other things being equal – we would nevertheless argue that rural residence remains a relative disadvantage. The growth sectors of contemporary Eastern Europe tend to be located elsewhere.

The transition from plan to market spelled problems for most East Europeans and particularly for the upper age cohorts. Pensioners – and, for that matter, others living on fixed incomes – found it particularly difficult to make ends meet in an emerging market economy without large scale government subsidies of basic services and commodities. The younger generation – the sons and daughters of those who were in their fifties when the communist regimes came tumbling down – were only slightly better off. Job security, pension rights, health care, work eligibility requirements and working conditions in general were all up for re-negotiation, and nothing could be taken for granted. Young people, on the other hand, had little to lose and possibly much to gain from the transformation of the Central and East European societies into market economies and liberal democracies. Similar comments apply to qualified as opposed to semi-qualified and non-qualified workers or employees, but it would be less than honest not to admit that the line of demarcation between these categories has a certain ambiguity to it. We have simply re-coded the occupational categories in the CEEB barometers in such a way as to give a certain edge to those active within the competitive private sector (Appendix 5.2).

We are now ready to present our two hypotheses in operational form. The loser hypothesis says that losers – the poorly educated, the rural dwellers, the upper age cohorts and the non-qualified – are more likely than winners to come out strongly against the human rights situation in their respective home countries. It casts dissatisfaction with the government's human rights record as part and parcel of a general feeling of *malaise* among East Europeans with the odds tilted against them in the transition from plan to market. But there is also a good case to be made for the counter-hypothesis which says that winners – the well educated, the city dwellers, the young and the qualified – are more likely than losers to monitor the human rights situation critically.

On the whole, however, the empirical evidence supports the loser hypothesis. There is a general trend for respondents with little education to be more negative towards the human rights record of their respective governments than those with higher education. Similar comments apply to age and occupation. In the vast majority of cases, dissatisfaction with the human rights situation at home consistently increases as we move from the young (15–35) to the middle aged (36–60) in the same way as it decreases as we move from non-qualified to semi-qualified or qualified workers.

But dissatisfaction with human rights does *not* tend to be a rural phenomenon, as the loser hypothesis would have it; it is in fact a distinctly urban phenomenon in all but four countries – the Czech Republic, Slovakia, Georgia and Russia. In Russia, there is a great deal of dissatisfaction with the way the government is handling the human rights situation (more than 50 per cent), but rural folks are only somewhat more likely than city dwellers to be dissatisfied. Similar comments apply to Georgia, which is marked by a general rate of dissatisfaction of around 30 per cent. We find the same general pattern in the Czech and Slovak republics, but in those instances we are talking about considerably more modest levels of dissatisfaction in the range of 9–14 per cent. Although the underlying causes of this behaviour might be the same in all four countries, it is obvious that they do not constitute a homogeneous group.

This also goes for the mainstream countries, complying with the winner hypothesis in the sense that dissatisfaction with human rights tends to be an urban phenomenon. We are dealing with a very heterogeneous set of countries, including Armenia and the Ukraine in the Commonwealth of Independent States as well as Estonia and Latvia. The two former have high levels of dissatisfaction and smallish differences between rural and urban residents; the two latter have modest overall levels of dissatisfaction but urban and rural residents at quite a distance from one another on the human rights item.

Table 5.3: 'No respect for human rights at all' by demographics.
Percentages

	RESPECT FOR HUMAN RIGHTS: 'UNACCEPTABLE'									
	Education		Rural/Urban		Age			Occupation		
	High	Low	Rural	Urban	15–35	36–60	61+	Un-qualified	Semi-qualified	Quali-fied
Albania	6.0 100	9.0 851	7.7 626	10.4 356	7.7 451	9.6 446	11.8 85	10.8 566	5.0 221	6.7 195
Armenia	45.1 224	40.8 770	40.9 587	43.0 407	37.4 404	43.5 382	47.1 208	44.6 653	34.9 272	42.0 69
Belarus	41.6 221	29.2 783	27.5 530	37.1 475	32.7 352	34.8 434	25.6 219	30.7 675	32.6 267	44.4 63
Bulgaria	21.2 165	21.0 784	18.8 554	24.3 395	15.2 349	24.2 413	25.1 187	23.8 659	11.7 205	22.4 85
Croatia	3.2 189	7.2 732	5.6 693	9.1 231	6.5 355	6.7 420	6.3 144	7.0 484	2.9 206	8.9 203
Czech Republic	4.2 95	11.8 879	12.4 524	9.5 453	9.6 408	12.7 418	10.7 149	12.5 511	6.7 180	11.2 278
Slovakia	8.9 112	14.8 900	14.3 481	14.1 533	11.8 466	15.5 401	18.5 146	15.9 611	11.4 167	11.0 219
Estonia	11.4 158	10.0 902	6.7 480	13.1 580	8.5 422	10.9 411	11.9 227	12.9 498	6.8 279	8.8 283
Hungary	9.9 111	15.0 827	12.6 525	16.7 413	11.8 287	13.6 396	18.4 255	15.0 600	14.6 171	12.4 161
Latvia	17.3 185	18.3 774	15.3 450	20.6 544	15.7 376	15.9 427	28.3 191	18.8 573	16.9 249	18.0 172
Lithuania	21.7 184	29.8 773	27.1 520	29.5 437	25.1 335	29.8 450	30.2 172	30.6 566	23.1 182	26.3 209
Mace-donia	8.1 74	22.0 905	20.8 553	21.1 426	22.1 416	22.5 408	13.5 155	22.0 700	14.0 114	21.3 164
Poland	8.7 92	13.0 856	12.3 718	13.5 230	9.4 309	13.2 484	16.8 155	12.3 634	8.8 137	16.4 177
Romania	7.4 148	12.5 1023	10.9 649	13.1 526	12.4 402	11.0 592	13.8 181	12.5 803	10.8 195	10.7 177
Russia	53.2 171	52.8 856	53.7 748	50.5 279	44.5 326	56.5 487	57.5 214	54.4 733	42.2 199	63.2 95
Slovenia	11.7 197	11.6 895	11.5 820	12.1 272	8.3 420	12.9 459	15.5 213	14.5 620	7.8 333	7.9 139
Ukraine	51.7 232	49.6 896	49.1 701	51.5 427	46.5 359	51.5 507	51.9 262	51.0 789	46.9 228	49.5 111
Georgia	26.4 220	28.6 761	28.9 533	27.4 453	22.6 451	31.4 408	37.8 127	30.3 521	25.7 377	26.1 88
Kazakh-stan	39.1 161	34.1 819	32.7 636	38.9 347	30.8 438	36.5 419	43.7 126	35.0 719	33.3 174	36.7 90
Yugo-slavia	15.1 166	12.3 767	11.6 664	15.3 274	13.8 377	12.2 434	11.0 127	12.9 582	10.7 206	14.7 150

Source: CEEB 7, 1996.

In Estonia and Latvia, the outcome may be attributed to the strong element of ethnic Russians within urban conglomerations. The vast majority of the Baltic Russians immigrated to the region while it was still part of the Soviet empire. They actually stand out as losers rather than winners in the sense that they ended up in some kind of involuntary exile (Lagerspetz and Vogt 1998; Smith-Sivertsen 1998). But Belarus, Bulgaria, Kazakhstan and Yugoslavia (Serbia) – four other countries featuring large differences between rural and urban residents – would have to be otherwise accounted for, perhaps in terms of the lingering impact of authoritarian or semi-authoritarian regimes on the mobilization of the countryside (Karasimeonov 1998; Linz and Stepan 1996).

A close inspection of the table alerts us to a few other subtleties in the data. The relationship between human rights and age is not always linear. The oldest respondents (61+) in our sample occasionally – in Belarus, Croatia, Macedonia and Yugoslavia – come out as more satisfied with the human rights record of their respective governments than the younger age cohorts. Such an outcome is by no means theoretically counterintuitive. In terms of material welfare, old people are among the most obvious losers of the current transition processes in Central and Eastern Europe. But in terms of immaterial values, they may be the true winners. Rights and freedoms, of which they were deprived when young, have now to some extent been restored. This may indeed be the perspective applied by old citizens of Belarus, Croatia, Macedonia and Yugoslavia at the time of CEEB 7 (1996), but the nature of the post-communist regimes in those countries should make us open to yet another interpretation. The relative satisfaction of old Belorussians, Croatians, Macedonians and Yugoslavs with the human rights record of their respective governments may be no more and no less than a standard expression of regime support, whether 'spontaneous' or not.

The relationship between human rights and occupation also displays curvilinear features. With the sole exception of Belarus, the unqualified in our trichotomy are consistently more dissatisfied than the semi-qualified, but they are not always more dissatisfied than the qualified. Russia, Belarus and Kazakhstan are in fact the most prominent cases of widespread human rights dissatisfaction among losers and winners alike. Table 5.3 also testifies to a great deal of between-country variation. Well educated East Europeans are more likely than East Europeans with poor education to express satisfaction with the human rights records of their respective governments, but this does not mean that they are all equally pleased. In Croatia a meagre 3.2 per cent of the well educated express dissatisfaction with the human rights record of the government. In the Ukraine and Russia, on the other hand, well over 50 per cent of the well-educated respondents come out strongly against the government's human rights performance.

Table 5.4: Respect for human rights: 'Unacceptable' among the well educated. Percentages

'Unacceptable' (0–10 per cent)	'Unacceptable' (11–25 per cent)	'Unacceptable' (26+ per cent)
Croatia 3.2 (PF)	Estonia 11.4 (F)	Georgia 26.4 (PF)
Czech Republic 4.2 (F)	Slovenia 11.7 (F)	Kazakhstan 39.1 (NF)
Albania 6.0 (PF)	Yugoslavia 15.1 (NF)	Belarus 41.6 (NF)
Romania 7.4 (F)	Latvia 17.3 (F)	Armenia 45.1 (PF)
Macedonia 8.1 (PF)	Bulgaria 21.2 (F)	Ukraine 51.7 (PF)
Poland 8.7 (F)	Lithuania 21.7 (F)	Russia 53.2 (PF)
Slovakia 8.9 (PF)		
Hungary 9.9 (F)		

Note: The *Freedomhouse* ratings (within brackets) are from 1996–97.
Source: CEEB 7, 1996.

In Table 5.4 we have simply divided all the countries in the previous table into three groups with respect to the proportion of intellectual dissent on the human rights issue. There is a group of countries such as the Czech Republic and Croatia, where but a minor fraction of the intelligentsia expresses all-out distrust in the government's ability and willingness to respect human rights. There is yet another group of countries including Georgia, Belarus and Russia with a substantial share of intellectual human rights dissent and a third group of countries such as Estonia, Yugoslavia and Lithuania with proportions of intellectual dissent hovering between these two extremes.

The outcome ties in with *Freedomhouse*, but the fit is far from perfect. The right-hand column of the table – featuring Georgia, Belarus, Russia and a few other countries with a substantial proportion of intellectual human rights dissent – only includes countries rated as 'partially free' or 'not free'. The two other columns are slightly more problematic. It is hardly surprising to find countries like the Czech Republic, Slovakia, Poland and Hungary or, for that matter, a South European country like Romania in the left-hand column. They all have democratic credentials that stretch at least a few years back and – with the exception of Slovakia – they are all listed as 'free' by *Freedomhouse*. Nor is it surprising to find the three Baltic states along with Bulgaria in the mid column. These countries also have respectable democratic credentials, and they are all considered 'free' by *Freedomhouse*. There is even a case to be made for positioning the Baltic countries slightly behind the other democracies in the region (Hellén, Berglund and Aarebrot 1998), but Slovenia and Bulgaria have ended up somewhat out of context.

More problematic, however, are the appearance of Albania and the Yugoslav successor states of Croatia and Macedonia with a shaky democratic record among the more or less well established transitional democracies of Central and Eastern Europe. The outcome is *not* a statistical artefact in the sense that there are too few well-educated Albanians,

Macedonians and so on in the sample to make for reliable analyses. It is real and reliable enough, and we would be inclined to interpret it in a historically comparative fashion. Post-communist Albania may not be a democracy, but it is a much better and safer place to live, particularly in terms of human rights, than Albania at the time of Enver Hoxha's die-hard neo-Stalinist regime. One swallow may not make a summer, but there may be times when even a little freedom makes a lot of difference.

Taking Freedom for Granted?

The current West European debate about democracy in Eastern Europe is frequently based on the implicit assumption that West European democracy may be taken for granted and serve as a model. This approach may be captured by substituting the West for the Soviet Union in an East German communist party slogan of the 1950s (Leonhard 1994): 'Who learns from the West learns how to triumph'. We believe things are slightly more complex.

Map 5.2: 'Not at all satisfied with democracy'. Over-time averages[2] (CEEB 2–8, 1991–97) Percentages

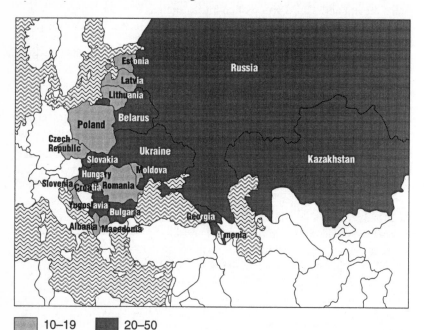

██ 10–19   ██ 20–50

Contemporary Western Europe is in fact beset by many of the problems encountered in the East European context, albeit in different forms and in a different order of magnitude. Most of Western Europe is in the midst of a transition process of sorts. Harsh economic realities undermine the welfare states, which were built from the 1950s and onwards on the dual assumption of continuous growth and the primacy of politics. The increasing inability of the welfare state to deliver on its outstanding promises erodes the legitimacy of the national political system as well as the attachments to political parties (Biorcio and Mannheimer 1995). This has not yet reached alarming proportions, but it is worth noting that Western Europe includes countries with levels of dissatisfaction with democracy comparable to some of the more extreme cases in the belt of democratic dissatisfaction in Eastern Europe, including Russia, Belarus, the Ukraine and stretching deep into Hungary, Yugoslavia and Bulgaria (Map 5.2; Berglund and Aarebrot 1997).

The focus in this section is on individual attitudes towards democracy in the post-communist countries of Central and Eastern Europe. More specifically, we are interested in two alternative explanations of satisfaction with democracy – political versus economic explanations. In both cases, the dependent variable is democratic legitimacy, measured in terms of citizens' assessment of the development of democracy in their respective countries. If we find *economic prospects* to be a more important indicator of democratic satisfaction than *political rights* – nowadays more or less taken for granted – we would have a strong case for the notion that Eastern Europe has reached the stable position where citizens can afford to take freedom for granted in the same way that West Europeans presumably do.

When analysing 1995 survey data from 18 post-communist countries in Central and Eastern Europe (*Central and Eastern Eurobarometer* No. 6), Hans-Dieter Klingemann and Richard Hofferbert test the following alternative hypotheses accounting for satisfaction with democracy:

1. The higher the citizen's estimate of the condition of individual human rights, the more positive the evaluation of democratic performance.
2. The more positive the citizen's estimate of personal economic conditions, the more favourable the evaluation of democratic performance.

Satisfaction with democracy – the dependent variable – is measured by the following question in the CEEB surveys: 'On the whole, are you very satisfied, fairly satisfied, not very satisfied, or not at all satisfied with the way democracy is developing in [your country]?'. The first independent variable in Klingemann and Hofferbert's analyses is identical with the CEEB human rights item, familiar from the previous section of this chapter. As will be remembered, it reads: 'How much respect is there for individual human rights nowadays in [your country]? Do you feel there is a lot of respect for individual human rights, some respect, not much respect or no respect at all?'. The second independent variable is based on yet another standard item from the *Central and Eastern Eurobarometers*. It reads: 'Over the next twelve months, do you expect the financial situation of your household will get a lot better, a little better, stay the same, get a little worse, or get a lot worse?'

Klingemann and Hofferbert's findings strongly suggest that citizens' human-rights situation is a more powerful predictor of democratic satisfaction than self-ascribed economic prospects (Table 5.5): 'It was not for groceries that the people of the Central and Eastern European countries took to the streets between 1989 and 1991. It was for freedom.' (Klingemann and Hofferbert 1998). We believe their findings to be true.

Table 5.5: Predicting democratic performance with assessments of human rights conditions and economic prospects (CEEB 6, 1995)

	Correlation		Multiple Regression		
	Human Rights (r)	Economic Prospects (r)	Human Rights (b)	Economic Prospects (b)	Adjusted R^2
Albania	.58	.38	.44	.42	.46
Macedonia	.65	.40	.55	.14	.45
Georgia	.60	.43	.58	.23	.43
Estonia	.55	.38	.43	.19	.35
Lithuania	.56	.36	.51	.16	.36
Czech Republic	.53	.34	.47	.18	.31
Slovakia	.54	.30	.49	.12	.32
Armenia	.51	.33	.41	.12	.30
Romania	.47	.32	.42	.14	.27
Croatia	.61	.26	.53	.16	.29
Bulgaria	.40	.26	.30	.14	.19
Latvia	.43	.32	.34	.19	.24
Russia	.38	.31	.31	.14	.21
Poland	.39	.29	.37	.20	.21
Hungary	.36	.33	.28	.19	.19
Belarus	.40	.26	.34	.13	.20
Ukraine	.33	.26	.35	.15	.17
Slovenia	.30	.23	.24	.15	.12
Mean Value	*.47*	*.32*	*.41*	*.18*	*.28*

Source: Klingemann and Hofferbert 1998.

However, we also believe that recollection of the 'bad old days' will not be a sufficient condition for system legitimacy in the future. As time goes by, citizens with personal experience of communist rule will be replaced by younger generations, who will take freedom and respect for human rights more or less for granted. Economic performance will thus become more important in order to explain satisfaction with democracy. In other words, the countries of Central and Eastern Europe will be more comparable to the welfare states in Western Europe in this respect. By analysing CEEB survey data from the 1990s, we will try to find out in which way the wind has been blowing. Are East Europeans more and more inclined to take freedom for granted as time goes by or does the past still weigh heavily upon them in the sense that the human rights issue retains its original salience?

Straightforward questions do not always get the straightforward answers they deserve. The full time series (Tables 5A.3–5A.7, Appendix 5.3) lends itself to a short and snappy summary on one count only. Klingemann and Hofferbert's findings stand confirmed in one table after an other. The human rights item does have a stronger impact on East Europeans' assessment of the development of democracy than economic prospects over time as well as across countries.

Table 5.6: Predicting democratic performance with assessments of human rights conditions and economic prospects (CEEB 3–7, 1992–96). Average correlation and regression coefficients*

	Correlation		Multiple Regression		
	Human Rights *(r)*	*Economic Prospects (r)*	*Human Rights (b)*	*Economic Prospects (b)*	*Adjusted R²*
Albania	.57	.50	.46	.30	.42
Macedonia	.49	.26	.40	.14	.26
Georgia	.48	.40	.44	.22	.32
Estonia	.50	.32	.40	.16	.28
Lithuania	.46	.28	.42	.13	.25
Czech Republic	.47	.33	.42	.18	.27
Slovakia	.43	.29	.34	.14	.23
Armenia	.48	.37	.36	.14	.28
Romania	.45	.28	.38	.14	.24
Croatia	.51	.30	.49	.18	.29
Bulgaria	.34	.30	.23	.19	.17
Latvia	.47	.32	.37	.16	.27
Russia	.41	.37	.30	.17	.25
Poland	.39	.29	.35	.18	.20
Hungary	.34	.28	.28	.16	.16
Belarus	.40	.26	.32	.12	.19
Ukraine	.39	.31	.34	.16	.21
Slovenia	.35	.22	.29	.13	.15
Mean Value	*.44*	*.32*	*.37*	*.17*	*.25*

*Note: The correlation regression statistics in this table represent averages of the full time series (CEEB 3–7, 1992–96) presented in Tables 5A.3–5A.7 in Appendix 5.3. The average scores were obtained by dividing the summed correlation and regression coefficients for, say, Albania by the number of surveys carried out in the respective countries – in most cases by five, but occasionally by less than five. Albania was included in all five surveys (CEEB 3–7), Croatia only in the two most recent (CEEB 6–7, 1995–96). The average scores for Albania were, therefore, divided by five, and the average scores for Croatia by two.

There are differences between countries and fluctuations over time, but they do not seem to comply with any of the standard patterns. The Central European countries do not form a distinct cluster; nor do the Baltic or, for that matter, the South East European countries. Nor is there any compelling evidence to the effect that human rights is in the process of losing salience. It occasionally does, but the pattern is by no means stable. This is also brought out by Tables 5.6–5.7. The former provides an aggregate picture of the relationship between development of democracy and its two key predictors – human rights and economic prospects – in each of the eighteen countries over time (Tables 5A.3–5A.7); the latter (Table 5.7) provides us with the corresponding country and time specific data for 1996 (CEEB 7).[3]

Table 5.7: Predicting democratic performance with assessments of human rights conditions and economic prospects (CEEB 7, 1996)

	Correlation		Multiple Regression		
	Human Rights (r)	Economic Prospects (r)	Human Rights (b)	Economic Prospects (b)	Adjusted R²
Albania	.72	.60	.60	.29	.57
Macedonia	.44	.24	.32	.10	.21
Georgia	.39	.40	.31	.26	.24
Estonia	.47	.30	.38	.16	.25
Lithuania	.51	.27	.48	.15	.29
Czech Republic	.47	.35	.41	.21	.28
Slovakia	.50	.29	.47	.13	.28
Armenia	.52	.42	.38	.17	.32
Romania	.41	.22	.37	.14	.21
Croatia	.50	.33	.45	.18	.28
Bulgaria	.26	.31	.14	.14	.13
Latvia	.41	.34	.31	.22	.22
Russia	.42	.39	.31	.19	.26
Poland	.39	.32	.35	.21	.20
Hungary	.34	.28	.28	.16	.16
Belarus	.45	.27	.36	.10	.22
Ukraine	.45	.35	.36	.17	.25
Slovenia	.41	.22	.35	.12	.18
Mean Value	*.45*	*.33*	*.37*	*.17*	*.25*

Albania and Bulgaria may serve to highlight the opposing trends in the data. In Albania, human rights seem to be gaining importance as time goes by. In Bulgaria it is the other way around. There are plenty of good reasons why this should be the case. Democracy has been – and remains – much more fragile in Albania than in Bulgaria; and Albanians are probably well advised not to take freedom for granted. But there are no strong theoretical reasons why the issue of human rights should be less salient in Bulgaria, Slovenia and Hungary than in the remaining fifteen East European countries, including other well established and largely successful transitional democracies in Central Europe, South Eastern Europe and the Baltic region (Table 5.6).

Nor is it intuitively obvious why Albania, Belarus, Lithuania, Slovakia and Slovenia as of 1996 should end up with scores (read: correlation and regression coefficients) significantly higher than their respective over-time averages (Tables 5.6–5.7). Similar comments apply to the group of countries – Macedonia, Georgia, Bulgaria, Croatia and Latvia – which ends up with human rights scores significantly lower than their respective averages. It might be argued that they – and the eight additional countries with 1996 human rights scores hovering around the country-specific averages for the 1990s – provide support for the notion that the human rights item is indeed losing salience as a determinant of attitudes towards the development of democracy. But it would not be a strong argument. It fails to account for the five countries that stand out as outliers; and it would seem to attribute undue importance to what are minor fluctuations around the country-specific averages for the 1990s. The case in favour of the notion that human rights loses salience as time goes by and freedom is being taken for granted is at best incomplete.

*

Table 5.3 drew attention to the importance of political generation in contemporary Eastern Europe, and separate analyses by age groups may indeed shed additional light on the attitudinal dynamics at work in all the eighteen countries in our sample. Tables 5.8–5.11 report the results of such analyses at two different points in time, 1992 and 1996. The focus is on the two age groups that were previously defined as clear cut winners and obvious losers in the transition process from plan to market – that is on the 15–35 age group who are in the labour market as opposed to those aged 65+, the bulk of whom are retired. Table 5.3 tells us that the old were considerably more likely than the young to express all-out distrust in the human rights record of the post-communist regimes as of 1996. Many of those in the upper age bracket also have personal memories and experiences of communist repression, occupation by Nazi Germany and even of the inter- and post-war experiments in democracy that may go towards highlighting the importance of human rights issues. We would, therefore, expect human rights to be, and to remain, a highly salient topic for the older generation throughout the current phase of transition. In a similar vein, we would expect human rights to be less salient to start with within the younger generation and to lose salience as time goes by and freedom is being taken for granted. The time series at our disposal (1992–1996) may very well be too short for valid generalizations, but to the extent that these five years do make a difference we would thus expect human rights to be less salient to the young as of 1996 than to the young as of 1992.

Table 5.8: Predicting democratic performance with assessments of human rights conditions and economic prospects (CEEB 3, 1992): age 15–35

	Correlation		Multiple Regression		
	Human Rights (r)	Economic Prospects (r)	Human Rights (b)	Economic Prospects (b)	Adjusted R²
Albania	.46	.31	.41	.18	.23
Macedonia	.43	.11	.35	–	.16
Georgia	.36	.37	.38	.24	.25
Estonia	.51	.28	.43	.13	.28
Lithuania	.34	.33	.26	.18	.19
Czech Republic	.42	.19	.43	–	.18
Slovakia	.49	.35	.29	.12	.28
Armenia	.43	.23	.35	–	.20
Romania	.39	.26	.31	.12	.17
Croatia	–	–	–	–	–
Bulgaria	.27	.32	.21	.20	.13
Latvia	.33	.32	.24	.16	.20
Russia	.29	.26	.26	.16	.15
Poland	.29	.25	.23	.16	.10
Hungary	.34	.26	.29	.16	.16
Belarus	.31	.21	.26	.12	.13
Ukraine	.21	.27	.10	.17	.08
Slovenia	.32	.21	.26	.13	.14
Mean Value	*.36*	*.27*	*.30*	*.16*	*.18*

Table 5.9: Predicting democratic performance with assessments of human rights conditions and economic prospects (CEEB 3, 1992): age 61–99

	Correlation		Multiple Regression		
	Human Rights (r)	Economic Prospects (r)	Human Rights (b)	Economic Prospects (b)	Adjusted R²
Albania	.65	.54	.45	.35	.52
Macedonia	.42	.27	.31	.17	.17
Georgia	.47	.24	.50	.13	.20
Estonia	.53	.40	.36	.15	.31
Lithuania	.39	.28	.33	.10	.17
Czech Republic	.44	.41	.32	.22	.26
Slovakia	.39	.24	.28	.15	.18
Armenia	.24	.35	.13	.22	.10
Romania	.46	.21	.36	.11	.24
Croatia	–	–	–	–	–
Bulgaria	.45	.49	.23	.34	.32
Latvia	.39	.51	.18	.27	.31
Russia	.48	.31	.40	–	.23
Poland	.47	.46	.39	.35	.37
Hungary	.35	.45	.20	.30	.24
Belarus	.40	.35	.26	.22	.25
Ukraine	.38	.41	.30	.20	.24
Slovenia	.25	.09	.24	–	.05
Mean Value	*.42*	*.35*	*.31*	*.22*	*.24*

Table 5.10: Predicting democratic performance with assessments of human rights conditions and economic prospects (CEEB 7, 1996): age 15–35

	Correlation		Multiple Regression		
	Human Rights (r)	Economic Prospects (r)	Human Rights (b)	Economic Prospects (b)	Adjusted R²
Albania	.69	.58	.59	.30	.55
Macedonia	.38	.12	.28	–	.14
Georgia	.25	.29	.24	.21	.13
Estonia	.46	.17	.43	–	.23
Lithuania	.50	.26	.44	.14	.25
Czech Republic	.42	.29	.38	.17	.22
Slovakia	.48	.24	.49	.11	.25
Armenia	.43	.38	.30	.18	.24
Romania	.47	.13	.42	–	.23
Croatia	.49	.24	.48	.10	.24
Bulgaria	.18	.29	–	.14	.09
Latvia	.44	.36	.33	.25	.24
Russia	.34	.35	.24	.20	.17
Poland	.36	.31	.34	.23	.19
Hungary	.43	.14	.44	–	.20
Belarus	.36	.27	.28	.11	.17
Ukraine	.39	.31	.28	.18	.17
Slovenia	.35	.13	.31	–	.13
Mean Value	*.41*	*.27*	*.37*	*.18*	*.21*

Table 5.11: Predicting democratic performance with assessments of human rights conditions and economic prospects (CEEB 7, 1996): age 61–99

	Correlation		Multiple Regression		
	Human Rights (r)	Economic Prospects (r)	Human Rights (b)	Economic Prospects (b)	Adjusted R²
Albania	.76	.69	.52	.43	.59
Macedonia	.53	.30	.43	.15	.33
Georgia	.62	.44	.48	.24	.41
Estonia	.41	.31	.28	.21	.20
Lithuania	.51	.37	.50	.25	.33
Czech Republic	.53	.62	.39	.47	.54
Slovakia	.61	.39	.54	.14	.40
Armenia	.64	.44	.52	.16	.50
Romania	.52	.38	.47	.27	.38
Croatia	.62	.49	.55	.31	.45
Bulgaria	.26	.36	.12	.20	.16
Latvia	.43	.32	.31	.19	.21
Russia	.55	.36	.45	.12	.36
Poland	.49	.34	.41	.14	.23
Hungary	.36	.38	.26	.24	.21
Belarus	.47	.25	.35	–	.18
Ukraine	.54	.47	.39	.23	.39
Slovenia	.34	.20	.31	.13	.11
Mean Value	*.51*	*.40*	*.40*	*.23*	*.33*

This is not how it works out, though. A simple eyeball inspection of the average correlation and regression coefficients is enough for us to reject the hypothesis that freedom is being taken for granted; and this is also the message conveyed by the country-specific coefficients. As we move from 1992 to 1996, human rights gain importance in both age groups in all but a few deviant cases. It remains the key predictor of attitudes to democracy identified by Klingemann and Hofferbert. But Tables 5.8–5.11 also serve as a reminder that we cannot afford to neglect material incentives in the form of self-ascribed economic prospects. This variable also gains importance as we move forward along the time axis; and it makes itself felt particularly strongly within the upper age bracket. In a few instances – which tend to coincide with the deviant cases above – economic prospects comes out as the top predictor of attitudes towards democracy. Tables 5.8 and 5.10 – which contain data on young East Europeans – include two such cases; Bulgaria (Table 5.10) and the Ukraine (Table 5.8). Tables 5.9 and 5.11 – which address themselves to those in the upper age bracket – count a total of six additional cases; Armenia (Table 5.9), Bulgaria (Tables 5.9 and 5.11), the Czech Republic (Table 5.11), Hungary (Table 5.9) and Latvia (Table 5.9). These five countries in different parts of Eastern Europe may very well turn out to be forerunners in the uneven race towards political normalcy in Eastern Europe. Only the future will tell. Until then, we will have to treat them as a socially, politically and economically rather heterogeneous group of outliers, deviating from the familiar pattern with human rights as the key predicator of attitudes towards democracy in Eastern Europe.

Conclusions

Human rights constitute an issue of crucial importance in contemporary Eastern Europe. Losers in the rough transition from plan to market tend to be somewhat more critical of the government's human rights record than the smaller group of winners. But there are also strong indications that human rights are approached in a meaningful historical perspective. Contemporary Albania may not be a democracy, but it nevertheless stands out as a better place to live in terms of human rights than early post-war Albania, when the country was dominated by a hard-line communist regime with all the attributes of totalitarianism; and, on the whole, Albanians tend to appreciate this regardless of their socioeconomic and demographic background (Table 5.3). This syndrome may incidentally go a long way towards accounting for the discrepancies between our freedom rating based on CEEB human rights data and that of *Freedomhouse* (Table 5.1).

The evaluation of the government's human rights record is closely intertwined with the respondents' assessment of the development of democracy. The evaluation of the government's human rights record is in fact a much more powerful determinant of the respondents' assessment of the development of democracy than self-ascribed economic prospects. This is readily apparent from findings, based on CEEB 6, presented by Klingemann and Hofferbert (1998) which stand confirmed when checked against the full data set in Tables 5A.3–5A.7 (Appendix 5.3).

There is no evidence that human rights lose salience as time goes by and freedom is being taken for granted. There are fluctuations around the average scores for the 1990s, but they do not lend themselves to such interpretations (Tables 5.6–5.7). Detailed analyses of young (15–35) versus old (61+) also fail to reveal but a few deviations (Tables 5.8–5.11) from the familiar pattern with human rights as the key predictor of attitudes towards democracy, but provide fruitful insights into the interaction between human rights and self-ascribed economic prospects among young versus old citizens. The bottom line is unusually straightforward, however. East Europeans do *not* take their recently acquired rights and freedoms for granted. In this sense, they would seem to agree with those Western analysts who keep reminding us that the third – and current – experiment in democracy in Central and Eastern Europe may very well end on a similar note as the inter- and post-war democratic experiments – in the breakdown of somewhat shaky democratic institutions.

NOTES

1. The table draws on data from 1996–97 for the twenty-seven Central and East European countries originally covered by *Freedomhouse* as well as the *Central and Eastern Eurobarometer*. The European Union (EU) has subsequently reduced the scope of its Central and East European surveys to EU candidate countries to the detriment of the CIS countries, Albania and the former members of the Yugoslav federation. The *Freedomhouse* ratings are, however, relatively stable over time as are the CEEB estimates. Slovakia, Yugoslavia (Serbia) and Azerbaijan are in fact the only countries to shift position as we move to more recent data (1999–2000) by *Freedomhouse*. The changes are all for the better. Slovakia is promoted from 'partially free' to 'free' and Serbia–Yugoslavia and Azerbaijan from 'not free' to 'partially free'. Similar comments apply to the CEEB data. As we move from CEEB 7 to CEEB 8, the human rights index remains stable in all candidate countries but two: Lithuania and Slovakia which improve their scores, Lithuania from a rock-bottom '4' to a decent '3' and Slovakia from a decent '3' to a respectable '2'.

2. The averages in Maps 5.1–5.2 have been calculated on the basis of all observations available, including CEEB 8 for the EU candidate countries.

3. It would admittedly have been nice to extend the time series to CEEB 8, the most recent *Central and Eastern Eurobarometer* currently available. This strategy was, however, rendered impossible by the removal of the item on economic prospects from the questionnaire.

REFERENCES

Beetham, David (1999), *Democracy and Human Rights*, Oxford, Polity Press in association with Blackwell.

Berglund, Sten and Frank H. Aarebrot (1997), *The Political History of Eastern Europe in the 20th Century: The Struggle Between Democracy and Dictatorship*, Aldershot, Edward Elgar.

Berglund, Sten, Tomas Hellén and Frank Aarebrot, eds, (1998), *Handbook of Political Change in Eastern Europe*, Aldershot, Edward Elgar.

Biorcio, Roberto and Renato Mannheimer (1995), 'Relationships Between Citizens and Political Parties', in Hans-Dieter Klingemann and Dieter Fuchs, eds, *Citizens and the State*, Beliefs in Government Volume 1, Oxford, Oxford University Press.

Central and Eastern Eurobarometer No. 3–7, Cologne, Zentralarchiv für Empirische Sozialforschung.

Freedomhouse Homepage, [http://www.freedomhouse.org/] 1999 05 03.

Hellén, Tomas, Sten Berglund and Frank H. Aarebrot (1998), 'From Transition to Consolidation', in Sten Berglund, Tomas Hellén and Frank Aarebrot, eds, *Handbook of Political Change in Eastern Europe*, Aldershot, Edward Elgar.

Karasimeonov, Georgi (1998), 'Bulgaria', in Sten Berglund, Tomas Hellén and Frank Aarebrot, eds, *Handbook of Political Change in Eastern Europe*, Aldershot, Edward Elgar.

Klingemann, Hans-Dieter and Richard I. Hofferbert (1998), 'Remembering the Bad Old Days: Human Rights, Economic Conditions, and Democratic Performance in Transitional Regimes', Discussion Paper FS III 98-203, Wissenschaftszentrum Berlin für Sozialforschung (WZB).

Lagerspetz, Mikko and Henri Vogt (1998), 'Estonia', in Sten Berglund, Tomas Hellén and Frank Aarebrot, eds, *Handbook of Political Change in Eastern Europe*, Aldershot, Edward Elgar.

Leonhard, Wolfgang (1994), *Spurensuche: 40 Jahre nach Die Revolution Entläßt Ihre Kinder*, Cologne, Kiepenheuer & Witsch.

Linz, Juan and Alfred Stepan (1996), *Problems of Democratic Transition and Consolidation: Southern Europe, South America and Post-Communist Europe*, Baltimore and London, Johns Hopkins University Press.

Smith-Sivertsen, Hermann (1998), 'Latvia', in Sten Berglund, Tomas Hellén and Frank Aarebrot, eds, *Handbook of Political Change in Eastern Europe*, Aldershot, Edward Elgar.

APPENDIX 5.1

Table 5A.1: Reasons why respect for human rights by country. *
Percentages

	Good ethnic rel.	Restored democr.	Freedom	Economic opportun.	Independ.	Ability to travel	Other positive
Albania	7.6	38.9	48.3	27.8	6.8	36.2	5.1
Armenia	34.0	34.1	38.2	34.6	20.2	7.3	22.3
Belarus	5.0	3.0	7.0	4.2	2.2	4.4	2.2
Bulgaria	5.2	8.9	21.9	11.2	2.4	8.4	3.8
Czech Rep.	1.8	17.9	26.2	9.7	1.4	18.4	5.2
Slovakia	4.1	15.1	19.6	9.8	6.4	15.5	5.6
Estonia	3.1	4.0	5.7	6.0	4.7	6.4	3.4
Georgia	3.3	6.6	11.8	6.3	8.3	6.2	0.5
Hungary	5.7	10.9	22.3	2.3	0.7	2.1	3.8
Latvia	4.0	4.6	13.8	13.8	15.1	11.2	3.3
Lithuania	4.8	12.1	12.5	7.3	4.9	8.2	2.8
Macedonia	10.1	8.3	16.2	5.9	4.1	1.4	4.3
Moldova	4.5	5.9	17.0	7.0	10.8	20.1	1.6
Poland	5.1	8.6	22.4	10.6	6.5	12.9	11.4
Romania	5.1	6.9	27.5	6.0	2.1	11.0	6.7
Russia	0.3	1.7	4.8	3.8	1.1	2.6	2.1
Slovenia	7.4	17.7	22.3	6.4	11.3	3.7	5.7
Ukraine	0.6	2.4	7.7	6.5	4.7	4.4	3.6

Note: In CEEB 3, 1992, respondents were prodded for the reasons why they felt the government had or did not have respect for human rights. The follow-up question to the human rights item (Appendix 5.2) was open-ended and the answers were subsequently classified into a number of relevant categories. The percentages have been computed with the total number of relevant respondents in the respective countries in the denominator. Thus, 48.3 per cent of those Albanians who feel the government has a lot or some respect for human rights, may be seen to refer to freedom by way of explanation. 38.9 and 36.2 per cent of them mention the 'restoration of democracy' and the 'ability to travel' respectively. This method of presentation paves the way for comparisons between, as well as within countries.

Table 5A.2: Reasons why no respect for human rights by country.*
Percentages

	Nation-al tension	Ethnic trouble	Right wing extr.	Econom. hard-ship	Political problem	Crime and violence	Nothing changed	Other negative
Albania	2.2	0.6	20.8	37.4	21.8	43.6	8.1	12.9
Armenia	9.3	11.1	6.0	26.4	14.8	17.6	8.0	20.2
Belarus	3.3	2.1	4.3	29.5	14.4	21.0	11.1	28.0
Bulgaria	4.4	0.5	2.4	21.6	10.6	20.7	6.0	8.2
Czech Rep.	4.4	2.4	1.9	9.8	6.6	15.4	7.6	16.1
Slovakia	12.5	2.9	2.0	18.7	8.9	22.5	8.4	19.5
Estonia	17.1	1.0	0.9	20.9	12.8	16.4	3.5	15.8
Georgia	26.7	24.9	9.0	38.6	27.6	50.7	11.0	8.1
Hungary	6.9	1.4	2.9	20.9	25.5	6.1	2.7	7.1
Latvia	17.7	7.2	4.8	36.2	18.0	23.9	14.3	13.9
Lithuania	2.4	2.0	3.9	19.4	6.1	9.5	5.3	19.0
Macedonia	14.8	2.6	1.9	16.3	8.2	2.6	2.9	13.1
Moldova	8.7	7.5	3.4	22.7	11.5	7.2	6.0	3.0
Poland	4.6	3.8	5.0	19.5	11.6	17.6	5.3	37.5
Romania	5.6	1.8	2.8	19.8	7.5	10.0	3.7	15.8
Russia	6.5	7.8	2.6	21.7	7.2	17.9	6.5	26.6
Slovenia	4.3	2.2	1.6	22.9	10.3	7.4	4.7	10.1
Ukraine	3.6	2.7	1.4	28.0	8.9	7.8	13.7	18.7

*Note: In CEEB 3, 1992, respondents were prodded for the reasons why they felt the government had or did not have respect for human rights. The follow-up question to the human rights item (Appendix 5.2) was open-ended and the answers were subsequently classified into a number of relevant categories. The percentages have been computed with the total number of relevant respondents in the respective countries in the denominator.

APPENDIX 5.2

RESPECT FOR HUMAN RIGHTS	
OLD VALUE	*RE-CODED VALUE*
1 A lot of respect	1 Acceptable
2 Some respect	1 Acceptable
3 Not much respect	1 Acceptable
4 No respect at all	2 Unacceptable
5 Don't know	System missing
0 No answer	System missing

EDUCATION LEVEL	
OLD VALUE	*RE-CODED VALUE*
1 Up to elementary	2 Low
2 Some secondary	2 Low
3 Secondary graduated	2 Low
4 Higher education	1 High
5 Don't know	System missing
6 Refused	System missing
0 No answer	System missing

TYPE OF COMMUNITY	
OLD VALUE	*RE-CODED VALUE*
1 Capital	1 Urban
2 Other big city	1 Urban
3 Provincial	2 Rural
4 Rural area	2 Rural
0 No answer	System missing

AGE	
OLD VALUE	*RE-CODED VALUE*
15–99	1 15–35
	2 36–60
	3 61–99

OCCUPATION	
OLD VALUE	RE-CODED VALUE
Private sector owner	1 Qualified
Private sector employee	1 Qualified
Civil servant	2 Semi-qualified
Student	2 Semi-qualified
Other paid work	2 Semi-qualified
State-owned enterprise	3 Unqualified
All agriculture	3 Unqualified
Pensioner	3 Unqualified
Housewife	3 Unqualified
Not working	3 Unqualified
No answer	System missing

APPENDIX 5.3

Table 5A.3: Predicting democratic performance with assessments of human rights conditions and economic prospects (CEEB 3, 1992)*

	Correlation		Multiple Regression		
	Human Rights (r)	Economic Prospects (r)	Human Rights (b)	Economic Prospects (b)	Adjusted R²
Albania	.48	.39	.40	.23	.29
Macedonia	.41	.16	.33	.10	.16
Georgia	.38	.37	.39	.23	.25
Estonia	.52	.32	.39	.12	.30
Lithuania	.38	.26	.32	.12	.18
Czech Republic	.44	.33	.39	.15	.23
Slovakia	.41	.30	.26	.14	.22
Armenia	.42	.31	.31	.13	.21
Romania	.40	.27	.31	.13	.19
Croatia	–	–	–	–	–
Bulgaria	.39	.43	.28	.26	.25
Latvia	.40	.37	.29	.16	.27
Russia	.36	.33	.27	.15	.19
Poland	.39	.32	.33	.20	.21
Hungary	.32	.31	.26	.18	.16
Belarus	.37	.25	.27	.13	.17
Ukraine	.32	.34	.23	.18	.17
Slovenia	.31	.20	.24	.12	.12
Mean Value	*.39*	*.31*	*.31*	*.16*	*.21*

*Note: Tables 5A.3–5A.7 present correlation and regression coefficients between the variables 'satisfaction with democracy'/'respect for human rights' and 'satisfaction with democracy'/'economic prospects'. In the multiple regression analysis, 'satisfaction with democracy' is the dependent variable. The variables included in the correlation and regression analyses have been re-coded. Thus, 'don't know' and missing cases are not included in the material. Scaling: human rights 1 = high, 4 = low; economic prospects 1 = high, 5 = low; democratic satisfaction 1 = high, 4 = low.

Table 5A.4: Predicting democratic performance with assessments of human rights conditions and economic prospects (CEEB 4, 1993)

	Correlation		Multiple Regression		
	Human Rights (r)	Economic Prospects (r)	Human Rights (b)	Economic Prospects (b)	Adjusted R^2
Albania	.52	.49	.39	.28	.36
Macedonia	.45	.14	.39	–	.20
Georgia	–	–	–	–	–
Estonia	.47	.27	.39	.14	.25
Lithuania	.43	.26	.41	.11	.22
Czech Republic	.46	.36	.39	.19	.27
Slovakia	.34	.27	.23	.14	.16
Armenia	.47	.44	.31	.17	.31
Romania	.45	.23	.36	–	.22
Croatia	–	–	–	–	–
Bulgaria	.34	.31	.26	.19	.17
Latvia	.55	.30	.44	.10	.31
Russia	.47	.44	.36	.19	.34
Poland	.36	.22	.34	.15	.18
Hungary	.32	.24	.26	.14	.13
Belarus	.42	.28	.35	.14	.22
Ukraine	.39	.33	.33	.16	.21
Slovenia	.43	.23	.36	.10	.20
Mean Value	*.43*	*.30*	*.35*	*.16*	*.23*

Table 5A.5: Predicting democratic performance with assessments of human rights conditions and economic prospects (CEEB 5, 1994)

	Correlation		Multiple Regression		
	Human Rights (r)	Economic Prospects (r)	Human Rights (b)	Economic Prospects (b)	Adjusted R^2
Albania	.56	.48	.45	.27	.41
Macedonia	.50	.36	.40	.19	.30
Georgia	.53	.39	.49	.16	.34
Estonia	.49	.35	.39	.18	.27
Lithuania	.41	.27	.36	.13	.19
Czech Republic	.44	.28	.43	.16	.23
Slovakia	.37	.29	.25	.15	.18
Armenia	.46	.33	.37	.12	.25
Romania	.53	.34	.46	.15	.32
Croatia	–	–	–	–	–
Bulgaria	.30	.19	.18	–	.11
Latvia	.54	.27	.45	.13	.31
Russia	.39	.38	.27	.18	.23
Poland	.40	.28	.34	.16	.20
Hungary	.35	.24	.33	.14	.15
Belarus	.35	.26	.28	.12	.16
Ukraine	.44	.25	.42	.12	.24
Slovenia	.28	.22	.25	.18	.11
Mean Value	*.43*	*.31*	*.42*	*.16*	*.24*

Table 5A.6: Predicting democratic performance with assessments of human rights conditions and economic prospects (CEEB 6, 1995)

	Correlation		Multiple Regression		
	Human Rights (r)	Economic Prospects (r)	Human Rights (b)	Economic Prospects (b)	Adjusted R^2
Albania	.57	.55	.44	.41	.45
Macedonia	.65	.40	.54	.15	.45
Georgia	.60	.42	.57	.23	.43
Estonia	.55	.37	.44	.18	.35
Lithuania	.57	.36	.52	.16	.37
Czech Republic	.53	.35	.48	.18	.32
Slovakia	.53	.29	.48	.12	.31
Armenia	.51	.34	.41	.13	.30
Romania	.46	.32	.41	.14	.26
Croatia	.51	.26	.53	.17	.29
Bulgaria	.40	.26	.31	.15	.20
Latvia	.44	.33	.35	.19	.25
Russia	.39	.31	.31	.14	.22
Poland	.39	.29	.37	.20	.21
Hungary	.35	.33	.28	.19	.19
Belarus	.40	.26	.34	.12	.20
Ukraine	.34	.27	.36	.15	.18
Slovenia	.30	.23	.25	.15	.12
Mean Value	*.47*	*.33*	*.41*	*.18*	*.28*

Table 5A.7: Predicting democratic performance with assessments of human rights conditions and economic prospects (CEEB 7, 1996)

	Correlation		Multiple Regression		
	Human Rights (r)	Economic Prospects (r)	Human Rights (b)	Economic Prospects (b)	Adjusted R^2
Albania	.72	.60	.60	.29	.57
Macedonia	.44	.24	.32	.10	.21
Georgia	.39	.40	.31	.26	.24
Estonia	.47	.30	.38	.16	.25
Lithuania	.51	.27	.48	.15	.29
Czech Republic	.47	.35	.41	.21	.28
Slovakia	.50	.29	.47	.13	.28
Armenia	.52	.42	.38	.17	.32
Romania	.41	.22	.37	.14	.21
Croatia	.50	.33	.45	.18	.28
Bulgaria	.26	.31	.14	.14	.13
Latvia	.41	.34	.31	.22	.22
Russia	.42	.39	.31	.19	.26
Poland	.39	.32	.35	.21	.20
Hungary	.34	.28	.28	.16	.16
Belarus	.45	.27	.36	.10	.22
Ukraine	.45	.35	.36	.17	.25
Slovenia	.41	.22	.35	.12	.18
Mean Value	*.45*	*.33*	*.37*	*.17*	*.25*

6. Civil Society

Not all modern societies are democracies. And not all non-modern societies are dictatorships. The standard work on transition to democracy, the four-volume *Transitions from Authoritarian Rule* edited by O'Donnell, Schmitter and Whitehead (1986), concludes that there is little, if any, correlation between socioeconomic development and political structure; that is a certain socioeconomic structure can generate and coexist with a number of political systems. Yet there is a good case to be made for the notion that modernity facilitates the transition to democracy. Economic development is often cast as a necessary, if not sufficient, prerequisite for democracy – this is in fact one of the underlying notions of the so-called convergence theory – and it would be entirely plausible to draw the somewhat paradoxical conclusion that the prospects for democracy are particularly bright in those former communist states of Central and Eastern Europe where the ruling Marxist–Leninist parties were especially successful in promoting socio-economic development and state-building (Berglund and Aarebrot 1997).

The communist call for modernization was universal, but as a rule it was more successful in Northern than in Southern Europe. The communist campaign against organized religion made itself felt throughout the Soviet bloc as well as in Yugoslavia, to say nothing of Albania, which proclaimed itself an atheist republic, but it was less than successful in predominantly Catholic countries like Poland and Lithuania. The managerial style of communist Eastern Europe required a powerful state machinery capable of mobilization as well as social control, but the kind of clientelism which had been practised for centuries in Southern Europe does not disappear during a few short decades. The many references to the sultanistic features of the Ceaușescu regime in Romania, and to the feudal heritage of post-communist Bulgaria, testify to the resilience of old patterns of governance (Linz and Stepan 1996).

The argument that socialism had run its course by 1989, having built more modern societies, should not be construed to mean that the transformation itself or its timing was predestined and inevitable in all, or any, of the East European states. Nor does it imply that the countries of Eastern Europe had become duplicates of Western societies. It takes time for modernization to change political culture. As Slavenka Drakulíc notes: 'Romania, like most ex-Communist countries, remains a country of peasants […] The values of a civil society are values created by citizens, and one or two generations of peasants living in the cities under a totalitarian regime had no chance of becoming citizens, politically or culturally' (Drakulíc 1994). In particular, the socialist societies did not include a middle class in the traditional sense; the middle strata were defined not by ownership but by educational achievement and access to state and party power structures. This fluidity of the class cleavage has indeed proved a destabilizing factor after the introduction of multi-party democracy.

Nevertheless, it remains true that the East European revolutions were the result of an alliance between intellectuals and the working class. The turning point came when the middle strata – even segments of the privileged *nomenklatura* – lost faith in the system. This was a gradual process, starting long before 1989; during the 1980–81 Polish crisis every third member of the communist party joined the Solidarity opposition movement, and the Hungarian and Czechoslovak crises of 1956 and 1968 witnessed large-scale defections from the ranks of the ruling parties. This loss of faith was particularly debilitating due to the nature of the ruling parties; by reference to Marxist–Leninist dogma, they defined themselves as leading parties, but now increasingly found themselves in a position where they could command the support, or even the compliance, of but a minority of the population. Without the backing of the Soviet Union, their fate was sealed.

But transition to democracy is not all; democracy also has to be consolidated, as Linz and Stepan (1996) and other students of the third wave of democratization keep telling us. A consolidated democracy, they argue, requires that a number of democratic 'arenas' be represented in the state. These arenas must interact and mutually reinforce one another, thereby creating a situation where democracy is not challenged – 'in a phrase, democracy has become the "only game in town"' (Linz and Stepan 1996, 5). This chapter deals with one of these arenas, civil society. The relevance of a well functioning civil society is beyond doubt. The importance of independent voluntary associations and civility for democracy has been a recurrent theme in modern political science ever since Alexis de Tocqueville's frequently quoted study of democracy in the United States of the early 19th century. It is a moot question: how many independent voluntary associations, and what kind of voluntary associations, are required to make democracy work? Of relevance are not only the number of organizations, but also the type of organizations they represent and, for that matter, the quality of organization they have.

What can be said, then, about the civil society arena in Central and Eastern Europe? The literature at hand admittedly does not provide any straightforward answers to such questions. The breakdown of communism in 1989–90 is often attributed to the gradual emergence of 'second societies', beyond the control of the communist regimes, in the countries of Central and Eastern Europe (cf. Hankiss 1988). Dissident movements like *Charter 77* in Czechoslovakia, the Hungarian Democratic Forum (HDF) in Hungary, Solidarity in Poland, the ecological movements of Bulgaria, East Germany and Russia and the popular fronts of the Soviet Baltic republics testify to the salience of civil society in the struggle for democracy of the late 1980s and early 1990s. But – as suggested by Jan Urban, a leading dissident in *Charter 77*, in a self-critical article written on the eve of the secession of Slovakia – we are nevertheless well advised not to exaggerate their importance.

> [I]n the summer of 1989 we received a copy of a secret paper for party propagandists, based on an analysis the StB (the Czechoslovak secret police) had prepared for the Politburo. In it, the StB estimated the hard core of 'anti-socialist opposition groups' to consist of about sixty people with some five hundred supporters and collaborators. Their estimate was right. And it remained right [...] We believed in the regime's invincibility until it *collapsed* on its own. We did not know how to organize ourselves to form a political opposition [...] We did not know the non-society we lived with. All we knew was our enemy and he – spiteful bastard – all of a sudden ran away. Without him we were left alone with an unknown atomized non-society – and with power over it. Had the Communists been able to bargain longer, or had they tried to resist, the new power elite would have learned at least something about how to organize political support and how important it is to institutionalize it [...] Blinded by the easiness of taking power, we did not think about its nature and institutions [...] Because of our own anti-political way of existing as political creatures before the change, we were bound to lose – unless we ourselves changed into politicians. By now we know we have failed (quoted by Linz and Stepan 1996, 321).

It would be unfair to describe the state of civil society in Poland and Hungary in such bleak terms. As of the late 1980s, Czechoslovakia and some of the other socialist countries stood out as a 'hibernating neo-Stalinist' regimes with little or no room for negotiated compromise, while Poland and Hungary were sliding towards authoritarianism with some, but by no means all, the trappings of institutional pluralism, including emerging multiparty systems (Berglund and Aarebrot 1997). Bulgaria, East Germany and the Soviet Union were probably not that far removed from Czechoslovakia in terms of civil society (Tempest 1997); and the sultanistic features of Ceauşescu's Romania served as a particularly effective barrier against all but anomic protest (Linz and Stepan 1996).

At the outset – back in 1989 – we would thus seem to have a small group of countries with a strong civil society (Poland and Hungary) and another considerably larger group of countries with civil society arenas ranging from weak to non-existent. A decade or more of successful experiments in democracy, likely to serve as an impetus for civil society, has elapsed since then. We would, therefore, be inclined to attribute more importance to the civil society arena in contemporary Eastern Europe than in Eastern Europe as of the early 1990s.

But this is by no means a foregone conclusion. In an article published in the spring of 1997, Clive Tempest argues that civil society never existed in Central and Eastern Europe, neither before nor after the velvet revolutions of 1989–91. The argument is based on an analysis of Poland, the 'quintessential example of the rebirth of civil society' and of Solidarity as the 'most cited symptom of this phenomenon'. It basically breaks down into three points.

- Poland remains characterized by tightly-knit circles of families and friends with deep roots in rural Poland that allow Poles to live: to make contacts with official society (the 'others'), to obtain scarce goods and to survive in an unfriendly social environment. In Tempest's own words, 'such descriptions hardly add up to the exalted vision of civil society beloved of western analysts'.
- Solidarity is dismissed as a by-product of the struggle against communism, inspired by the same Leninist principles as the Polish United Workers' Party:

[...] Jadwiga Staniszkis, the respected Polish philosopher and social analyst drew attention, in an oft cited article, to the similarity in the forms of reasoning between Solidarity theorists and the guardians of Leninist orthodoxy. They partook of the same 'cognitive radicalism i.e. striving towards a simplicity of form based on unambiguous opposition'. Genuinely liberal, pluralist thinking is said to require a bargaining, compromising mentality and Staniszkis argues that Solidarity was incapable of this as it was a product of Eastern European dualist and bricolage reasoning patterns. This was to help it to completely oppose communism, but it was neither a product of civic reasoning nor a grounding for civic reasoning (Tempest 1997, 137).

- In a similar vein, the Catholic Church, Solidarity's foremost ally, is discarded as an exponent of moral and religious supremacy.

Cardinal Glemp has been heard to remark on more than one occasion, that as they made the revolution, they had the right to decide the forms of society and culture. Hardly a form of accommodative and bargaining mentality, but one informed by an absolute moral certainty (Tempest 1997, 137).

These observations are astute, but nevertheless somewhat beside the point. Tightly-knit circles of families and friends are part of a clientelistic heritage that affects all of Eastern Europe, particularly the countries of South Eastern Europe. They are part of civil society to the extent that they are voluntary, regardless of whether they live up to the visions cherished by Western analysts. Solidarity was indeed marked by the struggle against the communist regime. Its stance against the communist regime was outright intransigent, but it was nevertheless the first free trade union based on mass membership that had emerged in Central and Eastern Europe for well over thirty-five years and as such an obvious candidate for inclusion among civil society organizations. Similar comments apply to the Catholic Church. It too is part of civil society in so far as it plays a social and/or political role; and nobody denies that the Polish Catholic Church does just that. It is in fact one of the most high profile branches of modern Roman Catholicism. The moral supremacist ambitions of some of its leaders, including Joseph Cardinal Glemp, is an entirely different story.

On a general level, however, it is easy to agree with Tempest. All civil society organizations do not necessarily promote liberal democracy. The clientelistic networks encountered in Eastern Europe are probably less ideal as democratic agents than the many voluntary associations on which de Tocqueville (1835–40; 1990) dwells in his account of American democracy in the early 19th century or the decline of which Robert Putnam deplores in his pessimistic account of the state of democracy in contemporary America (Putnam 1995), but they may nevertheless play a constructive role. The ideological intransigence of two sworn enemies, pitted against one another, may indeed have dire consequences for fledgling democracies, but this is not what happened in Poland. The communist party literally collapsed and re-emerged as a reformed socialist party. Solidarity disintegrated into a variety of political factions. Catholic conservatives have scored some parliamentary victories, including a restrictive abortion policy, but that falls considerably short of Catholic supremacy. Our verdict of the democratic potential of civil society in Poland and – through it – the other countries of Central and Eastern Europe is, therefore, much more optimistic.

*

Civil society is apparently a multifaceted concept with normative connotations. We will do our best to avoid the latter in the subsequent attempts at quantification that we are inclined to see as a *sine qua non* for the comparative study of civil society in Central and Eastern Europe. The index on civil society presented by Adrian Karatnycky, Alexander Motyl and Boris Graybow (1999) of *Freedomhouse* in a volume on *Nations in Transit* 1998 will serve as our point of departure. It is based mainly on information about the number of Non-Governmental Organizations (NGOs) in the respective countries, and on indicators tapping the legal and regulatory framework within which they operate, such as ease of registration, legal rights, government regulation, taxation, procurement, and access to information. Opinion polls are also taken into account in a dual effort to gauge the level of activity within the voluntary associations and the degree of hostility that characterizes the approach by government officials towards the NGOs. Trade unions constitute a particularly important component of the index: Are there free trade unions? How many workers belong to these unions? Is the number of workers belonging to trade unions growing or decreasing? (Karatnycky, Motyl and Graybow 1999). The index theoretically ranges from 1.00 to 7.00. '1' stands for a highly developed civil society and '7' for total lack of civil society. On the basis of this index, we have divided the countries of Central and Eastern Europe into the following four groups (Table 6.1).

Table 6.1: Civil society in Central and Eastern Europe

Hungary	1.25		
Poland	1.25	Russia	4.00
Czech Republic 1.50		Albania	4.25
		Georgia	4.25
Slovenia	2.00	Ukraine	4.25
Lithuania	2.00	Kyrgyz Republic	4.50
Estonia	2.25	Azerbaijan	5.00
Latvia	2.25	Bosnia	5.00
		Kazakhstan	5.00
Slovakia	3.00	Yugoslavia (Serbia)	5.00
Mongolia	3.25	Tajikistan	5.25
Armenia	3.50	Belarus	5.75
Croatia	3.50	Uzbekistan	6.50
Bulgaria	3.75	Turkmenistan	7.00
Macedonia	3.75		
Moldova	3.75		
Romania	3.75		

Source: Karatnycky, Motyl and Graybow (1999).

A simple eyeball inspection would seem to suggest that the index is not a bad starting point at all. It corresponds rather neatly with what one would be inclined to suspect, considering findings of earlier research in this field. For example, we know that there are a number of transitional democracies with poorly developed civil societies – that is voluntary associations and organized interest groups – in contemporary Central and Eastern Europe. Estonia, Latvia and the countries of South Eastern Europe are sometimes cited as cases in point (Berglund, Hellén and Aarebrot 1998). Then there are a few transitional democracies with moderately developed voluntary associations such as Poland, Hungary, the Czech Republic, Lithuania and Slovenia (Linz and Stepan 1996). Also, it is conventional wisdom that all these countries, however underdeveloped they seem to be when it comes to the civil society arena, are better off than the countries within the Commonwealth of Independent States like Russia, the Ukraine and Belarus.

Map 6.1: Civil society – the promising countries of Central Europe

Civil society index: 1.00–1.75 [ ]   2.00–2.75 [■]

Maps 6.1–6.2 show the countries of Central and Eastern Europe, with respect to the development of civil society. The lighter shaded area in Map 6.1 corresponds with the top rated countries of Table 6.1 (Hungary, Poland and the Czech Republic). The darker shaded area refers to the second best rated countries (Slovenia, Lithuania, Estonia, and Latvia). The same logic applies to Map 6.2; the lighter shaded area represents the countries in our third group (index 3.00–3.75), and the darker shaded area identifies the least promising cases (index 4.00–7.00). In short, we find a group of promising countries in Central Europe and the Baltic states, and a group of less developed countries in South Eastern and Eastern Europe. It should be noted that several countries covered by *Freedomhouse* are not included in the maps (Mongolia, Armenia, Georgia, the Kyrgyz Republic, Azerbaijan, Kazakhstan, Tajikistan, Uzbekistan, and Turkmenistan).

Map 6.2: Civil society– the less developed countries of South Eastern Europe and Eastern Europe

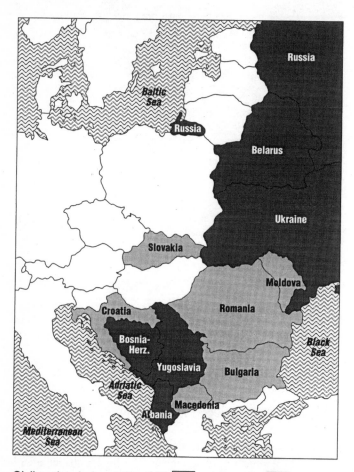

Civil society index: 3.00–3.75 ▢   4.00–7.00 ▮

For a first validity test of the *Freedomhouse* index, we turn to data from the International Social Survey Programme (ISSP) and the Central and Eastern Eurobarometer (CEEB). Neither of these data sets focuses explicitly on civil society, but they both contain information on trade union membership, religious affiliation and church attendance and other civil society relevant organizations. We will also explore the potential of other composite indices available to the analyst such as the Corruption Perceptions Index (CPI) developed by *Transparency International*.

Civil Society and Social Virtues

Trade union membership was one of the items included in the early CEEB and ISSP surveys. How does this variable fare with respect to the composite index developed by *Freedomhouse* which sets out to tap the development of civil society in general? The problem is that trade union membership *as such* tells us preciously little about the civil society arena in these countries. For example, consider Table 6.2.

Table 6.2: 'Is anyone in your household a member of a trade union?'
Percentages

	'Nobody'	*Number of cases*
Poland	85.2	1451
Bulgaria	80.7	1078
Latvia	80.5	1036
Slovakia	67.9	1370
Western Germany	62.5	1243
Slovenia	62.0	966
Lithuania	61.3	1000
Albania	56.3	1000
Hungary	49.7	987
Czechoslovakia	41.5	1076
Russia	38.2	832
Estonia	23.0	999
Eastern Germany	20.1	601
Romania	2.7	1000

Sources: CEEB 2, 1991; ISSP 1995 ('National Identity').

The pattern we are looking for (cf. Table 6.1) simply is not there. The fact that a given country has few members in its trade unions, does not necessarily give us even a snapshot of civil society conditions in that particular country. We should rather ask the respondents in each country how they perceive the trade unions. In the real world, survey data are a scarce commodity and usually do not include the questions of primary interest to secondary users. This time we are lucky, though. In ISSP 1993 ('Environment'), respondents in the Czech Republic and Bulgaria were asked to evaluate the trade unions in their respective countries. The Czech

Republic could be taken to be a representative of promising Central Europe, while Bulgaria may serve as a proxy for the poorly developed countries of Eastern Europe (cf. Maps 6.1–6.2). Will we find the same pattern again?

In the Czech Republic, a majority of the respondents feel that it would not be such a bad idea to give the trade unions more power (Table 6.3). Consequently, a majority of those polled feel that the Czech Republic benefits from the existence of trade unions (Table 6.4). In Bulgaria, on the other hand, the respondents are markedly less enthusiastic about giving trade unions more power than they already have (Table 6.3). Furthermore, those who feel that Bulgaria benefits from its trade unions are fewer than those who feel that trade unions are harmful. There also seems to be more of a polarized climate on this issue in Bulgaria than in the Czech Republic (Table 6.4). To the extent that we are willing to assume that a positive assessment of trade unions is indicative of a mature civil society, the Czech Republic stands out as the more developed of the two countries. Thus, here we find the pattern we are looking for. It is also worth noting that the impact of age on Tables 6.3–6.4 turned out to be of minor significance.

Table 6.3: 'Do trade unions in your country have too much or too little power?' Percentages

	Czech Republic	Bulgaria
Far too much	1.4	5.1
Too much	6.8	19.9
About the right...	26.7	20.7
Too little	50.2	32.6
Far too little	14.8	21.7
N	849	792

Source: ISSP 1993 ('Environment').

Table 6.4: 'How good are the trade unions in your country for the country as a whole?' Percentages

	Czech Republic	Bulgaria
Excellent	4.0	10.1
Very good	15.6	21.4
Fairly good	57.6	23.1
Not very good	18.8	21.2
Not good at all	3.9	24.2
N	865	822

Source: ISSP 1993 ('Environment').

The early CEEB surveys also asked respondents about their 'church attendance', yet another factor of possible civil society relevance: 'Do you participate in religious services several times a week, once a week, a few times a year, once a year or less, or never?' In Table 6.5, we have singled out the respondents that attend religious services most frequently, and those who state that they never attend religious services.

The outcome is a bit tricky to interpret. The first column tells us that the Catholic countries of Poland and Slovakia top the 'church attendance' ranking. Lithuania and Slovenia also have high scores. But Hungary ranks lower than expected considering that it too has a Catholic majority. The problem is that the figures in the first column are distorted by the third column, which includes those respondents who do not pledge allegiance to any religion and those who refrained from answering the question for some reason or other. Therefore, the second column is not merely the mirror image of the first.

Table 6.5: 'Attending religious services?' Percentages

	Once a week or several times a week	Never	No religion, do not know or no answer	N
Poland	62.1	3.3	6.2	999
Slovakia	33.7	6.8	18.1	734
Romania	21.4	7.3	2.8	1000
Lithuania	19.3	3.0	21.8	1000
Slovenia	17.7	10.2	34.9	1063
Armenia	15.2	15.7	21.2	918
Moldova	13.0	8.6	15.4	1000
Albania	12.2	34.0	9.1	1049
Macedonia	11.9	7.9	5.1	1002
Georgia	11.1	11.7	7.8	1038
Hungary	9.8	16.2	43.3	1000
Czech Republic	9.2	11.3	55.3	924
Ukraine	7.4	10.4	36.2	1400
Bulgaria	6.2	22.1	31.2	1312
Belarus	5.5	6.3	46.0	1030
Latvia	5.1	7.9	44.7	1000
Estonia	4.0	5.3	61.4	1000
Russia	3.0	11.6	55.2	1000

Source: CEEB 3, 1992.

The atheist/no answer category ranges from 2.8 per cent in Romania to 61.4 per cent in Estonia. If we were to count the valid percentages for each country, looking at church attendance among those who have stated that they actually belong to some religion, that is excluding the non-believers, the list would look a bit different. Hungary and the other countries with large numbers of non-believers would score higher on the attendance list. Still, Table 6.5 does not really convince us that 'church attendance' is an adequate indicator of civil society. Culturally determined behaviour is not the same thing as participation in voluntary associations; and CEEB stops short of prodding the churchgoers for the social networks to which they belong.

*

Part of what is conventionally referred to as civil society involves industrious citizens who take initiatives, trust one another and their political institutions, and participate in voluntary associations – in short, 'virtuous' citizens in the classical sense of the term. Have East Europeans in general developed some sort of 'social capital', or do they still represent that rather stereotyped notion of *Homo sovieticus*? In the 1993 ISSP survey ('Environment'), respondents were faced with the statement: 'It is just too difficult for someone like me to do much about the environment', and asked whether they agreed or not (Table 6.6).

Table 6.6: 'It is just too difficult for someone like me to do much about the environment.' Percentages

	West Germany	Slovenia	East Germany	Poland	Hungary	Czech Republic	Russia	Bulgaria
Strongly agree	7.1	8.8	10.6	14.4	20.3	21.8	27.5	47.0
Agree	21.0	35.4	29.8	43.9	31.7	34.9	26.1	29.3
Neither/nor	15.1	13.6	17.1	9.1	22.3	12.6	22.5	6.8
Disagree	32.4	37.7	30.0	28.7	19.9	22.3	13.7	8.1
Strongly disagree	24.4	4.4	12.5	3.9	5.7	8.4	10.2	8.8
N	985	997	1047	1520	1150	982	1761	1084

Source: ISSP 1993 ('Environment').

In Table 6.6, West Germany (the 'old' Federal Republic of Germany) as well as East Germany (former territory of the German Democratic Republic) are included as points of reference. Unfortunately, only a few of the new democracies in Central and Eastern Europe were polled by ISSP in 1993, and with the sole exception of Russia, none of the former Soviet republics. Still, the countries that are included roughly follow the pattern reported by *Nations in Transit 1998*, that is the countries of Central Europe are ahead of South Eastern and Eastern Europe, represented by Bulgaria and Russia (cf. Maps 6.1–6.2). In this particular survey, Bulgaria stands out as a country with a large number of citizens lacking the social virtues necessary to have an impact on environmental policy.

When controlling for age, we find that it is above all older respondents (50+) who feel that they are unable to do something about the environmental situation in their respective home countries. This tendency is manifest in all the countries in Table 6.7, which indicates that generation is an item of importance for civil society. It is probably safe to draw the conclusion that the younger generation will become 'virtuous citizens' much more quickly than the older age cohorts, which basically consist of people who have been subjects rather than citizens for most of their lives (cf. Almond and Verba 1963). Russia and Bulgaria once again stand out as worst off.

Table 6.7: 'It is just too difficult for someone like me to do much about the environment,' by age. Percentages

	West Germany			East Germany		
	18–29	*30–49*	*50+*	*18–29*	*30–49*	*50+*
Strongly agree	5.2	5.1	10.0	7.5	9.3	13.0
Agree	18.4	18.1	25.1	26.0	24.7	35.5
Neither/nor	16.0	14.3	15.4	22.5	16.2	15.5
Disagree	35.8	36.1	27.1	30.0	35.6	25.5
Strongly disagree	24.5	26.4	22.4	14.0	14.1	10.6
N	212	371	402	200	376	471

	Slovenia			Poland		
	18–29	*30–49*	*50+*	*18–29*	*30–49*	*50+*
Strongly agree	4.9	7.6	13.3	9.1	11.1	20.4
Agree	32.1	30.1	44.6	32.9	41.5	51.2
Neither/nor	19.9	14.8	7.5	14.3	10.1	5.8
Disagree	36.6	43.4	31.3	37.7	33.7	19.2
Strongly disagree	6.5	4.1	3.3	6.1	3.6	3.4
N	246	419	332	231	701	588

	Hungary			Czech Republic		
	18–29	*30–49*	*50+*	*18–29*	*30–49*	*50+*
Strongly agree	12.1	16.0	27.7	13.6	18.0	31.1
Agree	25.8	30.9	34.7	33.6	32.8	38.1
Neither/nor	26.8	23.4	19.6	14.5	15.3	8.4
Disagree	27.8	22.8	14.1	27.7	24.4	16.5
Strongly disagree	7.6	7.0	3.8	10.5	9.4	5.9
N	198	457	495	220	405	357

	Bulgaria			Russia		
	18–29	*30–49*	*50+*	*18–29*	*30–49*	*50+*
Strongly agree	33.0	40.8	57.0	23.3	26.2	32.8
Agree	35.2	33.8	23.7	26.4	26.8	24.8
Neither/nor	9.3	10.0	3.4	24.2	22.0	22.1
Disagree	11.0	9.3	6.2	14.0	14.3	12.2
Strongly disagree	11.5	6.3	9.8	11.8	10.7	8.0
N	182	400	502	417	820	524

Source: ISSP 1993 ('Environment').

The 1993 ISSP survey also included an item tapping the involvement of the respondents in voluntary environmental groups or organizations. Membership in these organizations may be seen as yet another civil society indicator and it does in fact produce the pattern familiar from Tables 6.1, 6.6–6.7 with the countries of Central Europe slightly ahead of South Eastern and Eastern Europe (Table 6.8).

Table 6.8: 'Are you a member of any group whose main aim is to preserve or protect the environment?' Percentages

	West Germany	Slovenia	Poland	Czech Republic	Hungary	East Germany	Russia	Bulgaria
Yes	5.6	3.7	3.5	3.2	3.0	3.0	2.4	1.9
No	94.4	96.3	96.5	96.8	97.0	97.0	97.6	98.1
N	994	1029	1636	1004	1166	1079	1927	1174

Source: ISSP 1993 ('Environment').

The pattern becomes less clear, however, when we look at the respondents' willingness to participate in different kinds of activities in order to protect or preserve the environment (Tables 6.9–6.11).

Table 6.9: Activity: 'In the last five years, have you signed a petition about an environmental issue?' Percentages

	West Germany	East Germany	Czech Republic	Russia	Slovenia	Poland	Bulgaria	Hungary
Yes	31.0	28.2	14.5	10.7	10.5	10.1	8.7	5.3
No	69.0	71.8	85.5	89.3	89.5	89.9	91.3	94.7
N	1004	1083	1005	1921	1031	1611	1179	1158

Table 6.10: Activity: 'In the last five years, have you given money to an environmental group?' Percentages

	West Germany	Poland	Russia	East Germany	Slovenia	Czech Republic	Hungary	Bulgaria
Yes	19.2	18.1	10.0	9.6	7.8	5.9	4.3	3.8
No	80.8	81.9	90.0	90.4	92.1	94.1	95.7	96.2
N	999	1610	1923	1063	1030	1005	1159	1179

Table 6.11: Activity: 'In the last five years, have you taken part in a protest or demonstration about an environmental issue?' Percentages

	East Germany	West Germany	Bulgaria	Czech Republic	Slovenia	Russia	Poland	Hungary
Yes	8.8	8.4	6.0	5.8	5.6	3.9	3.7	1.5
No	91.2	91.6	94.0	94.2	94.4	96.1	96.3	98.5
N	1066	995	1179	1003	1031	1923	1607	1163

Source (Tables 6.9–6.11): ISSP 1993 ('Environment').

Tables 6.9–6.11 provide interesting information about the attitudes towards environment protection in Central and Eastern Europe of the early 1990s. It is not a particularly hot issue in Hungary, nor, for that matter, in Bulgaria which had embarked on the transition from communism to democracy under the banner of *Ecoglasnost*. Environment protection seems to have a rather explosive potential in Russia. As of 1993, Russians actually scored higher than Hungarians did on all three items – signing petitions, donating money and participating in demonstrations about environmental issues (Tables 6.9 and 6.11). The rank order clearly is not what we expected. We can perhaps dismiss Tables 6.9–6.11 as *general* civil society indicators. For all we know, Hungarians and other Central Europeans with little interest in environment protection may be actively involved in an array of social movements of less relevance to Russians. This time around, we are not as lucky as in the previous case: questions about these movements are not included in any of the ISSP, nor for that matter in any of the CEEB, surveys. We are thus well advised to scan other databases for possible civil society indicators, preferably for indicators with a general scope.

*

The 1999 *Transparency International Corruption Perceptions Index* (CPI) by *Transparency International* has this potential. Corruption is the very opposite of civility. It is not condoned by 'virtuous citizens'; and widespread corruption is generally seen as a serious obstacle on the road towards a well functioning civil society. The CPI is based on the perceptions among businessmen, risk analysts and the public at large of the degree of corruption in countries throughout the world. It ranges between 10.0 ('highly clean') and 0.0 ('highly corrupt'). We have singled out the countries of Central and Eastern Europe for attention (Table 6.12).

Table 6.12: 1999 Transparency International Corruption Perceptions Index (excerpt)

Germany	8.0	Romania	3.3
Slovenia	6.0	Croatia	2.7
Estonia	5.7	Moldova	2.6
Hungary	5.2	Ukraine	2.6
Czech Republic	4.6	Armenia	2.5
Poland	4.2	Russia	2.4
Lithuania	3.8	Albania	2.3
Slovakia	3.7	Georgia	2.3
Belarus	3.4	Kazakhstan	2.3
Latvia	3.4	Kyrgyz Republic	2.2
Bulgaria	3.3	Yugoslavia	2.0
Macedonia	3.3	Uzbekistan	1.8

Source: www.transparency.de/

The Federal Republic of Germany is used as a point of reference; and compared to Germany, the countries of Central and Eastern Europe are actually more or less corrupt, but – on the other hand – they are far from being interchangeable. With a rock-bottom score of 1.8, Uzbekistan is far removed from Slovenia, which stands out as the least corrupt country of the entire region by virtue of a score of 6.0 on the CPI index. There is in fact enough diversity in the data to make for a trichotomy (Map 6.3).

Map 6.3: Corruption in Central and Eastern Europe

Corruption index: ☐ Low ▨ Medium ■ High

The first group of countries consists of Slovenia, Estonia, Hungary, the Czech Republic and Poland, all of them with CPI scores above 4. In the second group of countries we find Lithuania, Slovakia, Belarus, Latvia, Bulgaria, Macedonia and Romania, all of them featuring CPI scores in the range of 3.8–3.3. The third group counts highly corrupt countries such as Croatia, Moldova, Ukraine, Armenia, Russia, Albania, Georgia, Kazakhstan, the Kyrgyz Republic, Yugoslavia (Serbia) and Uzbekistan, all of them with CPI scores below 3. The picture of Eastern Europe conveyed by *Transparency International* ties in rather neatly with the data provided by *Freedomhouse* in *Nations in Transit* (Table 6.1). Hungary, Poland, the Czech Republic, Slovenia and Estonia come out on top, while countries like Russia, Ukraine, Yugoslavia (Serbia) and Albania end up at the bottom of the ranking list.

But the fit is far from perfect. Map 6.3 thus features Belarus in a prominent position along with Lithuania, Slovakia, Latvia, Bulgaria, Romania and Macedonia in the second group of countries with CPI scores of 3.8–3.3. This might seem counterintuitive. Belarus is no less plagued by pre-democratic clientelistic networks than the eleven countries listed as highly corrupt by *Transparency International*. Belarus has become increasingly isolated under President Alexander Lukashenko. His authoritarian and arbitrary rule has made Belarus somewhat of an outcast in the East European context. And it may be that trade with Western Europe has slowed down to the point that there were not enough observations for *Transparency International* to make an accurate assessment of the level of corruption. But there is also an alternative explanation. Communist style law and order with stiff penalties for those officials who get caught with their hands in the till might still prevail and serve as deterrent. We would at any rate be inclined to look at the 1999 *Transparency* rating for Belarus with some scepticism.

*

In most cases, *Freedomhouse* reports no changes in the civil society arena between 1997–98; and where changes have taken place, they have generally been for the better (Table 6.13). Six countries have improved their civil society ratings. Bulgaria has actually improved significantly, leaving the index group 4.00–7.00. Russia, on the other hand, has made the opposite journey, going from 3.75 to 4.00. Two other countries have had a negative development when it comes to the civil society arena, Ukraine and, most notably, Belarus.

In short, the general pattern stands confirmed. Lack of civil society is above all a problem for the countries of South Eastern and Eastern Europe. It would thus seem that the old demarcation line between East and West still manifests itself in contemporary Europe. It may be noted that we are not referring to the Cold-War East/West division line (Berglund, Hellén and Aarebrot 1998, 1–4) but to the fault-line separating Rome from Constantinople.

Table 6.13: Civil society in Central and Eastern Europe

	1997	1998	Development
Hungary	1.25	1.25	
Poland	1.25	1.25	
Czech Republic	1.25	1.50	0.25 ↘
Slovenia	2.00	2.00	
Lithuania	2.25	2.00	0.25 ↗
Estonia	2.25	2.25	
Latvia	2.25	2.25	
Slovakia	3.25	3.00	0.25 ↗
Mongolia	Missing	3.25	
Armenia	3.50	3.50	
Croatia	3.50	3.50	
Bulgaria	4.00	3.75	0.25 ↗
Macedonia	3.75	3.75	
Moldova	3.75	3.75	
Romania	3.75	3.75	
Russia	3.75	4.00	0.25 ↘
Albania	4.25	4.25	
Georgia	4.50	4.25	0.25 ↗
Ukraine	4.00	4.25	0.25 ↘
Kyrgyz Republic	4.50	4.50	
Azerbaijan	5.00	5.00	
Bosnia	Missing	5.00	
Kazakhstan	5.25	5.00	0.25 ↗
Yugoslavia	Missing	5.00	
Tajikistan	5.50	5.25	0.25 ↗
Belarus	5.25	5.75	0.50 ↘
Uzbekistan	6.50	6.50	
Turkmenistan	7.00	7.00	

Source: Karatnycky, Motyl and Shor (1997) and Karatnycky, Motyl and Graybow (1999).

The region of Central and Eastern Europe, taken as a whole, has served as an interface between East and West since at least the 10th century, when it became part of Christian European civilization. But with the onset of proto-industrialization in the 15th and 16th centuries, the distance to the European core again began to broaden. Since then, the bulk of Central and Eastern Europe has remained relegated to the periphery or at least the semi-periphery of the European economic system; only some parts (in particular, Bohemia) have occasionally been within the core (Wallerstein 1974, 99). There is no doubt that all of 'Eastern' Europe (as opposed to 'Western' Europe) has been part of the broad pattern of European civilization and culture for at least a millennium, but 'slightly differently, less intensively, less fully' than the West, 'with the result that East European participation in the European experience was only partial' (Schöpflin 1993, 11). In political terms, Central and Eastern Europe has been a transitional zone between the Western tradition of division of power and the Eastern tradition of concentration of power. This fault-line coincides with that between Western and Eastern Christianity; the Eastern tradition is at its strongest in territories once under Ottoman rule, and the Western tradition is strongest in areas marked by Lutheranism (Map 6.4).

Map 6.4: Historical religious cleavage lines in Central and Eastern Europe

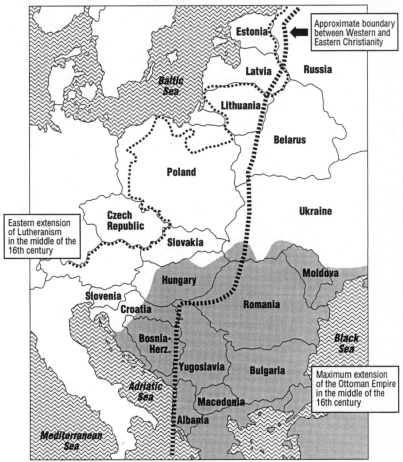

Source: Berglund, Hellén and Aarebrot (1998, 15).

This dichotomy between the German and Habsburg empires and their Russian and Ottoman counterparts, neatly coincides with the East/West fault-line between Central and Eastern Europe. The Western group shares traditions of Roman law, feudalism and relatively early national awakening; the Eastern group has a Byzantine heritage and a lack of strong feudal traditions, enabling ancient local authority relationships, such as kinship and clientelism, to survive longer. This tendency is stronger in the South than in the North. The North/South dichotomy is reinforced by the strength and autonomy of political authority versus religious leadership. The North/South dimension separates the Protestant and substantially secularized states from the Counter-Reformation Catholic states, non-secularized Orthodox states, and the Muslim states (Berglund and Aarebrot 1997).

All in all, a quick glance at the maps in this chapter tells us that the historical East/West divide remains relevant in contemporary Europe. The civil society arena is most developed in the Western Christianity territories, that is Central Europe (Map 6.1, Map 6.4). The Baltic states are characterized by their position at the crossroads of German, Russian, Polish and Scandinavian culture. Nevertheless, they are not a culturally homogenous group. In the late pre-modern and early modern era, the Lithuanian heartland was part of the Polish–Lithuanian commonwealth, at times ruling over vast tracts of land stretching down to the Black Sea; thus it has a tradition of itself being an imperial centre. Estonia and most of Latvia, on the other hand, have no pre-20th-century traditions of independence. They were ruled by the Teutonic Order, Denmark, Poland, Sweden, and eventually by aristocratic Germanic agents of the Russian Tsar. This gave them a more Western cultural tradition, and a mainly German nobility and bourgeoisie, as opposed to Lithuania's mainly Polish and Russian landowners and Jewish artisan, merchant and professional classes. Latvia and Estonia are predominantly Protestant while Catholicism is dominant in Lithuania. Still, all three states are part of the Western Christianity sphere. In the Eastern Christianity territories, the civil society arena is clearly less developed (Map 6.2, Map 6.4). Furthermore, the North/South dichotomy is detectable in Map 6.3. Corruption is perceived as a problem above all in the countries to the East of Poland, and to the South of the old Habsburg territories, that is in the former Ottoman territories. The Protestant/Counter-Reformation dichotomy could perhaps also be used to account for the differences between the Czech Republic and Slovakia.

It would seem, then, that the old demarcation line between East and West still manifests itself in contemporary Europe, and affects the possibilities of creating a well-functioning civil society arena. Such a conclusion could be criticized for being overly simplistic or potentially lending itself to determinism or ethnocentrism. Still, there is arguably some truth to the claims that 'Western Europe', including *Mitteleuropa*, has a long historical tradition of a markedly clear distinction between public and private, between state and society, whereas Eastern Europe, Russia in particular, lacks such a tradition. Civic virtues will perhaps not be a *Fremdkörper* in Russia and Eastern Europe for ever, but we would nevertheless expect the development of a stable and well functioning civil society to take less time in the countries of Central Europe. On a general level, that is at any rate what we would hypothesize.

Testing the Hypothesis

If our general hypothesis is correct, we would expect civil society in contemporary Russia to be plagued by problems, by now long removed from the agenda in the countries to the West of the historical fault-line (Map 6.4), such as outright repression and harassment by local authorities. We would therefore expect leaders of Russian civil society organizations to have a negative picture of the human rights situation in Russia and little trust in such institutions as the courts, the police and the army, but perhaps also in the political parties that have emerged after the breakdown of communism. We would furthermore expect civil society leaders to approach the democratic way of public decision-making, including referenda, general elections and political parties, with somewhat more than a fair share of suspicion.

This is where we would normally stop, albeit with the standard, almost ritualistic call on the scientific community to pick up the thread where we were compelled to leave it. But it so happens that we have access to up-to-date Russian civil society data. The data were gathered within the framework of a research project on local democracy in the East Baltic Sea region, sponsored by the Baltic Sea Foundation.[1] The questionnaires are in the process of being coded, as this chapter is being finalized. But we are currently in a position to present aggregate statistics on four out of five Russian regions. We will eventually be able to compare the Russian data with civil society data from Estonia, Latvia and Lithuania. For the time being, however, we will have to confine ourselves to Estonia as the sole point of reference.

Table 6.14: 'Organization suffered harassment or repression by local authorities?' Percentages

	Estonia	Russia
No problems with local authorities	72	52
Occasional bureaucratic or legal problems	22	35
Systematic bureaucratic problems and legal harassment	1	8
Repression, police actions, threats of violence	1	3
N	76	417

Note: There are percentages missing (DK, NA). The columns do not necessarily add up to 100 per cent.

Estonia is admittedly less than ideal as a representative of the Western tradition. Polish, Czech or Hungarian civil society data would have served us better, but Estonia does have more of a Western tradition than Russia by virtue of its exposure to Danish, Swedish and Germanic influences throughout history. And the differences between Russian and Estonian civil society leaders are indeed striking.

In Russia, one civil society leader out of ten reports systematic harassment and/or outright repression by local authorities. Estonia hardly features any such instances; Estonian civil society leaders live in a world with few or any of the problems facing their Russian colleagues. Russian civil society leaders tend to be strongly dissatisfied with the human rights situation at home; while Estonians tend to be content (Tables 6.14–6.15).

Table 6.15: 'How much respect is there for human rights nowadays in our country?' Percentages

	Estonia	Russia
A lot	25	2
Some	50	19
Not much	24	48
None at all	–	30
N	76	417

Note: There are percentages missing (DK, NA). The columns do not necessarily add up to 100 per cent.

In Russia, civil society leaders tend to distrust the courts, the police and the army. In Estonia, the prevailing mood is trusting. Parties are objects of distrust in both countries, but much more so in Russia than in Estonia (Table 6.16). And as a rule, Estonian civil society leaders attribute greater importance than Russians to the formal political process (Table 6.17).

Table 6.16: 'How much trust do you have in the following institutions?' Percentages

ESTONIA (N=76)	None at all	Little	Some	A lot
Courts	8	24	47	17
Police	8	30	50	11
Army	7	24	50	16
Federal/national authorities	5	22	55	16
Regional authorities	1	15	55	26
Local authorities	5	15	57	20
Political parties	22	41	24	8
RUSSIA (N=417)	None at all	Little	Some	A lot
Courts	15	50	28	6
Police	22	51	23	4
Army	19	34	41	5
Federal/national authorities	24	54	21	2
Regional authorities	17	51	26	3
Local authorities	9	46	35	6
Political parties	41	48	7	3

Table 6.17: 'There are a number of ways in which people can influence decisions. We have listed some of them and would like to get your opinion on their effectiveness': 'Very effective' percentages

	Estonia	Russia
Referendum, voting	46	17
People's meeting, public debates	15	7
Committees to solve specific issues	26	12
Movements, political parties, or groups with general objectives	28	12
Local self-government bodies (councils)	30	16
Trade unions	15	11
Parliamentary elections	37	21
Personal contact with decision makers	62	49
N	76	417

Thus far at least, our hypothesis about the lingering impact of the historical East/West divide would seem to be corroborated. Russia does lag behind Estonia. But, on a slightly more optimistic note, it may also be noted that the situation in Russia is not entirely bleak. More than 50 per cent of Russian civil society leaders do not report any problems with the local authorities. About a third have a lot or some trust in what may be referred to as the repressive organs of the state such as the courts, the police and the army (Table 6.16); and a clear-cut majority of Russian civil society leaders attributes at least some effectiveness to referenda, voting and political parties.

NOTE

1. Within the framework of this project on *Democratisation: Local and Transnational Perspectives* in the East Baltic Sea region, Russian, Estonian, Latvian and Lithuanian local civil society leaders were interviewed. Interviews were carried out in a limited set of regions (in the Russian case: five regions); and the data are not statistically representative in the same sense as a national opinion poll. The regions to be surveyed were, however, selected with great care so as to include urban as well as rural, prosperous as well as depressed areas.

REFERENCES

Almond, Gabriel A. and Sidney Verba (1963), *The Civic Culture: Political Attitudes and Democracy in Five Nations*, Princeton, New Jersey, Princeton University Press.

Berglund, Sten and Frank Aarebrot (1997), *The Political History of Eastern Europe in the 20th Century: The Struggle Between Democracy and Dictatorship*, Aldershot, Edward Elgar.

Berglund, Sten, Tomas Hellén and Frank Aarebrot, eds, (1998), *Handbook of Political Change in Eastern Europe*, Aldershot, Edward Elgar.

Central and Eastern Eurobarometer (CEEB) No. 2, Cologne, Zentralarchiv für Empirische Sozialforschung.

Central and Eastern Eurobarometer (CEEB) No. 3, Cologne, Zentralarchiv für Empirische Sozialforschung.

Drakulíc, Slavenka (1994), 'Lav Story: Romania's dirty little secret', *The New Republic*, 25 April.

Hankiss, Elemer (1988), 'The "Second Society": Is There an Alternative Social Model Emerging in Contemporary Hungary?', *Social Research* Vol. 55, No. 1–2.

International Social Survey Programme (ISSP) (1993), 'Environment', Cologne, Zentralarchiv für Empirische Sozialforschung.

International Social Survey Programme (ISSP) (1995), 'National Identity', Cologne, Zentralarchiv für Empirische Sozialforschung.

Linz, Juan and Alfred Stepan (1996), *Problems of Democratic Transition and Consolidation: Southern Europe, South America and Post-Communist Europe*, Baltimore and London, Johns Hopkins University Press.

Karatnycky, Adrian, Alexander Motyl and Charles Graybow, eds, (1999), *Nations in Transit 1998*, New Brunswick and London, Transaction Publishers.

Karatnycky, Adrian, Alexander Motyl and Boris Shor, eds, (1997), *Nations in Transit 1997*, New Brunswick and London, Transaction Publishers.

O'Donnell, Guillermo, Philippe C. Schmitter and Laurence Whitehead, eds., (1986), *Transitions from Authoritarian Rule*, Baltimore and London, Johns Hopkins University Press.

Putnam, Robert D. (1995), 'Bowling Alone: America's Declining Social Capital', *Journal of Democracy* (January 1995).

Schöpflin, George (1993), *Politics in Eastern Europe 1945–1992*, Oxford, Blackwell.

Tempest, Clive (1997), 'Myths from Eastern Europe and the Legend of the West', *Democratization* Vol. 4, No. 1, Spring 1997.

Tocqueville, Alexis de (1990 [1835–1840]), *Democracy in America*, 2 volumes, New York, Vintage Books.

Transparency International Corruption Perceptions Index (1999), (www.transparency.de/).

Urban, Jan (1992), 'The Powerlessnes of the Powerful', unpublished manuscript, Prague.

Wallerstein, Immanuel (1974), *The Modern World System: Capitalist Agriculture and the Origins of the European World-Economy in the Sixteenth Century*, London, Routledge.

7. Changing Perspectives on Political Challenges

The major impression conveyed by the previous chapters is one of progress. The new democracies of Central and Eastern Europe are indeed up against challenges, but generally speaking they seem to be increasingly able to cope with them. But this generally optimistic conclusion must come with a warning attached to it. Few Western academics, including our fellow political scientists, succeeded in predicting the fall of communism in 1989–90, even though they knew a lot about the challenges facing the Soviet bloc. The democratic regimes that were installed in Eastern Europe after the demise of communism have remained in place only for a decade. We thus have a rather narrow basis for generalizations about the region and our conclusions should therefore be read with some caution.

Two different paradigms or modes of understanding have dominated the debate on the new democracies in Central and Eastern Europe.

1. The *renascence* paradigm based on three assumptions: (i) democracy was anathema to the defunct communist regimes; (ii) free elections would regenerate the political system in accordance with historical patterns specific to each country; and (iii) the introduction of the market economy would improve living conditions more or less automatically – failing which the West would promptly bail out Eastern Europe by introducing a new Marshall style scheme.

2. The *integrationist* paradigm calls for a more active approach. Taking advantage of the window of opportunity now open to Eastern Europe, integrationist politicians actively promote membership in the European Union, NATO and other organizations of regional or international cooperation, fully realizing that this entails obligations as well as privileges. These politicians are more concerned with future strategic options than with the political structures of the past. This has made it possible for former dissidents and reformed communists alike to embrace the integrationist cause. Within the framework of this

171

paradigm, we would expect mass politics to be built upon contemporary rather than historical cleavages and economic success to be based upon competitive skills rather than *quid pro quo* benefits from the West.

These paradigms are not really competing. It may be better to look upon them as sequential. The former mode of understanding dominated East European politics in the early 1990s, the latter prevailed towards the end of the decade.

The integrationist and renascence paradigms are relevant for our understanding of how democratic systems adapt to political challenges. Table 7.1 provides a brief overview. The intense formation of political parties prior to the founding elections was in many ways a matter of a revival of the past. There was an abundance of parties with ideological and historical roots in the inter-war era and of parties with organizational ties to the various anti-communist fronts or movements. A combination of skilful electoral engineering and sheer luck prevented party fragmentation from overburdening the first freely elected parliaments. In most countries, only a handful of the many political parties competing for the favour of the voters gained parliamentary representation. This renascence mode of understanding was replaced by growing national consensus around the integrationist approach in the late 1990s. Contemporary parliamentary politics tends to be oriented towards consensus and coalition building. As the years have gone by, European integration has become less of a dividing issue than it was at the outset. In many instances, it has provided the basis for coalitions across the left/right divide. Volatility, whether measured in terms of fluctuating electoral results or in terms of frequent modifications of the party trees, does not *ipso facto* lead to fragmentation.

The challenge of nationalism can be seen as an integral part of the renascence paradigm. Nationalism was readily employed as a mobilizing force, fuelled by border changes that date back to the First and Second World Wars and by widespread national grievances long repressed by communist ideologues. With the demise of communism, nationalist mobilization once again became politically acceptable. Nationalism is far less compatible with the integrationist paradigm. In a sense, the wish to be accepted by the international community and to be part of the process of European integration effectively reduces the ability of East European leaders to play the nationalist card. In fact, the truth of the matter is that such restraint was as much self-imposed as a response to external expectations.

The party systems of the communist era had a variety of forms, ranging from Soviet style one-party systems to the Polish kind of hegemonic party system (Berglund and Dellenbrant 1994; Wiatr 1964), but the number of parties was limited indeed. Central and Eastern Europe could not by any stretch of imagination be characterized as fragmented. The development of

Central and Eastern Europe in 1989–90 was in many ways reminiscent of that of West Germany and Italy in the immediate aftermath of the Second World War. A dictatorship had been defeated and given way to a number of political entrepreneurs. In the founding elections, an array of political formations, in some cases more than one hundred, competed for the favour of the newly enfranchised voters. Most of the parties that emerged in early post-communist Central and Eastern Europe failed to gain parliamentary representation, but there were certainly enough parties in the first freely elected parliaments to make coalition building into a complicated affair. Creative electoral engineering, mainly in the form of threshold clauses, has successfully reduced the number of parties in parliament, but the political landscape has not yet stabilized. Parties come and disappear after elections, in some countries more often than in others. This volatility notwithstanding, the broadening range of possible coalitions stands out as the most important change under the recent integrationist paradigm. Politics today makes strange bedfellows also in Central and Eastern Europe. As the options for possible coalitions increase, so does the understanding of the need for national consensus, further enhanced by the European process of integration. But consensus is presently mainly as an elite phenomenon, and it is questionable to what extent it will be embraced by the masses. For the time being, atomization and alienation from the realm of official politics seem to be the order of the day.

Table 7.1: Challenges are affected by the two paradigms

	Renascence paradigm	Integrationist paradigm
Party Fragmentation	Intense formation of political parties, many of which were self-proclaimed heirs of pre-war party formations.	Consensus and coalition building, often across cleavage lines such as the left/right divide.
Nationalism	Nationalism as a mobilizing tool at least in some countries.	Hopes for internationalization limit the scope of national mobilization.
Human Rights	Dualism: Human rights activism under communism was a strong legitimizing force for new leaders, but in some cases the eagerness to purge the former *nomenklatura* was not in line with human rights norms.	International norms have often been accepted for purposes of international integration. It remains a central predictor of satisfaction with democracy.
Civil Society	Moderately developed in Central Europe, weak in Eastern Europe. This possibly reflects the long-standing fault-line between Western and Eastern Christianity; the importance of pre-democratic networks in Central Europe should not be underestimated.	Progress in the entire region, but differences between regions remain. European integration may possibly further the development of civil society organizations.

Under the early renascence paradigm, the human rights situation in Central and Eastern Europe was characterized by imbalanced dualism. On the one hand, human rights activism under communism was an important legitimizing platform for emerging political elites. On the other hand, there were some rather embarrassing cases of exaggerated eagerness to purge former *nomenklatura* to the detriment of the very same human rights.[1] More recently, international norms have been adopted throughout the region, often for purposes of international integration. The harmonization of the citizenship laws of Estonia and Latvia from the principle of *ius sanguini* to the more common European standard of residency is a good case in point (Aarebrot and Knutsen 2000). It remains to be seen if and to what extent these new standards are felt as an imposition, accepted in order to facilitate European integration, or if they reflect a genuine change of hearts.

The importance of civil society organizations for the renascence of democracy in Eastern Europe should not be overestimated. With the notable exception of the Solidarity trade union in Poland, mobilization against the communist regimes took the form of loosely organized groups, fronts, or movements throughout the entire region. The systematic building of independent civil society organizations seemed to be redundant at the time. During the 1990s, the civil society arena has developed, but seldom beyond a moderate level. It is becoming increasingly clear that European integration will call for the countries of Central and Eastern Europe to create organizational counterparts to the strong and established civil society organizations in the EU countries. It is still too early to say whether these civil society organizations will have a real impact on their societies beyond mirroring their Western counterparts.

All in all, the overwhelming impression is that the four challenges were much more pronounced in the early 1990s than they are now. Today's challenges are best described as dormant. Party fragmentation has been successfully checked, but there is an undercurrent of social atomization and alienation from party politics throughout the entire region. On the contemporary political agenda, nationalism has been subordinated to the issue of European integration, but it would be naïve to assume that it has ceased to exist. East Europeans are indeed concerned about human rights standards; in many respects they are even more important than material considerations. Civil society organizations are developing, but in all but a few countries they remain weakly or moderately developed. Belarus and possibly Yugoslavia represent the most conspicuous deviations from the overall trend. The authoritarian regime of Alexander Lukashenko has in fact turned the clock backwards to the point that Belarus no longer can be classified even as a transitional democracy[2]; and the Belgrade regime seems to be facing mounting legitimacy problems as Slobodan Milosevic gradually loses his grip on power.

Table 7.2: The geography of differences: synthesis of the four challenges

Country grouped by analytical region.	Party fragmentation (founding election minus latest election). See Tables 3.2–3.3	Nationalism. Assessment of the current nationalist challenge to democracy. Table 4.16	Human rights. Proportion of well educated respondents answering 'unacceptable' to query about respect for human rights. Table 5.4	Civil society. Assessment of civil society strength according to Nations in Transit 1998. See Table 6.13	Number of significant challenges.
Central Europe					
Estonia	Reduction	Still potentially problematic	Medium	Moderately strong	1
Latvia	Reduction	Still potentially problematic	Medium	Moderately strong	1
Lithuania	No change	Weak	Medium	Moderately strong	0
Poland	Strong reduction	Weak	Low	Strong	0
Czech Republic	No fragmentation	A potential challenge constrained by integration	Low	Strong	0
Slovakia	No change	A potential challenge modified by integration	Low	Medium	1
Hungary	Reduction	Weak	Low	Strong	0
Slovenia	No change	None	Medium	Moderately strong	0
South Eastern Europe					
Romania	Strong reduction	A potential challenge modified by integration	Low	Medium	1
Bulgaria	No change	Weak	Medium	Medium	0
Croatia	Reduction	Nationalist challenge present	Low	Medium	1
Bosnia-Herzegovina	The party system remains fragmented by ethnicity	Totally dominant	Human rights situation problematic	Weak	4
Macedonia	No change	Very important	Low	Medium	1
Yugoslavia	No change, but mounting problems of legitimacy	Very important	Medium	Weak	3
Albania	No change	Weak	Low	Weak	1

Table 7.2: continued

CIS Countries					
Russia	No change	Present but limited	High	Weak	3
Ukraine	Increase	Present but limited	High	Weak	4
Belarus	Problems of legitimacy	Present but limited	High	Weak	4
Moldova	No change	Potential challenge		Medium	2
Georgia	Reduction	Strong	High	Weak	3
Armenia	No change	Weak	High	Medium	1
Kazakhstan	No change	Moderate	High	Weak	2

In Table 7.2 we make an attempt to summarize some of the major highlights from the four previous chapters on challenges to democracy. A simple eyeball inspection of each of the four columns helps us to get an idea of the profiles of the individual countries. In Central Europe the number of parties represented in parliament has generally been reduced since the founding elections or remained the same, at a relatively moderate level. A similar trend makes itself felt also in the CIS countries and in the Balkans, but less convincingly so than in the more mature Central European party systems. Nationalism has not developed into a challenge in any of the countries where its impact was weak at the outset. In those countries, where national sentiments served as a mobilizing force at the time of the founding elections, the challenge has since been reduced to the realm of the potential. Bosnia-Herzegovina, Macedonia, Yugoslavia and Georgia are exceptions for rather obvious reasons, plagued as they have been by armed rebellions and civil wars through the 1990s. Using the percentage of the well educated respondents who find that the government has little or no respect for human rights as an indicator of systemic arbitrariness, we find high levels of dissatisfaction only in the CIS countries. In the rest of Central and Eastern Europe, including the Balkans (*sic*), the levels of dissatisfaction range from medium to low. The development of civil society organizations has been tentative in Central and Eastern Europe. According to *Nations in Transit* 1998, it is at its weakest in the CIS countries, the former Yugoslav Federation and Albania, and at its strongest in the Baltic countries and Central Europe, including Slovenia.

Summarizing the impact of the four challenges, we arrive at a classification of all the countries in the region. We have defined party fragmentation as an important challenge, whenever the number of parties represented in parliament has increased significantly after the founding election. Nationalism is deemed significant in countries where this issue is at least potentially problematic. Human rights constitute a challenge in countries where 25 per cent or more of the well educated find the government's respect for human rights to be unacceptable. The civil society

Figure 7.1 highlights the importance of institutional factors for the system's ability to deal successfully with challenges. Russia and Albania may serve as examples. The former faces more challenges than the latter, but we would nevertheless be hard put to argue that Albania is leading in terms of democratic consolidation. Relatively more solid institution building tips the balance in Russia's favour. In general terms, we must attribute as much importance to internal institution building as to social and attitudinal challenges in order to ascertain the level of democratic consolidation.

The debate about the prospects for democracy in Central and Eastern Europe has been largely normative. Western experts and their East European clients have more often than not perceived the challenges as unique to the region. In this volume we have taken a rather different approach. Challenges can be analysed empirically through comparisons between countries within the region. Such comparisons may also serve as a reminder that problems of democratic governance are in fact all-European, or to quote our Saviour 'And why beholdest thou the mote that is in thy brother's eye, but considerest not the beam that is in thine own eye?' (Matthew, 7, 3).

NOTES

1. The most absurd case of cleansing was probably the Czechoslovak clause barring from political office anyone listed in the archives of the communist security forces, including suspected dissidents targeted by these very forces.

2. Serbia is yet another exceptional case in the sense it has not developed beyond the transitional stage. The former communist party has remained in power in a new nationalist guise, but competitive elections have been held and opposition parties and media are active.

REFERENCES

Aarebrot, Frank H. and Terje Knutsen, eds, (2000), *Politics and Citizenship on the Eastern Baltic Seaboard*, Kristiansand S, Høyskoleforlaget.
Berglund, Sten and Jan Åke Dellenbrant, eds, (1994), *The New Democracies in Eastern Europe: Party Systems and Political Cleavages*, 2nd edn, Aldershot, Edward Elgar.
Karatnycky, Adrian, Alexander Motyl and Charles Graybow, eds, (1999), *Nations in Transit 1998*, New Brunswick and London, Transaction Publishers.
Putnam, Robert D. (1995), 'Bowling Alone: America's Declining Social Capital', *Journal of Democracy* (January 1995).
Wiatr, Jerzy (1964), 'One-party Systems: The Concept and Issues for Comparative Studies', in Erik Allardt and Yrjö Littunen, eds, *Cleavages, Ideologies and Party Systems*, Åbo, The Westermarck Society.

Name Index

181

Subject Index